PERSUASION AND LEGAL REASONING IN THE ECTHR RULINGS

This book analyses the case law of the European Court of Human Rights (ECtHR) from the point of view of argumentative tools used by the Court to persuade the audience – States, applicants and public opinion – of the correctness of its rulings. The ECtHR judgments selected by the authors concern justification of some of the most difficult issues. These are matters related to human life, human dignity and the right to self-determination in matters concerning one's private life. The authors looked for paths and repetitive patterns of argumentation and divided them into three categories of argumentative tools: authority, deontological and teleological. The work tracks how ECtHR judges aim to find a consensual, universal and, at the same time, pragmatic and axiologically neutral narrative on the collisions of rights and interests in the areas under discussion. It analyses whether the voice of the ECtHR carries the overtones of an ethical statement and, if so, to which arguments it appeals. The book will be of interest to academics and researchers working in the areas of jurisprudence, human rights law, and law and language.

Aleksandra Mężykowska is an associate professor within the Department of Constitutional Law and European Research at the Institute of Law Studies of the Polish Academy of Sciences and an expert in the Treaty and Legal Department of the Ministry of Foreign Affairs. Her research interests focus on constitutional and human rights law with particular emphasis on the issues related to the application of the European Convention on Human Rights (protection of property rights and reforms of the control system created on the basis of the Convention).

Anna Młynarska-Sobaczewska is a professor within the Department of Constitutional Law and European Research at the Institute of Law Studies of the Polish Academy of Sciences. Her research interests focus on the theory of constitutional law (legitimacy of public authorities and constitutional adjudication) and human rights (right to privacy, freedom of press and freedom of artistic creativity). Her research often looks at the relationship between language, persuasion and legal reasoning, as well as legitimising the dimension of legal instruments.

Persuasion and Legal Reasoning in the ECtHR Rulings

Balancing Impossible Demands

Aleksandra Mężykowska and Anna Młynarska-Sobaczewska

Routledge
Taylor & Francis Group
LONDON AND NEW YORK

First published 2023
by Routledge
4 Park Square, Milton Park, Abingdon, Oxon OX14 4RN

and by Routledge
605 Third Avenue, New York, NY 10158

Routledge is an imprint of the Taylor & Francis Group, an informa business

British Library Cataloguing-in-Publication Data
A catalogue record for this book is available from the British Library

ISBN: 978-1-032-44622-6 (hbk)
ISBN: 978-1-032-45222-7 (pbk)
ISBN: 978-1-003-37599-9 (ebk)

DOI: 10.4324/9781003375999

Typeset in Galliard
by Apex CoVantage, LLC

Publication financed under the program of the Minister of Science and Higher Education under the name "DIALOG" in the years 2019–2023 as part of the project "Excellence in Legal Research. Promoting Polish Achievements in the Area of Legal Sciences Abroad" implemented under the leadership of Celina Nowak by the Institute of Law Studies of the Polish Academy of Sciences.

DIALOG

Contents

Introduction

In all probability, a reader who picks up this book will do so reluctantly, thinking: *"oh no, not that again: another volume on the right to medically assisted procreation/abortion/euthanasia."* And if this reader decides to give it a try, he or she will probably do so just to find out what world-view stance the authors are trying to justify and what their objections to the developed lines of jurisprudence are. We must immediately disappoint such readers. Our book does not discuss how the boundaries of the right to medically assisted procreation, abortion and euthanasia should be set. For we do not know any better than the European Court of Human Rights (ECtHR, the Court) and we do not intend to define what the right to life and the right to privacy mean in these contexts. We refrain from assessing the correctness of the position taken in the ECtHR rulings in question. We will do so neither from the standpoint of European Convention on Human Rights (ECHR, Convention) standards, nor from a moral or political perspective.

The reasons that prompted us to analyse the Court's jurisprudence in selected groups of cases concerning moral issues arising in the public and scientific debate was the controversy surrounding their legal resolvability, or rather irresolvability, and their transgression of the boundaries of rationality in defining the limits and content of the right to decide about one's own life or the existence of human beings brought into the world. Thus, this is not a book analysing the jurisprudence from the perspective of the scope and content of the right to life or the right to privacy itself nor of their limits. Our work critically discusses the Court's jurisprudence in the respected areas even less.

Rather, its aim is tracking and tracing, demonstrating what the Court is actually trying to justify and what it is trying to convince us of as recipients of its rulings. To put it simply, this book does not focus on what the Court has ruled, but instead addresses the ways in which it seeks to convince audiences of its decisions in cases that are exceptionally complex, as they concern the deepest essence of humanity, with its attendant pain, fear and disappointed hope. Our intention was to explore how the Court carries out its argumentation.

The courts in general face a difficult task adjudicating cases that raise moral questions. Especially courts like the Court of Human Rights, which operates in conditions of pluralism of values, has a composition that is ideologically and

DOI: 10.4324/9781003375999-1

politically diverse, and is composed of judges representing various legal traditions and moral and social attitudes. At the same time, the Court addresses its judgments to a wide range of people from all European States, which are, after all, even more profoundly diverse.

Meanwhile, the advancement of medical science, as well as the changing attitude to the right to privacy and deciding about one's own life and the increase in the number of claims connected with it, mean that the jurisprudence in the areas selected by us is developing with particular dynamism in the present millennium. It has already been a significant group of judgments, which makes it possible to reconstruct certain patterns repetitively used by the Court argumentative tools, to find specific regularities in it and to develop a kind of classification of ways of reasoning. Consequently, we use our work to analyse judicial reasoning.

We acknowledge that the environment in which ECtHR judgments are delivered and where their justifications must fit in does not only consist of the domain of human rights as norms determining the status of individuals. It is also a world of universally accepted, even inherent, pluralism of values, with no single moral axiological order or universally accepted religious belief system. In a nutshell, it is the place where morals become a private issue. Thus, the limits of human freedom and privacy are set only by a norm – in our case, the norm of the Convention – and the limitation must be justified by the threat or violation of the legitimate aims indicated therein, behind which the world of certain universal values can be deciphered with some effort. What is more, it is also the world of pragmatism, in which the assessment of reality is based on quantifiable facts and supporting evidence, judgments concern real possibilities and the measure of actions is their effectiveness. Therefore, we found it extremely interesting to examine how the reasoning concerning the limits of human life – a value that is not only ultimate, but transcendent – is situated in this paradigm. Also, how do ECtHR judges find a consensual, universal, and at the same time pragmatic and axiologically neutral narrative on the scope and permissibility of the independent delimitation of life. We analyse whether the narrative contained in Court justifications reveals directions, paths or repetitive patterns of thinking concerning what a human being may do in relation to his or her own life and to human beings whom he or she has brought into the world – or is trying to bring into the world. This includes an analysis of whether the ECtHR's statements carry any ethical connotation, and how any such ethical connotation is structured – that is, to what arguments it appeals: are such arguments deontic or pragmatic (teleological); and do they refer to a certain axiological order, social practice or rather remain in a closed circle of self-referential legal norms of the Convention? And, finally, can the Court's justifications be treated as an attempt to set a certain moral minimum for the community of people under the ECtHR's jurisdiction in matters involving decisions on issues that are so difficult to argue and evoke the highest emotions?

One of the most intriguing questions which came up in the course of our study and which we tried to answer is: what is the relationship between the known and frequently described tools and methods of interpretation and ways of reasoning which in our assumptions play the role of convincing about the rightness of the accepted decision? Is it possible to define some kind of hierarchy between them (does interpretation precede argumentation, or is it the other way round) or is there any regularity in their co-application?

The analysis of judicial reasoning in the examined cases was carried out in order to find what arguments are used by the Court and what patterns and categories can be identified in this reasoning. For the purpose of such analysis, we drew on methods of research characteristic of rhetoric – the art of persuasion.

We have decided to select three groups of issues which, in our view, are associated with the greatest number of "unsolvable" problems in the light of current social and scientific debates. Accordingly, we focused our research on issues relating to medically assisted procreation, abortion and euthanasia. In these circumscribed areas, we have carefully picked rulings that are ground-breaking, trendsetting and, at the same time, well-known to the public and representatives of legal doctrine. However, our analysis should not be regarded as a comprehensive presentation of the Court's jurisprudence in the area under examination.

The focus of our analysis was the reasoning used by the Court to justify its decision. We sought to examine its external nature according to the terminology used by theorists of legal argumentation, which is presented in Chapter 1. In other words, to what extent it serves to convince the recipient. We revisited the interpretative tools used in the judgments, searching for argumentative devices in them. We have also attempted to find other, extra-legal patterns of argumentation that derive from a reliance on external, extra-legal reasoning. We studied their nature, recurrence in the judgments under review and the function they perform in terms of persuading the audience. Our approach stems from rhetoric and is therefore different from classically approached legal analyses of jurisprudence. This allowed us to distinguish three main groups of arguments: referring to authority, deontological and teleological. Thus, we singled out a set of rhetorical instruments appealing to external authority, relegating the burden of evaluation and valuation to the entity endowed with the attribute of being right by virtue of its authority or knowledge. The second category consists of arguments that remain within the ambit of the assessment of rightness based on the internal order of legal and human norms. The third group includes measures that appeal to the effects of adjudication, thus focusing on the analysis of social practice and projecting potential consequences. We have chosen to designate the most repetitive patterns or modes of argumentation used by the Court in order to persuade the addressee of its ruling rendered in morally sensitive cases as argumentative tools. However, we refer to these terms as argumentative patterns, devices, instruments or ways of argumentation interchangeably.

We also analyse whether the Court's preference for one or another argumentative tool leads to a limitation or expansion of the scope of the right at issue, whether it is possible to determine how the choice of tools of judicial reasoning affects the entire system of the conventional protection of human rights, and what it means for the predictability of the scope and content of the rights covered by the guarantees of the Convention, for the effectiveness of their judicial protection, the universal determination of their content and the proportionality of the limitations.

The search for answers to these questions has led us to this publication, which presents ways of judicial reasoning in three categories of cases. We show that interesting regularities can be found in the cases we reviewed, evidencing the use of specific argumentative ways and patterns for similar or identical purposes with similar intentions.

Our publication is divided into five chapters. The first two chapters introduce our theoretical assumptions and classification of ways of reasoning, as well as the issue of the relation between interpretative and rhetorical (argumentative) tools. In the following three chapters, which form the core of our study, we analyse the ECtHR's case law in three groups of cases: adjudication in cases concerning admissibility of medically assisted procreation, abortion and end-of-life situations. Each of these chapters starts with an overview of the range of cases and rulings analysed, which are then presented in a structured order according to the selected ways of judicial reasoning. At some points, the analysis is supplemented by threads raised by the arguments of the domestic courts, especially when these arguments exist in dialogue with the ECtHR rulings. Our work is rounded off with a conclusion on the function of the discussed tools of argumentation.

Even if the reader does not share our opinion as to the division of argumentation tools we have proposed, we hope that this study will provoke reflection and initiate open discussion on the rhetorical use of these tools in jurisprudence. Our particular selection of cases allowed us to show these argumentative devices from a unique angle. We believe that they can be found in a number of other cases as well, although the Court probably does not need to look that far and produce such far-reaching rhetorical devices in all of them. When it comes to the cases analysed in our book, the Court was confronted with the task of rationalising that which does not submit to rationality, of presenting the taboo in secular terms, and of finding a compromise between issues that are not subject to gradation and concession – to universalise something that is utterly particularistic and as personal as can be imagined. In our view, such matters also deserve to be analysed from this perspective.

We would like to thank all those who believed in our project, the reviewers and contributors during the first stage of our work who were available for more than two years to talk and read about our ideas and submitted their comments, questions and feedback. Special thanks go to Dr Daniel Fenwick for his extremely valuable comments made following the first editing of initial chapters of our work, and to Dr Adam Czarnota (UNSW) for his comments and guidance in the earlier stages of developing our concept. More than anything, however, we would like to thank Professor Celina Nowak, who was the first to believe in our idea and decided to make this project happen. Their knowledge, inquisitiveness and kindness were a great support to us. Finally, all potential mistakes and shortcomings are ours.

1 Challenges of judicial reasoning in beginning and end-of-life cases

The most sensitive cases

Even a cursory glance at social life lets us notice that certain cases decided by national and international courts stir up emotions to a far greater extent than others, usually those of greater practical relevance for the vast majority of people. Back in 2005, the whole world was witnessing the dispute over the life of Terri Schiavo; several years later, public opinion was following the case of Alfie Evans' parents' struggle to keep him alive. In 2019, masses of people took to the streets in Poland, outraged by the decision of the Constitutional Tribunal to declare the clause allowing the termination of pregnancy in the event of a fatal foetal abnormality to be unconstitutional. The wave of large-scale protests lasted for months, and yet the direct outcome and the problem itself in each of these cases concerns an extremely delicate situation, albeit of quite marginal significance for the majority of people. Deciding on such matters in court is challenging and requires penetrating not only the law, but the principles and values of people's and communities' lives as well. This makes it exceptionally difficult and responsible, but it is even more difficult to accomplish with legal reasoning. In cases involving the adjudication on interference in the beginning and end-of-life, disagreements on principles or conflicts of interest among members of the society are profound and conditioned by the most deeply rooted worldviews and moral views. This makes finding and even defining publicly proclaimed standards and moral or legal agreements on the limits of the rights to be decided upon an extremely delicate task.[1] At the same time, it is fascinating to see how the courts, and in particular the court established to resolve disputes under the European Convention on Human Rights (ECHR), attempt to find the determining factors and criteria to be applied and the values to be shared by the community when the cases raise such serious ethical and social controversies. In other words, how it tries to rationalise

1 Joseph Raz, "Why interpret." *Ratio Juris* 9(4) (1996): 350, Scott Veitch, *Moral Conflict and Legal Reasoning: Contradictions between Liberalism and Liberal Legalism,* (Hart Publishing, 1996), 191–199; Judith Shklar writes about the ideology of agreement, see Judith Shklar, *Legalism,* (Harvard University Press, 1964), 101, 106.

DOI: 10.4324/9781003375999-2

what does not lend itself to rationalisation and find consensus where it seems there are only serious controversies. At the same time, judges do not always articulate the substantive reasons which justify their conclusion[2] and even tend to avoid it, which is perfectly clear from the reasoning of those cases.

The purpose of our book is to identify the ways of legal reasoning adopted by the European Court of Human Rights (ECtHR) in judgments which contain an element of defining the limits of the right to decide about the beginning or end of human life. Judgments concerning the termination of life not resulting from natural death and undergoing medically assisted procreation and abortion have been commented on numerous times, therefore it is not our intention to analyse them or to assess their compliance with a chosen legal or moral standard. Instead, our study deals with tools of argumentation, in particular concerning the limits of life within the framework of the right to self-determination – an element of personal/bodily autonomy and right to privacy. The common denominator in these cases is the definition of the limit of an autonomous decision to live one's own life or that of a person one calls into the world, which touches directly upon human life and the obligation to protect it.

The issue of life and its meaning is both highly controversial and closely linked to dignity[3], a fundamental category of human rights. Not only does it address the termination or inception of life itself, but also its evaluation and assessment of the social significance of the decision to interfere with its course. What constitutes a life worth protecting and what does not, what are the limits of human autonomy in deciding about one's own life and that of others, and who has the right to make such judgments[4] – these are fundamental questions not only for the order of human rights, but also for the existence of human society governed by certain rules.

The transcendental nature of life and death in human culture meant that the area of deciding about life and death used to be considered taboo until recently. It was a deep and fundamental cultural prohibition, the violation of which could threaten the entire social and axiological structure[5] – the fabric necessary for the continued existence of a given community. The preservation of life as a value with a metaphysical context, a destiny beyond human intentions[6], was classically excluded not only from the interference of the courts, but of any entity, which was a fundamental principle of modern legal cultures. On the other hand, human autonomy, and thus the ability to decide about

2 John Bell, *Policy Arguments in Judicial Decisions,* (Oxford University Press, 1983), 35.
3 Michael Rosen, *Dignity: Its History and Meaning,* (Harvard University Press, 2012), 6–7.
4 Alain Zysset, *The ECHR and Human Rights Theory: Reconciling the Moral and Political Conceptions,* (Routledge Research in Human Rights Law, 2016), 4, James Griffin, *On Human Rights,* (Oxford University Press, 2008), 33.
5 Michael Perry, *Toward a Theory of Human Rights: Religion, Law, Courts,* (Cambridge University Press, 2008), 12.
6 Charles J. Dougherty, "The common good, terminal illness and euthanasia." *Issues in Law and Medicine* 9(2) (1993–1994): 159.

oneself, implies the right to decide about the end of one's own life or about parenthood. The progress of medicine and the rapid evolution of social and moral attitudes towards life and death decisions have resulted in the law stepping in where, until now, religion and unquestionable social norms ruled indivisibly, addressing the taboo mentioned above.

Both sides of this equation, that is the protection of life and the right to self-determination, are cornerstones of the human rights order. Protecting them is a fundamental objective of the European Convention on Human Rights. Therefore, when these two values and rights collide, incredibly serious controversies arise with advocates defending each of them. The legal framework under which the cases in question are decided is extremely simple and laconic in terms of the Convention. It consists of the rights guaranteed by Articles 2 and 8 of the ECHR, respectively. The right to life, guaranteed first in the ECHR order,[7] is also guaranteed by the constitutional norms of most contemporary States.[8] Prohibition of interference in matters of termination of life is affirmed explicitly in Protocol No. 6 and Protocol No. 13 of the ECHR by outlawing the death penalty, indicating a closed link to respect for inalienable human dignity.[9] In turn, individual freedom and autonomy enjoys protection under Article 8 of the Convention as a fundamental component of the right to privacy,[10] the meaning of which has evolved and continues to develop dynamically and expand in scope. The right to privacy is also strongly emphasised

7 Article 2. Right to life:

1 Everyone's right to life shall be protected by law. No one shall be deprived of his life intentionally save in the execution of a sentence of a court following his conviction of a crime for which this penalty is provided by law.
2 Deprivation of life shall not be regarded as inflicted in contravention of this Article when it results from the use of force which is no more than absolutely necessary:

a in defence of any person from unlawful violence;
b in order to effect a lawful arrest or to prevent the escape of a person lawfully detained;
c in action lawfully taken for the purpose of quelling a riot or insurrection.

8 By way of example, the constitutional norms guaranteeing the protection of life include: Article 23 of the Belgian Constitution, § 7 of the Finnish Constitution, Article 6 of the Charter of Fundamental Rights of the Czech Republic, Article 5(2) of the Greek Constitution, Article 15 of the Spanish Constitution, Article 40(3)(2) of the Irish Constitution, Article 2 of the German Constitution, Article 24(1) of the Portuguese Constitution or Article 38 of the Polish Constitution.

9 Preamble: *The member States of the Council of Europe, signatory hereto, Convinced that everyone's right to life is a basic value in a democratic society and that the abolition of the death penalty is essential for the protection of this right and for the full recognition of the inherent dignity of all human beings . . .*

10 Art. 8. Right to respect for private and family life:

1 Everyone has the right to respect for his private and family life, his home and his correspondence.
2 There shall be no interference by a public authority with the exercise of this right except such as is in accordance with the law and is necessary in a democratic society in the interests of national security, public safety or the economic well-being of the country, for the prevention of disorder or crime, for the protection of health or morals, or for the protection of the rights and freedoms of others.

and guaranteed in constitutional orders.[11] The evolution of the scope of this right in ECtHR jurisprudence has led to the inclusion of a very wide range of elements into the Article 8 guarantee,[12] including an individual's physical and social identity and the right to personal development, and to establish and develop relationships with other human beings and the outside world.[13] Hence the content of the right to privacy has been shaped to encompass the right to decide about one's own body and life (both in the physical sense and in the sense of family life), which leaves a great deal of room for interpretation.

Both these rights belong to the unquestionable[14] and fundamental rights since the beginning of the modern human rights system.[15] At the same time, however, neither the Convention nor the Constitutional norms provide answers to the questions of how to solve the dilemma when the values they guarantee collide. Thus, the openness of the norms of human rights places individual decisions in the courts' hands, including the ECtHR, which is tasked with indicating their scope and assessing whether the interference with the law was justified. But the openness of these norms also causes jurisprudence to reveal certain helplessness in resolving such disputes, where, as A. Zysset puts it, the room for disagreement is exponential and there is a need to respond to practice.[16]

It is not always possible to balance social, moral, or customary norms with the interests and rights of persons who wish – and are, according to their own judgment, entitled – to decide on their own life or the life of another being they bring into existence within the framework of the guaranteed right to privacy, on account of the protection of the rights of persons other than the

11 The protection of private life is guaranteed among others under Article 22 of the Belgian Constitution, Article 18 of the Spanish Constitution or the general right of personality under Articles 5(2), 13 and 1(2) and 2(1) of the West German Basic Law, Article 47 and others of the Polish Constitution.

12 Among many others: B. v. France, appl. no. 13343/87, judgment of 25.03.1992, par. 63; Burghartz v. Switzerland, appl. no. 16213/90, ECtHR judgment of 22.02.1994, par. 24; Dudgeon v. the United Kingdom, appl. no. 7525/76, judgment of 22.10.1981, par. 41; and Laskey, Jaggard and Brown v. the United Kingdom, appl. nos. 21627/93, 21826/93, 21974/93, judgment of 19.02.1997, par. 36.

13 Mikulić v. Croatia, appl. no. 53176/99, judgment of 7.02.2002, par. 53, Friedl v. Austria, appl. no. 15225/89, report of the European Commission of Human Rights on 19.05.1994, par. 44.

14 It should also be mentioned that the right to life is guaranteed under Article 2 as an absolute right, while the right to privacy (like the other rights protected under Articles 9 to 11 of the Convention) may be subject to limitations meeting the conditions indicated in paragraph 2 of Article 8. That is, in cases provided for by law and meeting the proportionality test, namely necessary in a democratic society for the protection of legitimate aims: national security, public safety or the economic well-being of the country, the protection of order and the prevention of crime, the protection of health and morals, or the protection of the rights and freedoms of persons.

15 It is worth mentioning that they are already granted under the Universal Declaration of Human Rights of 1948, which in Article 3 declares every human being's right to life, liberty and security of person, and in Article 12 the prohibition of arbitrary interference with one's private and family life.

16 Zysset, *The ECHR and Human Rights Theory*, 4.

person concerned. Consequently, there is a tension between two parties: the autonomous individual as a subject of rights versus the community, sometimes demanding that this autonomy be limited in the decision to live. This in turn means that the position of the court, which must give greater weight to the interests of one of the parties, is extremely difficult to justify and substantiate within a judicial decision. Courts, particularly the European Court of Human Rights which is called upon to decide on complaints concerning such cases, are therefore forced to use subtle and complicated ways of reasoning based on repeated arguments. These arguments are also present in other ECtHR rulings, often deriving from well-known interpretative devices and methods. However, we attempt to show that they are particularly evident in situations of substantiating judgments of great weight involving a particular clash of interests and values, with the simultaneous attempt on the part of the Court to avoid taking a clear position on issues of moral character.

We try to demonstrate that the ways of legal reasoning applied in such sensitive cases are quite unique and evident precisely in those selected cases, where the conflict of arguments and the necessity to explain what escapes rationalisation is particularly present and clearly visible. We will try to show that ways of reasoning draw on interpretive as well as rhetorical methods. This will allow us to look at some interpretive instruments as not only targeted to interpretation of legal norms themselves, but primarily as tools of explanation and justification of the Court's decisions. The ways of reasoning presented herein largely deviate from pure deduction and legal syllogism in order to convince of the decision made by referring to commonplaces and pragmatic arguments, appealing to basic and neutral criteria: duty of care, protection of common sense and recognising shared community standards. It is therefore legal and extra-legal reasoning, rationalising things that are extremely difficult to reason about – that is, transcendental and ethical issues. In this way, interpretation begins to concern not only law but also social practice,[17] and the meaning given to human rights replaces the ethical order in the world of pragmatic, liberal and secularised values.[18] It is also an expression of a restrained – often without even taking a stand on merits – yet consensual search for boundaries,[19] finding not only what is explainable, but also what is acceptable at the time of judgment, often with an indication of, or an attempt to indicate, the evolution of the law to which the judgment relates.

17 Ronald Dworkin, "Social rules and legal theory." *Yale Law Journal* 81 (1972): 860–867; Ronald Dworkin, *Taking Rights Seriously*, (Bloomsbury Publishing, 2013), 77.

18 Romuald Haule, "Some reflections on the foundation of human rights – Are human rights an alternative to moral values?" *Max Planck Yearbook of United Nations Law* 10 (2006): 369, 377, https://doi:10.1163/187574106X00083.

19 Jean-Paul Costa, "On the legitimacy of the European court of human rights' judgments." *European Constitutional Law Review* 7(2) (2011): 177.

Legal reasoning in morally sensitive cases – an outline of its structure and functions

Legal reasoning has become a focus of both philosophy and jurisprudence – as well as a basis for research in specific disciplines of law. As we understand it, it is an action of the court based on the interpretation of norms, which at the same time constitutes practical legal argumentation, towards particular understanding of legal text as a special reason (justification) for a legal decision.[20] For that reason, the interpretation made by the court performs an argumentative function, since the conclusions of that reasoning must be acceptable by the audience or constituency to which such argumentation is directed.[21] Reflecting on legal reasoning requires recognising its components, that is constructing the facts, framing the case, setting the standard of review,[22] describing the applicable principle or test used by the court to reach its decision, as well as parsing the precedent and determining the meaning and extent of the subsequent impact. It is not just a matter of presenting a solution based on a purely logical analysis following strictly defined rules by means of strictly specified premises. The purpose of legal reasoning is to present an argument to convince the audience (and so it also performs a rhetorical function) of the correctness of the decision taken and its elements. This premise describes legal reasoning particularly well regarding the application of human rights, which are open-ended and do not allow for the employment of linguistic or systemic methods as a sufficient solution. In this case, we do not have a fully coherent set of axioms.[23] The methods of the syllogism and its structure are therefore completely inadequate.[24] Courts, especially the ECtHR, are forced to argue more in dialogue, showing arguments, values, principles, and interests and weighing them to convince people of their decisions.[25] Furthermore, there are no universally successful solutions that can convince everyone, so the choice of methods and techniques is particularly interesting.

20 Neil MacCormick, "Argumentation and interpretation in law." *Ratio Juris* 6(1) (1993): 16.

21 Chaim Perelman, "Law and rhetoric." in Chaim Perelman, Harold J. Berman *Justice, Law and Argument. Essays on Moral and Legal Reasoning* (Springer Dordrecht, 1980), 120–121, https://doi.org/10.1007/978-94-009-9010-4; Miami Paso, "Rhetoric meets rational argumentation theory." *Ratio Juris* 27(2) (2014): 236; Donald H. Hermann, "Legal reasoning as argumentation." *Northern Kentucky Law Review* 12(3) (1985): 510. More about attitudes of judges who do not always articulate the substantive reasons which justify their conclusion. See: Bell, *Policy Arguments in Judicial Decisions*, 35.

22 Patricia Wald, "The rhetoric of results and the results of rhetoric." *University of Chicago Law Review* 62(4) (1995): 1386, 1391–1392, 1395–1397.

23 Chaim Perelman, *The New Rhetoric and the Humanities. Essays on Rhetoric and its Applications* (Springer Netherlands, 1979), 10; Hermann, "Legal Reasoning." 471.

24 Paso, "Rhetoric." 237. Neil MacCormick, *Legal Reasoning and Legal Theory*, (Oxford University Press, 1994), 100; Aleksander Peczenik, *The Basis of Legal Justification*, (Lund University Press, 1983), 45–6.

25 Bartosz Brożek, Jerzy Stelmach, *Metody prawnicze*, (Wolter Kluwer, 2006), 167–8; Evelin Feteris, Harm Kloosterhuis, "Law and argumentation theory: Theoretical approaches to legal justification." *SSRN Electronic Journal* (2013), http://dx.doi.org/10.2139/ssrn.2283092.

As R. Alexy argues, legal reasoning must follow the rules of practical discourse while drawing on principles common to the empirical and analytical sciences.[26] When purely legal rules do not suffice, legal discourse must resort to the rules of general practical discourse, through which validity and rationality can be attained,[27] or rather demonstrated. This theory of legal reasoning makes it possible to reconstruct its procedural conditions, crucial for analysing and assessing the correctness and usefulness of reasoning as the ability to persuade an audience. Reflecting on legal reasoning requires recognising its components, that is, constructing the facts, framing the case, setting the standard of review,[28] describing the applicable principle or test used by the court to reach its decision, as well as parsing the precedent and determining the meaning and extent of the subsequent impact. According to Alexy[29] and similarly MacCormick, justification proceeds simultaneously on two levels: internal, which is deductive and logical, though invariably equipped with a system of values, which serve as pillars of justification; and external,[30] which justifies why these particular norms have been selected.[31] The assumptions often come from outside the legal system, where the material aspects are central. Checking whether the formal findings can be considered acceptable consists in demonstrating the validity of these findings from the internal point of view.[32] In our study, we seek to examine legal reasoning primarily from the perspective of external justification, which, in our view, largely dominates argumentation. Consequently, interpretation and its tools are used to convince (justify) far more often than used to be the case. Arguments derived from interpretative methods serve to demonstrate the validity and acceptability of the decisions taken and are subordinate to them. The nerve of presented justifications, as

26 Robert Alexy, *Theorie des juristischen Argumentation. Die Theorie des rationalen Diskurses als Theorie des juristischen Begrundung*, (Frankfurt am Mein, 1991), 225–32; Brożek, Stelmach, *Metody . . .*, 195–96,

27 Robert Alexy distinguished five types of rules: fundamental rules, rules of reason, rules on the burden of argumentation, rules of rationale and rules of transition. Aulis Aarnio, Robert Alexy, Aleksander Peczenik, “Grundlagen der juristischen Argumentation.” in Werner Krawietz, Robert Alexy, *Metatheorie juristischer Argumentation*, (Wolter Kluwer, 1983), 42.

28 Wald, “The rhetoric.” 1386, 1391–2, 1395–7.

29 Alexy, *Theorie des juristischen*, 285.

30 Herbert L.A. Hart, Leslie Green, *The Concept of Law*, (Oxford University Press, 2012), 89–90, 104; Aulis Aarnio, *On legal reasoning*, (Turku, 1977); Robert Alexy, Neil MacCormick, *Rhetoric and the Rule of law. A Theory of Legal Reasoning*, (Oxford University Press 2005); Aleksander Peczenik, *On Law and Reason*, (Kluwer, 1989); Jerzy Wróblewski *Legal Syllogism and Rationality of Judicial Decision*, (Rechtstheorie, 1974), see more: Paso, “Rhetoric.” 238.

31 Paso, “Rhetoric.” 239.

32 Alexy identifies six groups of rules and forms of external justification: 1) rules and forms of interpretation of law, 2) dogmatic interpretation, 3) lawmaking judgments, 4) practical argumentation, 5) empirical argumentation and 6) special forms of legal arguments (such as *a simili, a contrario, a fortiori, ad absurdum*). Alexy, *Theorie de Juristischen*, 285 et seq; Stelmach, Brożek, *Metody prawnicze*, 197, similarly Feteris, Kloosterhuis, “Law and argumentation theory.” 13–4.

we strive to prove herein, is not deduction and syllogism, but a reasoned and acceptable solution of interpretative problems, and presentation of a coherent version capable of convincing to the adopted solution.[33] This means that courts are not actually explaining reality – facts and legal rules – but creating a story about how the facts and allegations put forward can be presented in a way that will support their decision.[34] However, this type of legal reasoning – based on acceptability and belief in the fairness of the decision taken – requires a connection to the accepted standards in place in the socio-cultural community to which it applies,[35] and thus the values that this community shares. When understood as an argumentative action, legal reasoning harbours a certain element of moralistic assumption.[36] Making the right decision requires identification of a "particular conception of community morality as decisive of legal issues; this conception holds that community morality is the political morality presupposed by the law and institutions of the community."[37] It is therefore necessary to define public morality and to reach a certain agreement as to its content.[38] This problem remains to be solved, especially in the cases we are about to address. That is why it will be all the more interesting to analyse how the Court (and national courts) seek to recognise and protect this conviction of a minimum moral community. These issues are not always presented directly, resulting in reconstruction problems in a special category of cases of an exceptionally difficult nature.

So, let us pause for a moment and think about the use of this category in the process of judicial reasoning.

33 Elizabeth Fajans, Mary R. Falk, "Against the tyranny of paraphrase: Talking back to texts." *Cornell Law Review* 78 (1993): 163–74 (citing J. A. Berlin, "Contemporary composition: The major pedagogical theories." in *The Writing Teacher's Sourcebook*, eds. Gary Tate, Edward P.J. Corbett, (Oxford University Press, 1988), 47, 55–8).

34 Dworkin writes about moral reasoning. According to him, it is interpretation, but it is not collaborative or explanatory interpretation. It belongs to conceptual interpretation. As he further wrote: *we account for agreement and disagreement about cases not by finding shared criteria of application but by supposing shared practices in which these concepts figure . . . we develop conceptions of these concepts through interpretation*. R Dworkin, *Justice for Hedgehogs*, (Harvard University Press, 2013), 157, 180.

35 These two criteria should be met in parallel in a just argument: 1) anthropologic-relativists – argumentation must be in agreement with the standards applied in the community where the argumentation takes place; 2) critical – rationalistic – argumentation must correspond to rules of discussion that are conducive to the solution of a difference of opinion and acceptable to the parties involved. The first leads to the epistemo-rhetorical approach (identification of the kind of audience that will accept the arguments, what beliefs, customs are shared), the second – pragma-dialectical (ideal model of discussion, need to be constructive in expression). Frans H. van Eemeren, Rob Groothenhorst, *A Systematic Theory of Argumentation*, (Cambridge University Press, 2004), 18–20.

36 Hermann, "Legal Reasoning." 467–8.

37 Dworkin, *Taking Rights Seriously*, 154.

38 Dworkin requires that the validity of such a consensus be examined, (ibidem 251–61).

Morality and the difficulty of using this category by the courts

As far as the legal reasoning of the judgments under review is concerned, it is particularly complicated to apply such standards and values – and, at the same time, it is inevitable to make certain moral assessment on account of the need to decide on an issue belonging to the sphere of the limits of human life. This lies at the heart of moral considerations and judgments in any axiological order. It raises fundamental moral questions, believed by many philosophers to be based on religious grounds, including: Who are we? Where do we come from? What is our origin, our beginning? As well as: Where and how does our destiny manifest itself? What should our end be and what is the meaning of suffering? And finally: What value is there in human life; does it ultimately have meaning or not?[39]

Such an assessment is not confined to declaring the right and wrong of a particular act of an individual person: the applicant. It is, admittedly, an extremely difficult assessment, though not the only one. The assessment to be made when adjudicating these cases is much more in-depth and must reach far into the future. It is, first of all, the assessment of existing moral attitudes, which are accepted and recognised as the fabric of society, but also the assessment of how the possible outcome will affect further attitudes and the shape of social life.

Although the premise of morality as a legitimate aim of restricting rights and freedoms is explicitly expressed not only in the ECHR[40] but also in a number of constitutional orders and in the legislation of many States, the ECtHR's comments on morality are sporadic and cautious. Truth be told, the notion of morals appears in numerous judgments, although rather as an indication of a certain background of the solution, indicating that the problem has a moral nature in addition to the legal one, and the Court hardly ever elaborates on this thought.[41] The concept of morals or public morals appears in judgments in the context of quoting norms of national legislation[42] or an international

39 Perry, *Toward a Theory*, 12.

40 The clause is referred to in articles 6.1, 8.2., 9.2, 10.2 and 11.2 concerning, respectively, the right to a fair trial, the right to respect for "private and family life, the freedom of thought, conscience and religion, the freedom of expression, and the freedom of assembly and association. Moreover, the clause is mentioned at art 2.3 of the Fourth Additional Protocol to the Convention, concerning freedom of movement. Connected to health, and the connection is not accidental (the mentally ill, homosexuals). Renee Koering-Joulin "Public Morals." in *The European Convention for the Protection of Human Rights: International Protection Versus National Restrictions*, ed. Mireille Delmas-Marty, (Martinus Nijhoff Publishers, 1992), 83.

41 The term "morals" was found in 5,654 records in the ECtHR database HUDOC; the term "public morals" was found in 145 records.

42 Miljević v. Croatia, appl. no. 68317/13, judgment of 25.06.2020, par. 3; Kahadawa Arachchige and Others v. Cyprus, appl. nos. 16870/11, 16874/11 and 16879/11, judgment of 19.06.2018, par. 36 in reference to the provisions of the Aliens and Immigration Law; Sekmadienis Ltd. v. Lithuania, appl. no. 69317/14, judgment of 30.01.2018 (with multiple references to the concept in judgments, decisions, opinions of national authorities); Kącki v. Poland, appl. no. 10947/11, judgment of 4.07.2017, par. 21, also Kania v. Poland, appl. no. 49132/11, judgment of 19.07.2016, par. 31; Maciejewski v. Poland, appl. no. 34447/05, judgment of 13.01.2015, paras 48, 51, Cichopek and others v. Poland, appl. nos. 15189/10, 16970/10, 17185/10, 18215/10, 18848/10, 19152/10, 19915/10, 20080/10,

agreement it appears in.[43] The notion is also often quoted as having been used by one of the parties to the proceedings.[44] It does appear in the arguments of judges submitting dissenting opinions, too.[45]

In principle, the Court uses the concept of morals as referred to in the Convention when pointing to the need to recognise local determinants that necessitate protection on account of this legitimate aim. In the judgments on morally sensitive issues analysed in our monograph, the premise of morality is generally never directly used as a justification for limiting the rights and freedoms of individuals.

In a handful of judgments, the Court has commented on the applicability of morals as a legitimate aim, under Articles 8, 9 and 10 of the Convention. This was the case in the freedom of expression case (*Handyside v. UK*[46]), which gave rise to the doctrine of the margin of appreciation. On morality (in the sense of mores), the ECtHR expressed itself in this doctrine very cautiously, developing an approach which accepted the discretion of the State in this respect.[47] In *Müller and Others v. Switzerland*,[48] the Court indicated that the adjective "necessary (in democratic society)" implies the existence of a "pressing social need," thus indirectly connecting it to the issue of common

20705/10, 20725/10, 21259/10, 21270/10, 21279/10, 21456/10, 22603/10, 22748/10 and 23217/10; ECtHR decision of 14.05.2013, paras 94–6 (reffering to Polish Constitutional Court conclusions), Gukovych v. Ukraine, appl. no. 2204/07, judgment of 20.10. 2016, par. 28; Djundiks v. Latvia, appl. no. 14920/05, judgment of 15.04.2014, par. 37; Ciulla v. Italy, appl. no. 11152/84, judgment of 22.02.1989, par. 19.

43 Article 22 of the American Convention on Human Rights. See: Garib v. the Netherlands, appl. no. 43494/09, judgment of 6.11.2017, par. 94.

44 Samsonov v. Russia, ECtHR judgment of 9 June 2020, appl. no. 38427/11, par. 21 (government's reasoning); Beizaras and Levickas v. Lithuania, ECtHR judgment of 14 January 2020, appl. no. 41288/15, par. 148, third-party argumentation; Unifaun Theatre Productions Limited and Others v. Malta, ECtHR judgment of 15 May 2018, appl. no. 37326/13, par. 69 – government's reasoning; Dubská and Krejzová v. the Czech Republic ECtHR judgment of 15 November 2016, appl. nos. 28859/11 and 28473/12, par. 91 – the applicants' argumentation; Oliari and Others v. Italy ECtHR judgment of 21 July 2015, appl. nos. 18766/11 and 36030/11, par. 120 – applicants arguments; X. v. the United Kingdom, Decision of the Commission of 03 March 1978, appl. no. 7525/76, arguments of both parties based on the nomenclature used in British law.

45 Navalny v. Russia, appl. nos. 29580/12 and four others, judgment of 15.11.2018, par. 10. It is worth noting that the use of this concept appears particularly frequently and vividly in the dissenting opinions of Judge Sajo: Babiarz v. Poland, appl. no. 1955/10, judgment of 10.01.2017, par. 16 dissenting opinion by Judge Sajo; Parillo v. Italy, appl. no. 46470/11, judgment of 27.08.2015, dissenting opinion by Judge Sajo, par. 5; Hämäläinen v. Finland, appl. no. 37359/09, judgment of 16.07.2014, joint dissenting opinion of Judges Sajó, Keller and Lemmens, par. 13.

46 Handyside v. United Kingdom, appl. no. 5493/72, judgment of 7.12.1976.

47 "It is not possible to find in the domestic law of the various Contracting States a uniform European conception of morals" (par. 48).

48 Müller et al. v. Switzerland, appl. no. 10737/84, judgment of 24 .05.1988, paras. 30 and 39.

shared values and attitudes.[49] The Court reached a similar conclusion many years later in *Islamische Religionsgemeinschaft E.V. v. Germany*.[50]

The Court upheld the position on pressing social need and margin of appreciation in cases concerning private life, including *Dudgeon v. UK*,[51] defining morals as the "moral ethos or moral standards of a society as a whole,"[52] forming the "moral fabric of society" and, at the same time, refraining from making any value-judgment as to the morality of challenged activities.[53] Conversely, in *Laskey, Mr Jaggard and Mr Brown v. UK*,[54] the Court *did not find it necessary to determine* whether the interference with the applicant's right to privacy could have been justified on the ground of the protection of morals. At the same time, this finding should not be understood as calling into question the prerogative of the State on moral grounds to seek to deter acts of the kind in question. In its most recent judgment in the *Sekmadienis* case,[55] the Court acknowledged that in the area of morals, neither a European nor an international consensus had been developed.[56]

In the aforementioned cases, there is a trend towards creation of a well-established case law in which the Court justifies its rulings with reference to moral grounds, accords to the States a wide margin of appreciation, and thus leaves the final assessment of moral or customary (decent) behaviour to national legislatures and jurisdictions. The Court acknowledges the existence of a locally established benchmark of morality and, by extension, the right of domestic authorities to take measures and define the limits of permissible interference. The Court avoids (using the phrase "it is not necessary," for instance) any approximation or even interpretation of the concept and scope of morality. It is also notable that while applying the premise of morality, the Court often turns to the argument of protecting certain group of persons, usually weaker, unprepared or defenceless – and as such more vulnerable, such as children or juveniles.[57]

The reasons for this reluctance to present a concept of morality are quite obvious. The first is the ideological assumption of liberalism, which excludes the application of a single and unified moral order existing in society, assuming a wide range of individual freedom. The concept of morality – as a system of universally shared views on what is right and wrong, and therefore also the

49 Par. 32.
50 Islamische Religionsgemeinschaft E.V. v. Germany, appl. no. 53871/00, ECtHR decision of 5.12.2002, 12.
51 Dudgeon v. UK, paras. 51, 52.
52 Par. 47.
53 Par. 54, 57.
54 Laskey, Jaggard and Brown v. UK, appl. nos. 21627/93, 21628/93 and 21974/93, judgment of 19.02.1997, par. 51.
55 Sekmadienis Ltd v. Lithuania, appl. no. 69317/14, judgment of 30.01.2018.
56 Sekmadienis Ltd v. Lithuania, par. 55.
57 Koering. "Public Morals." 87. Handyside v. the UK par. 52, indirectly: Muller v. Switzerland, (age-free admission to an exhibition, par. 36).

stigmatisation of behaviour considered reprehensible in society for reasons other than an explicit prohibition by law – is regarded with suspicion as being ideologically motivated. The risk of revealing one's worldview, the risk of ***moral majoritarianism*** in the world of equitable (recognised as equal) attitudes and views on morality, is therefore the source of the difficulties here. The only truly justifiable reason for restricting the enjoyment of a sphere of freedom or right in the light of the liberal conception of society is the harm suffered by other people, so it is hardly surprising that the legitimate aim incorporating this thought, namely "the protection of the rights and freedoms of others," is most often referred to by the Court in the judgments discussed in this book.

A decision of the Court permitting limits to a right on grounds of protecting morals would inevitably result in interference with the autonomy of the individual, being inevitably arbitrary as based on the moral views and assessments, which also take into account the ideological and political views of judge.[58] Furthermore, such a determination would require finding a compromise – a shared mindset among the judges sitting in the Court – and agreement as to the decision and shared justification, and this proves to be extremely difficult in the panel representing different viewpoints.

Finally, such cases, in which it comes to reflecting on the need to limit the rights of the individual due to the protection of the interest of the community as well as for the sake of protecting the world of common shared values, most clearly expose the clash of two attitudes: individualistic and, on the opposite side, sociocentric,[59] according to which every community is equipped with certain moral standards the observance of which is unconditionally required by the society conceived as a coherent whole, and any infringement thereof, even if it is not an attack against the person directly harmed, is an act against the whole of society and is detrimental to its foundations. These attitudes towards what morality is and what duties or rights it imposes on people, as well as towards the scope of the power of the State authorities, are irreconcilable. A fragile compromise can only be reached by reducing the role of the State to identifying the social norms that members of society actually consider moral

58 Dworkin, *Taking Rights Seriously*, 151.

59 This rift was outlined with extraordinary clarity in the discussion of the Report of the Departmental Committee on Homosexual Offences and Prostitution (the so-called Wolfenden Report) by Lord Patrick Devlin (Patrick Devlin, "Morals and the Criminal Law"); in Patrick Devlin, *The Enforcement of Morals* (Oxford University Press, 1970); and the polemic by Herbert L.A Hart, who starting from the purist foundations of liberalism, argued that the only reason for the restriction of individual rights could be self-defence, and that the disintegration referred to by Devlin is an abstract creation, unproven by experience – and may even be a desirable effect. See, Herbert L.A. Hart, *Law, Liberty and Morality* (Oxford University Press, 1982). Kamil Jesiołowski, "The Concept of Public Morality of Lord Patrick Devlin and the Jurisprudence of the European Court of Human Rights." *Archiwum Filozofii Prawa i Filozofii Społecznej* 1 (22) (2020), 37–51, https://doi.org/10.36280/AFPiFS.2020.1.37.

and enforcing these norms.[60] It is obviously an incredibly challenging, even crippling task in today's world. And the ECtHR's judgments in this type of case must deal with this predicament.

The reasons previously outlined clearly reveal one fundamental doubt: whether moral issues can be presented as objective and susceptible to legal reasoning at all. The legislator puts this legitimate aim in the hands of judges by means of an open-ended phrase, appealing to an even transcendent order, far beyond the text of law. The court becomes a legislator to a greater degree than in other situations. It must discover the meaning of a norm of an intrinsically extra-legal origin and character. The reasoning of the court reflected in the judgment, and thus the argumentative methods employed, must be persuasive and consistent with the sentiments echoed by all members of the community. The judgment is made not on behalf of the judges themselves, but on behalf of society as a whole, the State. Therefore, the court does not judge whether something is moral according to its individual criteria, but rather whether certain behaviours and norms within society are moral with the aim of preserving the social fabric (preserving cultural and moral patterns, trust, loyalty, respect, harmonious coexistence). In other words, it is not a moral judgment similar to the one we make individually. It has the *erga omnes* dimension and its effects extend far beyond the assessment of individual behaviour. It relates to the decision on whether such behaviour should be permitted in society. The judgment pronounced in the ruling must, in view of the openness and indeterminacy of the concept of morality, satisfy certain qualities: it must be predictable, rational and reflect a social view, and, finally, it must constitute a reasoning in the name of the whole society.[61]

The next problem is of a more technical nature, but, despite this designation, it is an insurmountable and fundamentally important issue even more so than those previously mentioned. It is the impossibility of making a logical and rational argument in matters concerning morality in general.[62] Considerable attention has been paid to the issue of the mind's helplessness and inability to rationally explain what we are intuitively or emotionally sure of, brilliantly described by D. Hume in the past[63] and more recently by J. Haidt, among others.[64] Moral assessment and its justification are two separate processes. Assessment (usually instantaneous and intuitive) must be rationalised;

60 Broadly clarified (among others) in: Patrick Devlin "Law, Democracy and Morality." *University of Pennsylvania Law Review* 110(5) (1962).

61 Jeremy Waldron, "Judges as moral reasoners." *International Constitutional Law Review* 7(1) (2009): 19.

62 Koering-Joulin "*Public Morals*." 83, 97. The author writes about essentially flexible and relative concept and logical fuzzines of the concept.

63 David Hume, *A Treatise of Human Nature. Book III: Morals*, The Project Gutenberg eBook 2002, www.gutenberg.org/files/4705/4705-h/4705-h.htm#link2H_4_0083.

64 Jonathan Haidt, *The Righteous Mind: Why Good People are Divided by Politics and Religion*, (Knopf Doubleday Publishing Group, 2012).

that is, explained. But this rationalisation is derivative and sometimes unreliable. This is perfectly evident in formal situations, such as judicial decisions, where the elucidation of the grounds for an action is characterised by longing for deontology of clearly defined rules, a system of overriding imperatives and prohibitions elicited by careful reasoning.[65] However, such deontology sometimes fails due to the impossibility of reconstructing a coherent system of principles that would provide basis for the solution. This is clearly visible when the right to life is confronted with the human right to self-determination in extreme situations, such as when the collision concerns values which are difficult to resolve using a neutral worldview: the protection of life *per se* and the right to self-determination.

However, the substantive and technical difficulties mentioned here cannot obscure the necessity to justify the delimitation of the realisation of human rights and to find the best reasons to support and justify the limits and content of institutional human rights protection system.[66] Occasionally, such a justification is unavoidable[67] in an international court setting. As Zysset puts it:

> The human rights . . . concretisation in the case law implies that the ECtHR addresses and specifies their underlying interests in substantive terms. Judicial law specifies the normative content of human rights. As a result, the normative basis that serves the role played by ECtHR law is already within the realm of practice as a form of justification the qua judicial reasoning.[68]

As Dworkin noted, the very claims based on these rights constitute a kind of moral judgment about what the State authorities should do.[69] Human rights, on the other hand, have replaced references to morals in public discourse for years now, referring to them as ideologically dubious and unclear. It is much safer and more acceptable to say that a particular course of action violates human rights than that it is immoral. Such a practice is used very often nowadays. The European Convention on Human Rights is, in practice, the most comprehensive judicial implementation of the liberal concept of human rights in the contemporary world. At the same time, the ECtHR case law is a constant search for a consensual vision of individual interests for all people living in States – interests embodied in the claims of applicants. Finding such a common, acceptable agreement on the limits of the right to decide about one's own life and a life brought into existence is a sensitive issue and

65 For more on the need to rationalise moral judgments in a situation of disagreement about the moral sensitivity, see Jurgen Habermas, *Truth and Justification*, (The MIT Press, 2005), 241.
66 John Rawls, *Political Liberalism*, (Columbia University Press, 1993), 224.
67 Allen Buchanan, "Human Rights and the Legitimacy of the International Order." *Legal Theory* 14(1) (2008): 41, Zysset, *The ECHR and Human Rights Theory*, 6.
68 Zysset, *The ECHR and Human Rights Theory*, 22.
69 Dworkin, *Taking Rights Seriously*, 257.

is extremely complicated if based solely on the order of human rights and a neutral worldview. This brings us to the question of whether justifications for the scope and content of rights in situations where legal arguments are insufficient appeal to moral rather than sociological reasons. We assume, in line with the conclusion convincingly presented by A. Zysset, that both paths of argumentation become complementary[70] – social practice tends to justify ethical attitudes and moral grounds indicate the extent of permissible behaviour and the risk of unacceptable conduct that may be present in society.

Our study seeks to precisely identify and analyse the argumentative tools used in such cases. It is not our intention to question the method of classical, logical and dogmatic analysis and interpretation. We simply want to draw attention to the specific nature of certain arguments of an origin and character that transcend the legal order used to support the position taken and the decision made. We discuss the legal reasoning of ECtHR assessments drawing primarily on the views and concepts used by N. MacCormick.[71] There we refer to the unclear line between interpretation and argumentation and its types observed in his texts, as well as to Raz's concept of legal interpretation[72] and to the tools of argumentation already described in the literature (such as *slippery slope, secondary effects*) and the well-known instruments of interpretation (margin of appreciation), indicating the types and patterns of legal reasoning – the creation of narratives or stories about the limits of the right to self-determination in matters of life and death. To some extent, we also refer to the theory of legal rhetoric, looking for components for constructing argumentation in legal reasoning. We will attempt to show how interpretative instruments perform an argumentative function, and how extensively the ECtHR utilises references to interpretations of social practice, creating a certain fabric or matrix of consensual thinking about the limits of Convention rights in an attempt to convince the general public about the rightness of the decisions made.

The reference to the basics of legal rhetoric and legal reasoning prompts us to start our analysis by indicating two key elements from the perspective of the effectiveness of argumentation: recognition of who the reasoning is addressed to (audience) and commonplaces (starting points) of argumentation.

Audience – who is to be convinced

Given the fact that the process of legal reasoning is not limited to a logical operation, the judge must make choices and weigh values for the decision to be fair and legally correct. They must demonstrate these values and make them justified as intersubjectively acceptable.[73] The key problem in legal reason-

70 Zysset, *The ECHR and Human Rights Theory*, 12.

71 MacCormick, "Argumentation and Interpretation." 17–8, 25.

72 Raz, "Why Interpret." 350–2.

73 Feteris, Kloosterhuis, "Law and Argumentation Theory." 9.

ing is to identify who is to be convinced by the argument. As Perelman puts it, convincing someone requires contact of minds and this, in turn, requires recognition of the characteristics of the audience. Legal reasoning means organising argumentation, but also – and above all – turning towards the legal audience.[74]

Each court has its own concept of this audience, dependent on historical, cultural and social factors.[75] When it comes to the judgments of the ECtHR, this vision is quite straightforward under the assumptions of the Convention. It is the community subject to the legal order of the Convention, that is comprising the individuals living in the States participating in the Council of Europe. At this point the first difficulty (mentioned previously) in referring to the audience in such a way appears, namely the lack of a coherent vision of social, moral, ethical and ultimately legal order among such a diverse group. Claims acceptable in one community may not be acceptable in another, making the need for dialogical reasoning all the more urgent.[76]

However, the audience is only secondarily constituted by the individuals of these States. The ECtHR finds its first and most important recipients predominantly in the organs of States: governments, courts and parliaments (legislators).[77] Not only must the Court win understanding among this audience, it must also constantly direct its efforts towards gaining recognition and confirming the legitimacy of its decisions. This is due to the special status of this international court, established at the will of the parties and forever dependent on this will.

In general, the authority of the international court dealing with human rights issue – as well as that of the entire human rights system in the international order – is based solely on the mutual agreement of States. This agreement, expressed most often in the form of a treaty, has to be maintained and in fact developed if it is to fulfil its main function: the protection of human rights in an ever-changing political and social environment. The ECtHR is established as a universally respected judicial body with the ultimate authority to interpret rights under the ECHR, which is expressed in its powers in relation to domestic public institutions.[78]

74 Michael H. Frost, *Introduction to Classical Legal Rhetoric: A Lost Heritage*, (Ashgate Publishing. Ltd. 2005), 57 et seq.
75 Feteris, Kloosterhuis, "Law and Argumentation." 8.
76 Paso, "Rhetoric." 243.
77 Costa, "On the Legitimacy of the European Court of Human Rights' Judgments." 175.
78 George Letsas, *A Theory of Interpretation of the European Convention on Human Rights*, (Oxford University Press, 2009), 10. Samantha Besson, "European Human Rights, Supranational Judicial Review and Democracy – Thinking Outside the Judicial Box." Popelier, Patricia and Van de Heyning, Catherine and Van Nuffel, Piet. *Human rights protection in the European legal order: The interaction between the European and the national courts*, (Intersentia, 2011), 107, A. Zysset, *The ECHR and human rights theory*, 11.

However, the question of the recognition of authority of the international judicial organ is far from being trivial[79] or excessively cautious. At least in Poland, the year 2021 confirmed that such concerns were well founded. The judgments of the ECtHR questioning the new shape of Poland's judiciary and deeming the introduced amendments incompatible with the requirements of an independent court in the meaning of the Convention received a response from the Polish Constitutional Tribunal, which is currently strongly influenced by the ruling government. It declared that Article 6 of the Convention is in turn incompatible with the Polish Constitution to the extent that the notion of court used in this provision includes the Constitutional Tribunal.[80] This only proves the escalating conflict between the Polish domestic authorities (including some courts) and the ECtHR, as well as the Court of Justice of the European Union (CJEU), but it is extremely telling in terms of the need for legitimacy – the imperative of mutual recognition between domestic and international bodies. Such doubts and undermining of the legitimacy of the international court to determine the scope of national norms were also present in other countries, such as the Netherlands, Germany, Great Britain, Belgium and Russia, although for other reasons and in different context than in Poland.[81]

This legitimacy relies on two pillars that have to be developed by the ECtHR. The first is the States' agreement on the meaning of the Convention norms. This meaning is subject to evolution,[82] but the development of the meaning and scope of human rights must still be acceptable to the authorities of the countries that are members of the Council of Europe. This can be achieved through judicial restraint and respect for domestic authorities, norms and social practice. The second pillar – addressing the audience – also implies the need to examine and communicate within legal reasoning the values of a jointly acknowledged social and legal practice and norm. Here, the issue consists of an agreement on the content and exercise of rights. This search for a consensus on the specific meanings of norms holds a uniquely prominent place in the ECtHR's judgments, and so it does in the legal reasoning of the decisions discussed in this book.

79 Fiona de Londras, Kanstantin Dzehtsiarou, "Managing Judicial Innovation in the European Court of Human Rights." *Human Rights Law Review* 15(3) (2015): 527 and literature quoted therein.

80 Polish CT Judgment of 24 November 2021, Ref. No. K 6/21.

81 Janneke Gerards, "The prism of fundamental rights." *European Constitutional Law Review* 8 (2012): 173. There is no better way of describing this problem than in the words of the author: "Many politicians and some scholars do not seem to be eager to accept that forty-seven judges in Strasbourg can decide on the content and meaning of fundamental rights, such as the right to life, the freedom of religion, or the right to property."

82 On the meaning of the original consent, see Londras, Dzehtsiarou: "Managing Judicial Innovation." 524, 542.

It is through diligent and prudent examination of the limits of acceptability of the developments in the meaning of human rights under the Convention that the Court can avoid the risk *that it turns into a purely academic church of human rights believers who say that we preach the new Gospel of human rights*[83] and will therefore not lose its power to influence the domestic order of States. Its rulings will be respected and enforced, and it will therefore retain a special power to decide on the content of rights. This does not mean that the Court does not deliver judgments that are unpopular with respondent States. On the contrary, many of the decisions, including those discussed herein, are of such a nature. However, the Court, being a court acting in recognition of the position not only of the applicant, but also of the authorities of the State, has to face the already designed, specific and sensitive issue of legitimacy and the limits of acceptability of its position in its reasoning.[84]

Among the attentive observers and addressees of the ECtHR's decisions, there are also right-bearers and a particularly influential group, human rights NGOs (often appearing in cases before the ECtHR as third parties). These entities usually have a very firmly grounded position on the content of the rights being decided by the ECtHR, and the potential of their influence can be enormous.

In view of the subtleties of the Convention and the expected resonance of the judicial decisions, all these recipients need to be persuaded rather than forced. This is why the analysis of the European consensus with the doctrine of the margin of appreciation are featured so prominently in the reasons behind ECtHR decisions. A proper recognition of what solution is acceptable and whether it is acceptable at all serves as the basis for the decisions in these cases. Engaging in dialogue between national courts and the ECtHR in the reasoning of judgments is therefore not only a game of arguments and pre-empting possible objections, but also a way of addressing a particular type of audience.

An important element of the audience is also this internal part, namely the other judges, or at least the majority who approved of a particular decision. The collegial nature of the decisions makes it necessary to resort to compromises which have been reached through voting and convincing.[85] This is yet another factor that leads to avoiding formulations and judgments that are not equally agreed upon, thus smoothing the edges, lacking strong individual judgments and individual perspectives. If this fails, these differences will be fully showcased in the dissenting voices and there is no shortage of such voices regarding the sensitive issues discussed in this book.

83 Dzehtsiarou, Interview with Judge of the ECtHR Egbert Myjer (2009) in: Londras, Dzetsiarou, "Managing Judicial Innovation." 529.

84 Ibidem, 544.

85 This is also indicated by Patricia Wald. See: Wald, "The Rhetoric." 1377 et seq.

Commonplaces in ECtHR legal reasoning

Commonplaces (*loci communes, loci, xonoi* in Greek, *topics*) play a particular role in the art of argumentation as statements or formulations concerning values that are generally accepted[86] and considered worthy of attention and protection.[87] They constitute the foundation which the author of reasoning must be aware of in order to have a chance of successful persuasion. Also, in legal reasoning, judges begin their arguments using certain starting points; these often consist of certain undisputed facts or principles such as fairness, equity, good faith or freedom. The idea behind their use is to make the audience sympathetic to such statements of values, principles and other kinds of abstracts. They are often linguistically characterised by the use of positive phrases such as true, just, good and unquestionable value. The second feature is the reference to commonly recognised criteria, such as common sense and duty of care,[88] or reason, tradition, consensus (widely shared values) and predicting progress.[89] Commonplaces are created and characterised by their generality and even indefinability, hence their usefulness in a variety of circumstances and their remarkable adaptability.

In the particularly morally sensitive cases discussed in this book, several such commonplaces can be distinguished, but two, deriving from the protection of the public interest, deserve particular attention. The notion of the public interest proves to be problematic when making any attempt to define it. Attempts to define it have failed to produce unequivocal findings so far, and it seems accurate (albeit pessimistic) to conclude that the public interest has no *a priori* content to be revealed. We accept a rather simple (and, in general, consistent with liberal assumptions) explanation, according to which the public interest usually exists in opposition to the private interest[90] and may be presumed to be what people would choose if they saw clearly, thought rationally, and acted disinterestedly and benevolently.[91] By appealing to the public interest perceived in this way, we get reference to common sense as well as the need for the survival of the community as a whole. In this sense, the public interest has great normative and persuasive potential.[92] Within the

86 Feteris, Kloosterhuis, "Law and Argumentation." 7.

87 Perelman, *The New Rhetoric and the Humanities*, par. 21.

88 Bell, "Policy Arguments." 36–43.

89 John H. Ely, *Democracy and Distrust. A Theory of Judicial Review*, (Harvard University Press, 1980), 56.

90 Wiliam Lucy, "Private and public: Some banalities about a platitude." *After Public Law*, eds. Cormac Mac Amhlaigh, Claudio Michelon and Neil Walker, (Oxford University Press, 2013), 58–9.

91 Walter Lippman, "The Public Interest." *The Public Philosophy*, (Routledge, 1955), 42.

92 On rhetorical approach to the concept of public interest, a.o.: Øyvind Idlhlen, Ketil Raknes, "Appeals to the 'Public Interest': How public relations and lobbying create a social license to operate." *Public Relations Review* 46(5) (2020), https://doi.org/10.1016/j.pubrev.2020.101976.

system of human rights protection contained in the Convention, the term is used explicitly to justify interference with two rights: to peaceful enjoyment of possessions (Article 1 of Protocol No. 1) and to liberty of movement and freedom to choose residence (Article 2[1] and [4] of Protocol No. 4).[93] However, other rights, guaranteed in Articles 8–11, are limited by a range of more specific "legitimate aims" and the public interest can be regarded as identical to the set of legitimate aims contained in those four articles of the Convention as a general statement of how to give justification in situations when protection of individuals' interests or choices are overridden by considerations of collective utility.[94] In the context of the ways of legal reasoning in question, the focal question is whether, in the situation of deciding between an individual choice as to the creation or termination of life, there are interests which may limit personal preferences and goods[95] and whether these can be objectively weighed against the rights of the person asserting his or her rights.[96] Conflict resolution, or striking a balance between the common (public) interest and the individual interest, will always be as valid and convincing as the justifications for the decisions that resolve these conflicts.

If we were to assume that the public interest refers to interests which all members of the public have in common and that it is ***any action which is conducive to the fulfilment of goals which the public wants for itself as a whole,***[97] then those goods which are important for collective existence, the broadly defined

93 Aileen McHarg, "Reconciling human rights and the public interest: Conceptual problems and doctrinal uncertainty in the jurisprudence of the European court of human rights." *The Modern Law Review* 62(5) (1999): 684.

94 ibidem: 671–2, 674–8.

95 On the public interest as a way of overcoming selfish preferences: Charles Frankel, *The Democratic Prospect,* (Harper Harper, 1962), 200.

96 As a category referred to by the courts on the issues discussed in this regard, the public interest may be regarded as identical in meaning to one of the notions of the common good, understood as the creation of conditions for the development and self-fulfilment of every person within the community. The common good is a classical philosophical notion, but considered suspicious in this context as ideologically connoted within Christian philosophy and less republican (although this connotation is at least equally strong). Still, it is worth keeping in mind, if only for the reason that Jacques Maritain, one of the designers of the Universal Declaration of Human Rights, referred to it. Maritain held that the common good means a good life for all, taking into account their diversity (multitude), and he emphasised that the most essential element of the common good is the free development of individuals in the community, taking into account the guarantees of their freedom. Glenn N. Schram, "Pluralism and the Common Good." *The American Journal of Jurisprudence* 36(1) (1991): 119. Even in classical philosophy (Thomas Aquinas), we can find reflections on the evaluation of suicide from the point of view of the common good (suicide is unnatural, ungrateful and antisocial – as directed against the common good) (St Thomas Aquinas, *Summa Theologica*, after: Daniel P. Sulmasy, "Four Basic Notions of the Common Good." *St John's Law Review* 75 (2001): 308.

97 Virginia Held, *The Public Interest and Individual Interests* (New York: Basic Books, 1970), McHarg, "Reconciling Human Rights and the Public Interest." 675–6.

collective welfare, will fall into the category of public interest.[98] This model requires strongly persuasive methods which must seek first to define collective goals and then to determine the means and scope of restriction. This often presupposes the existence of some *pre-existing moral theory or overarching moral principle to guide and justify* – something that is particularly challenging in matters that divide society and concern taboos or issues closely related to personal, private life. There is inevitably a risk of weighing individual values and goods against the values and goods of the general public, juxtaposing different needs and interests.[99] This problem is all the more serious when it comes to protecting life and deciding about one's own fate – values that are highly individual and of the highest priority.

The Court's refraining from justifying the restriction of the right to privacy on the premise of "public morality" brings about a return to the legitimate aim of protecting the rights and freedoms of others, and this seemingly does not involve the identification of the public interest to be protected. The Court's position does not stop at interpreting this premise as designed to protect other specific persons whose interests are in potential conflict with those of the applicants. It is aimed at protecting generally defined interests of society which manifest themselves in the need to care for certain groups in a given social context either actually or potentially exposed to the infringement of their rights whose interests collide with those of the applicants. In the cases pertaining to the area studied in our monograph, we acknowledge that the public interest expressed in the legitimate aim of "rights of others" is primarily identified by the designation of groups of vulnerable persons and groups of persons deserving special attention.

The first commonplace we would like to draw attention to is the reference to the concept of vulnerable groups. The protection of human rights has long recognised the need to single out certain groups to be afforded special protection on account of their status and in relation to certain categories of rights, usually guaranteed under specific acts.[100] However, for several years now, the ECtHR has begun to distinguish the category of "vulnerable groups" in its jurisprudence, also pursuant to the Convention. These are collectives whose members, for various, mainly stereotypical and historical reasons, fall victim to discrimination or insufficient care by the State. The open category of these groups stems from the evolution of case law; the literature indicates

98 McHarg, "Reconciling human rights and the public interest." 677. On the difficulty of defining the scope of public interest, see: Bell, "Policy Arguments." 130.

99 Claudio Michelon, "The public, the private and the law." *After Public Law*, eds. Cormac Mac Amhlaigh, Claudio Michelon and Neil Walker, (Oxford University Press 2013), 87–90.

100 For more, see Marc Bossuyt, "Categorical Rights and Vulnerable Groups: Moving away from the Universal Human Being." *The George Washington International Law Review* 48 (2016): 721 et seq.

that the ECtHR has so far considered such groups to be the Roma,[101] asylum seekers,[102] convicts (in particular juveniles or prisoners with disabilities), mentally ill persons,[103] persons living with HIV[104] and victims of domestic violence.[105] In addition to the groups already identified,[106] a review of the Court's case law reveals that it also employs such a concept in relation to ethnic religious or political minorities.[107]

Distinguishing these vulnerable groups resulted from the Court's application of the group-centred analysis[108] through the use of a conceptual grid

101 Chapman v. UK, appl. no. 27238/95, judgment of 18.01.2001, paras 93, 96. As O'Boyle pointed out, the Court has similarly referred to the vulnerability of the Roma children in respect of their education in: D.H. v. Czech Republic, appl. no. 57325/00, judgment of 13.11.2007; Orsus and others v. Croatia, appl. no. 15766/03, judgment of 16.03.2010, paras 102 and 110; and Sampanis v. Greece, appl no. 32526/05, judgment of 11.12.2012. Similar concern for the treatment of Roma is expressed in V.C v. Slovakia, appl. no. 18968/07, judgment of 8.11.2011 (the problem of forced sterilisation of a woman, paras 146, 177).

102 Tarakhel v. Switzerland, ECtHR judgment of 4 November 2014, appl. no. 29217/12; M.S.S. v. Belgium and Greece, ECtHR judgment of 21 January 2011, appl. no. 30696/09 (unprivileged and vulnerable population par. 251).

103 Alajos Kiss v. Hungary, appl. no. 38832/06, judgment of 20.05.2010, par 42; Mifobova v. Russia, appl. no. 5525/11, judgment of 5.02.2015, par. 54; Zagidulina v. Russia, appl. no. 11737/06, judgment of 2.05.2013, par. 52. See also, Michael O'Boyle, "The Notion of 'Vulnerable Groups' in the Case-Law of the European Court of Human Rights." report delivered for Conference on The Constitutional Protection of vulnerable groups: a judicial dialogue, Santiago Chile 2015, 6.

104 Kiyutin v. Russia, appl. No. 2700/10, judgment of 10.03.2011, par. 48; Centre for Legal Resources on behalf of Valentin Campenau v. Romania, appl. no. 47848/08, judgment of 17.07.2014, par. 103. A thorough overview of these categories and cases: Bossuyt, "Categorical rights and vulnerable groups." 717–8, 726–34, O'Boyle, "The Notion of 'Vulnerable Groups." 8.

105 Opuz v. Turkey, appl. No. 33401/02, judgment of 9.06.2009 – vulnerable individuals (woman affected by her husband's violent behaviour) – paras 160–76, 199–202.

106 In turn, Alexandra Timmer, "A Quiet Revolution: Vulnerability in the European Court of Human Rights." *Reflections on a New Ethical Foundation for Law and Politics,* eds. Martha Finneman and Anna Grear, (Routledge, 2013) – classifies such groups as vulnerable: children, persons with mental disabilities, persons in detention, women in domestic violence or precarious reproductive health situations, persons who are accused who lack legal capacity, demonstrators, journalists, detention and expulsion of asylum seekers, Roma, people with impaired health, 152–61.

107 The ruling concerns Uzbeks who were threatened with expulsion from Russia to Kyrgyzstan: Gayratbek Saliyev v. Russia, appl. no. 39093/13, judgment of 17.04.2014, par. 62; Kadirzhanov and Mamashev v. Russia, appl. No. 42351/13 and 47823/13, judgment of 15.12.2014; Khamrakulov v. Russia, appl. no. 68894/13, judgment of 16.04.2015, par. 66; Eshonkulov v. Russia, appl. no. 68900/13, judgment of 15.01.2015, par. 34–5; Khalikov v. Russia, appl. no. 66373/13, judgment of 15.01.2019, par. 42–3; Mukhitdinov v. Russia, appl. no. 209999/14, judgment of 21.05.2015, par. 45–6 (cf. Bossuyt, "Categorical rights and vulnerable groups." 732–3).

108 Lourdes Peroni, Alexandra Timmer, "Vulnerable groups: The promise of an emerging concept in European human rights convention law." *International Journal of Constitutional Law* 11 (2013): 1058.

including phrases such as "specific type of disadvantaged and vulnerable minority,"[109] "a member of a particularly underprivileged and vulnerable population group,"[110] "particularly vulnerable group in society"[111] and "vulnerable group with a history of prejudice."[112] In these cases, the Court examined the situation of each individual applicant and assigned him or her to a certain group based on personal characteristics. Next, it sought to generalise his or her features on the basis of the characteristics attributed to that group, notably past discrimination and a history of legal or social disadvantage for a particular reason (race, gender, sexual orientation, mental capacity or disability), from which it inferred the need for special attention and imposed a positive obligation of special care on the State, not so much on account of individual characteristics, but on account of inclusion in that category having a specific legal and factual position and current mistreatment.

The application of the category produces three consequences. First, it increases the weight of the harm in the proportionality analysis. Second, it allows for narrower margin of appreciation in restricting the exercise of rights. Finally, it allows the Court to formulate special positive obligations incumbent upon States – to secure and to protect – to recognise a harm, past wrongs and award just-satisfaction.

The concept of "vulnerable groups" has not been received favourably in the relevant literature.[113] The case law of the ECtHR, which makes reference to the need to protect vulnerable groups, is notable for its inconsistency and incoherence for at least several reasons.[114] First of all, the Court failed to indicate the criteria for considering that a particular group would be eligible for inclusion in the vulnerable category.[115] Moreover, the case law does not take into account all the groups for which it seems necessary to extend the concept of "vulnerable groups."[116] In addition, the literature takes a critical view of the consequences of the application of such a category; the criticisms concern the imposition of additional positive obligations on States, including the need for special treatment.[117] This situation is de facto exacerbating the responsibility

109 Orsus and Others v. Croatia, par. 147.

110 M.S.S. v. Belgium and Greece, par. 251.

111 Alajos Kiss v. Hungary, par. 42.

112 Kiyutin v. Russia, par. 63–4.

113 Positive: Peroni and Timmer, "Vulnerable Groups." generally negative – Marc Bossuyt, "Belgium condemned for inhuman or degrading treatment due to violations by Greece of EU Asylum Law, M.S.S. v. Belgium and Greece, Grand Chamber European Court of Human Rights, January 21, 2011." *European Human Rights Law Review* (2011): 581, 597 and Bossuyt, "Categorical Rights and Vulnerable Groups."

114 Peroni, Timmer, "Vulnerable Groups." 1056–85.

115 Ibidem, 1064.

116 Ibidem, 1070.

117 Bossuyt, "Categorical Rights and Vulnerable Groups." 739–40. M. Bossuyt specifically draws attention to the singling out of the Roma and asylum seekers as vulnerable groups in the decisions in Orsus and Others v. Croatia and M.S.S. v. Belgium. According to the Court,

of the State. Finally, as Bossuyt points out, applying protection to vulnerable groups leads to the departure from the general concept and source of human rights and to the creation of specific rights of women, children, asylum seekers, the Roma population and others.[118] Meanwhile, human rights have been based on the universal and equal protection of every human person,[119] so it is legitimate to ask whether the axiological integrity of the protection system, as established by the Universal Declaration, the Convention and the International Covenants, is being maintained.[120] Additionally, in a certain perspective and situation, basically every person can be included in the group of the vulnerable. This concept is therefore being criticised on dogmatic, axiological and purely practical grounds.[121] However, it is not without considerable argumentative potential, especially in terms of reasoning about the narrowness of the margin of appreciation and the obligations incumbent on States whenever the Court sees the need to do so. However, the condition for classifying a person as vulnerable has so far been a test at the individual level as well as at the collective level, with a view to identifying significant vulnerability and thus justifying different degree of protection.[122] This means that a person qualified as a member of the vulnerable group must demonstrate the characteristics which make him/her vulnerable in his/her own situation, as well as in the situation of the group. It is necessary to specify the harm and the person who is affected along with the reasons for this particular vulnerability.

Meanwhile, in the cases discussed, the categories of the persons that we decided to name "persons deserving special protection" – although semantically similar – serve a rather different purpose. It is to concretise the public interest in limiting the rights of the applicants; that is, to indicate that the individual claims and interests of a person demanding recognition of his/her right to private life in a certain scope must be curtailed because of the necessity to protect the rights of other persons identified as those requiring such protection. This group's interest is different from and often opposed to that of the applicant and is the effect of a certain hypothesis adopted by the Court; however, it is supposed to embody the need to protect society by allowing (or to the contrary) the complainant to engage in certain activities. Reference to the protection of such a category will be particularly evident in the cases of end-of-life situations and artificially assisted procreation.

the applicants were entitled in those cases to more favourable treatment than other groups because they were classified by the Court as vulnerable groups. Cf. Bossuyt, p. 730. Also the Report of Michael O'Boyle.

118 Bossuyt. "Categorical Rights and Vulnerable Groups." 717–8.

119 Ibidem, 720.

120 This risk is highlighted by Bossuyt, "Categorical Rights and Vulnerable Groups." 741.

121 Peroni and Timmer define the risks of using this category as the fear of essentialising, stigmatising, victimising and paternalising. Peroni, Timmer, "Vulnerable Groups." 1072.

122 Bossuyt."Categorical Rights and Vulnerable Groups." 735.

Another commonplace phrase used in the cases reviewed in this study is the concept of best interest (of patient, of child). This concept has its origins in domestic legal systems. At the level of international law, the concept of "best interest of the child" was introduced in the 1959 Declaration of the Rights of the Child, which stipulates that "the best interests of the child shall be the paramount consideration" in the enactment of laws relating to children, as well as "the guiding principle of those responsible for (the child's) education and guidance."[123] The Committe on the Rights of the Child, that monitors States' compliance with the provisions of the Convention distinguished three potential levels of relationships in which the welfare of the child/children must be balanced against other interests: against the opposing interests of other children, against the interests of parents/carers, and against wider societal interests or the interests of other groups.[124] Several international conventions have also subsequently incorporated this provision.[125]

ECtHR has developed a vast body of case law related to best interests of child, despite the fact that ECHR does not contain an obligation to consider to directly consider this legal concept. The concept of best interest must be viewed in the context of the third function identified by the Committee – as a procedural rule[126] and as an element in the assessment of the proportionality of interference.[127]

The principle of taking action to pursue "best interests" has been replicated in other branches of law, particularly where it comes to decisions affecting unconscious patients or other "vulnerable individuals."[128] One such area includes provisions, particularly under the *common law* system, which apply to

123 In the framework of the Convention on the Rights of the Child, the UN Committee on the Rights of the Child understands Article 3 (1) as a "threefold concept.": a substantive right, an interpretative principle and a rule of procedure. Committee on the Rights of the Child, General comment No. 14 (2013) on the right of the child to have his or her best interests taken as a primary consideration (art. 3, para. 1) (available: https://www2.ohchr.org/english/bodies/crc/docs/gc/crc_c_gc_14_eng.pdf).

124 "The principle of the best interests of the child – What it means and what it demands from adults." Lecture By Thomas Hammarberg, Commissioner For Human Rights, Council of Europe, Warsaw, 30 May, 2008, CommDH/Speech (2008) 10, 6 (available: https://rm.coe.int/16806da95d).

125 Among others: the 1979 Convention on the Elimination of All Forms of Discrimination against Women and UN Convention on the Rights of Persons with Disabilities and the Convention on the Rights of the Child.

126 Milka Sormunen, "Understanding the Best Interests of the Child as a Procedural Obligation: The Example of the European Court of Human Rights." *Human Rights Law Review* 20 (2020): 754.

127 John Eekelaar, "The Role of the Best Interests Principle in Decisions Affecting Children and Decisions about Children." *The International Journal of Children's Rights* 23(3) (2015): 16 (https://doi.org/10.1163/15718182-02301003).

128 Helen Stalford, "The broader relevance of features of children's rights law." *Children's Rights Law in the Global Human Rights Landscape: Isolation, inspiration, integration?*, eds. Eva Brems, Ellen Desmet and Wouter Vandenhole, (Routledge Taylor Francis Group, 2017), 38.

situations where the patient cannot make an informed decision about further treatment.[129] This transposition of the "best interest" concept to areas of law other than the protection of children's rights has been rightly criticised in various publications. One of the main arguments cited in this context is that it provides a guideline for resolving potential disputes – which are often notable for their specificity – between conflicting interests of the persons involved.[130] Since it is widely accepted that, in such disputes, greater weight is given to the interests of the child for a variety of reasons, this is where the unjustifiability of applying the concept to other areas is derived, among other things, because it presupposes the "superiority" of one interest over another. Furthermore, given that one of the utilitarian functions of the child's "best interest" concept is, as Stalford puts it, that investing in children's interests maximises the welfare of society as a whole, translating it to other areas is highly problematic.[131] There is no doubt, however, that it carries a significant persuasive value, due to the very use of the phrase, linguistically connoted in an unambiguously positive way, almost unquestionable in its semantics. Indeed, it is difficult to disagree that the primary objective of the proceedings should be to secure the "best interest" – although, as it has already been pointed out, at a deeper level the application of such a directive is burdened with paternalistic approach. The second doubt relates to the transfer of the entity assessing this "best interest," especially the "best interest of the patient" in the event of the use of an order of care, when the court can easily be relieved by others, especially medical personnel, who are entrusted with the task of qualifying certain behaviours and procedures as being in the "best interest," as is highly evident in cases concerning the end-of-life.

The two phrases in the argumentation referring to the need to protect "vulnerable groups" and "best interest" are, in our view, fine examples of commonplaces employed in ECtHR rhetoric. They have some fixed meaning, but it is sufficiently fluid that it can be successfully adapted to suit the needs of the argument. For this reason, they are excellent argumentation tools to be used by judges. Both commonplaces also have clearly positive connotations in everyday language. Everyone seems to agree that the ultimate rationale is "best interests" and that a vulnerable group should be afforded special protection. They are therefore perfect examples of what has been called:

129 This concept is understood as a guideline for decision-making on behalf of incapacitated patients, but includes more than just medical issues, such as the legitimacy and necessity of performing certain medical procedures, but also more broadly ethical, social and moral issues. See, Helen J. Taylor, "What are 'best interests'?" 180–4.

130 Stalford, "The broader." 39.

131 Ibidem, 39.

> A persuasive argument is one that responds to the concerns and priorities of the particular person one is trying to persuade, one that resonates with his or her worldview and self-understanding.[132]

Their persuasive power is thus enormous, and their use is relatively effortless. In the cases discussed in our book, both these phrases were used frequently and eagerly in justifications, although the contexts and even the functions they perform are constantly changing.

Bibliography

Aarnio, Aulis. *On Legal Reasoning*. Turku, 1977.

Aarnio, Aulis, Robert Alexy and Aleksander Peczenik. "Grundlagen der juristischen argumentation." In *Metatheorie Juristischer Argumentation*, edited by Werner Krawietz, Robert Alexy. Duncker & Humblo, 1983.

Alexy, Robert. *Theorie des juristischen Argumentation. Die Theorie des rationalen Diskurses als Theorie des juristischen Begrundung*. Suhrkamp Verlag, 1991.

Alexy, Robert and Neil MacCormick. *Rhetoric and the Rule of Law. A Theory of Legal Reasoning*. Oxford University Press, 2005.

Bell, John. *Policy Arguments in Judicial Decisions*. Oxford University Press, 1983.

Besson, Samantha. "European human rights, supranational judicial review and democracy – Thinking outside the judicial box." In *Human Rights Protection in the European Legal Order: The Interaction between the European and the National Courts*, edited by Patricia Popelier, Catherine Van de Heyning and Piet Van Nuffel, 97–145. Intersentia, 2011.

Bossuyt, Marc. "Belgium condemned for inhuman or degrading treatment due to violations by Greece of EU Asylum Law, M.S.S. v. Belgium and Greece, Grand chamber European Court of Human Rights." *European Human Rights Law Review* (2011): 581–596.

Bossuyt, Marc. "Categorical rights and vulnerable groups: Moving away from the universal human being." *The George Washington International Law Review* 48 (2016): 717–742.

Brożek, Bartosz and Jerzy Stelmach. *Metody Prawnicze*, Wolter Kluwer, 2006.

Buchanan, Allen. "Human rights and the legitimacy of the international order." *Legal Theory* 14(1) (2008): 39–70.

Clark, Sherman J. "The character of persuasion." *Ave Maria Law Review* 1 (2003): 61–79.

Costa, Jean-Paul. "On the legitimacy of the European Court of Human Rights' judgments." *European Constitutional Law Review* 7(2) (2011): 173–182.

Devlin, Patrick. "Law, democracy and morality." *University of Pennsylvania Law Review*, 110(5) (1962): 635–649.

Devlin, Patrick. "Morals and the criminal law." In *The Enforcement of Morals*, edited by Patrick Devlin, 24–48. Oxford University Press, 1970.

Dougherty, Charles J. "The common good, terminal illness and euthanasia." *Issues in Law and Medicine* 9(2) (1993–1994): 151–165.

Dworkin, Ronald. *Justice for Hedgehogs*. Harvard University Press, 2013.

132 Sherman J. Clark, "The Character of Persuasion." *Ave Maria Law Review* 1 (2003): 61.

Dworkin, Ronald. "Social rules and legal theory." *Yale Law Journal* 81 (1972): 855–890.
Dworkin, Ronald. *Taking Rights Seriously*. Bloomsbury Publishing, 2013.
Eekelaar, John. "The role of the best interests principle in decisions affecting children and decisions about children." *The International Journal of Children's Rights* 23(3) (2015): 3–26.
Eemeren, Frans H. van and Rob Groothenhorst. *A Systematic Theory of Argumentation*. Cambridge University Press, 2004.
Ely, John H. *Democracy and Distrust. A Theory of Judicial Review*. Harvard University Press, 1980.
Fajans, Elizabeth and Mary R. Falk. "Against the tyranny of paraphrase: Talking back to texts." *Cornell Law Review* 78 (1993): 163–205.
Feteris, Evelin and Harm Kloosterhuis. "Law and argumentation theory: Theoretical approaches to legal justification." *SSRN Electronic Journal* 16(29) (2013): 307–331.
Frankel, Charles. *The Democratic Prospect*. Harper, 1962.
Frost, Michael H. *Introduction to Classical Legal Rhetoric: A Lost Heritage*. Ashgate Publishing Ltd., 2005.
Gerards, Janneke. "The prism of fundamental rights." *European Constitutional Law Review* 8 (2012): 173–202.
Griffin, James. *On Human Rights*. Oxford University Press, 2008.
Habermas, Jurgen. *Truth and Justification*. The MIT Press, 2005.
Haidt, Jonathan. *The Righteous Mind: Why Good People are Divided by Politics and Religion*. Knopf Doubleday Publishing Group, 2012.
Hart, Herbert. L.A. *Law, Liberty and Morality*. Oxford University Press, 1982.
Hart, Herbert. L.A. and Leslie Green. *The Concept of Law*. Oxford University Press, 2012.
Haule, Romuald. "Some reflections on the foundation of human rights – Are human rights an alternative to moral values?" *Max Planck Yearbook of United Nations Law* 10 (2006): 367–395.
Held, Virginia. *The Public Interest and Individual Interests*. Basic Books, 1970.
Hermann, H. Donald. "Legal reasoning as argumentation." *Northern Kentucky Law Review* 12(3) (1985): 467–510.
Hume, David. *A Treatise of Human Nature* (Book III: Morals). The Project Gutenberg eBook 2002, www.gutenberg.org/files/4705/4705-h/4705-h.htm#link2H_4_0083.
Idlhlen, Øyvind and Ketil Raknes. "Appeals to the 'public interest': How public relations and lobbying create a social license to operate." *Public Relations Review* 46(5) (2020): 1–8.
Jesiołowski, Kamil. "The concept of public morality of lord patrick devlin and the jurisprudence of the European Court of Human Rights." *Archiwum Filozofii Prawa i Filozofii Społecznej* 1(22) (2020): 37–51.
Koering-Joulin, Renee. "Public morals." In *The European Convention for the Protection of Human Rights: International Protection Versus National Restrictions*, edited by Mireille Delmas-Marty, 83–98. Martinus Nijhoff Publishers, 1992.
Letsas, George. *A Theory of Interpretation of the European Convention on Human Rights*. Oxford University Press, 2009.
Lippman, Walter. "The public interest." In *The Public Philosophy*, edited by Walter Lippman, 41–46. Routledge, 1955.
Londras de, Fiona and Kanstantin Dzehtsiarou. "Managing judicial innovation in the European Court of Human Rights." *Human Rights Law Review* 15(3) (2015): 523–547.

Lucy, Wiliam. "Private and public: Some banalities about a platitude." In *After Public Law*, edited by Cormac Mac Amhlaigh, Claudio Michelon and Neil Walker, 56–82. Oxford University Press, 2013.

MacCormick, Neil. "Argumentation and interpretation in law." *Ratio Juris* 6(1) (1993): 16–29.

MacCormick, Neil. *Legal Reasoning and Legal Theory.* Oxford University Press, 1994.

McHarg, Aileen. "Reconciling human rights and the public interest: Conceptual problems and doctrinal uncertainty in the jurisprudence of the European Court of Human Rights." *The Modern Law Review* 62(5) (1999): 671–696.

Michelon, Claudio. "The public, the private and the law." In *After Public Law*, edited by Cormac Mac Amhlaigh, Claudio Michelon and Neil Walker, 83–100. Oxford University Press, 2013.

O'Boyle, Michael. "The notion of 'vulnerable groups' in the case-law of the European Court of human rights." *Report Delivered for Conference on the Constitutional Protection of Vulnerable Groups: A Judicial Dialogue*, Santiago Chile, 2015.

Paso, Mirjami. "Rhetoric meets rational argumentation theory." *Ratio Juris* 27(2) (2014): 236–251.

Peczenik, Aleksander. *On Law and Reason.* Kluwer, 1989.

Peczenik, Aleksander. *The Basis of Legal Justification.* Lund University Press, 1983.

Perelman, Chaim. "Law and rhetoric." In *Justice, Law and Argument. Essays on Moral and Legal Reasoning*, edited by Chaim Perelman and Harold J. Berman, 120–124. Springer, 1980.

Perelman, Chaim. *The New Rhetoric and the Humanities. Essays on Rhetoric and Its Applications.* Springer, 1979.

Peroni, Lourdes and Alexandra Timmer. "Vulnerable groups: The promise of an emerging concept in European Human Rights Convention Law." *International Journal of Constitutional Law* 11 (2013): 1056–1085.

Perry, Michael. *Toward a Theory of Human Rights: Religion, Law, Courts.* Cambridge University Press, 2008.

Rawls, John. *Political Liberalism.* Columbia University Press, 1993.

Raz, Joseph. "Why interpret." *Ratio Juris* 9(4) (1996): 349–363.

Rosen, Michael. *Dignity: Its History and Meaning.* Harvard University Press, 2012.

Schram, Glenn N. "Pluralism and the common good." *The American Journal of Jurisprudence* 36(1) (1991): 119–124.

Shklar, Judith. *Legalism.* Harvard University Press, 1964.

Sormunen, Milka. "Understanding the best interests of the child as a procedural obligation: The example of the European Court of Human Rights." *Human Rights Law Review* 20 (2020): 745–768.

Stalford, Helen. "The broader relevance of features of children's rights law." In *Children's Rights Law in the Global Human Rights Landscape: Isolation, Inspiration, Integration?*, edited by Eva Brems, Ellen Desmet and Wouter Vandenhole, 36–51. Routledge and Taylor Francis Group, 2017.

Sulmasy, Daniel P. "Four basic notions of the common good." *St John's Law Review* 75 (2001): 303–310.

Taylor, Helen J. "What are 'best interests'? A critical evaluation of 'best interests' decision-making in clinical practice." *Medical Law Review* 24(2) (2016): 176–205.

"The principle of the best interests of the child – What it means and what it demands from adults." *Lecture by Thomas Hammarberg, Commissioner For Human Rights, Council of Europe*, Warsaw, 30 May, 2008, CommDH/Speech. https://rm.coe.int/16806da95d.

Timmer, Alexandra. "A quiet revolution: Vulnerability in the European Court of Human Rights." In *Reflections on a New Ethical Foundation for Law and Politics*, edited by Martha Finneman, Anna Grear, 147–170. Routledge, 2013.

Veitch, Scott. *Moral Conflict and Legal Reasoning: Contradictions between Liberalism and Liberal Legalism*. Hart Publishing, 1996.

Wald, Patricia. "The rhetoric of results and the results of rhetoric." *University of Chicago Law Review* 62(4) (1995): 1371–1419.

Waldron, Jeremy. "Judges as moral reasoners." *International Constitutional Law Review* 7(1) (2009).

Wróblewski, Jerzy. *Legal Syllogism and Rationality of Judicial Decision*. Rechtstheorie, 1974.

Zysset, Alain. *The ECHR and Human Rights Theory: Reconciling the Moral and Political Conceptions*. Routledge Research in Human Rights Law, 2016.

2 Ways of judicial reasoning – outline

Interpretation and argumentation under the European Convention on Human Rights

The Court's legal reasoning in an individual case is mostly based, as we already said, on the interpretation of norms. However, at the same time, the interpretation usually constitutes practical argumentation in law or at least is a starting point for further arguments. Therefore, the issues of interpretation and argumentation are closely related and often overlap each other.

The interpretation of human rights treaties is not limited to the application of classical methods, such as textual, functional or intentional interpretation. There are also other specific instruments of interpretation that can be applied therein.[1] It stems primarily from the fact that these agreements govern not only vertical (relation of State to an individual) but also horizontal (relations between individuals) relations and seek to give effect to the rights and freedoms of individuals falling under the jurisdiction of individual States and thus define relations between individuals and public authorities, such as obligations of an objective nature.[2]

The attempt to discern specific instruments for the interpretation of human rights norms faces particular challenges due to the lack of a uniform conceptual grid.[3]

1 Soering, par. 87, Tyrer v. UK, par. 31. The interpretation of the Convention should serve the fullest possible fulfilment of its provisions, Airey v. Ireland, par. 44, Siurdur A. Sigurjonsson v. Iceland, par. 24–5. More about interpretation of the ECHR, see Letsas, *A Theory of Interpretation*.

2 Cezary Mik, "Metodologia interpretacji traktatów z dziedziny praw człowieka." [Methodology of the interpretation of human rights treates] *Toruński Rocznik Praw Człowieka i Pokoju* 1 (1992–1993): 12.

3 There exists a lack of terminological uniformity in terms of the concepts used to describe the various interpretative procedures carried out by the bodies empowered to do so, in particular the European Court of Human Rights. This lack of terminological uniformity seems to be due to several reasons. Firstly, due to the fact that this problem is not referred to in the very texts of the agreements, including the ECHR; secondly, due to the fact that the process of interpretation is of a changing and dynamic nature, and the independence of the controlling

DOI: 10.4324/9781003375999-3

Therefore, we will use the notion of interpretative techniques or tools to denote any interpretative process of a special character in relation to classical interpretative methods.[4] Such tools and techniques will therefore include a wide range of concepts described in relevant literature to date. These will include general principles, concepts and tools,[5] concepts/theories,[6] doctrines,[7] concepts, doctrines and principles.[8] The catalogue of interpretative tools or techniques will include, *inter alia*, the following institutions indicated in literature as being used by the ECtHR in its interpretation: the doctrine of the margin of appreciation, the principle of effectiveness, the principle of consensus (that is, the consensus between States), the principle of proportionality and fair balance, the comparative method, the balancing method, the concept of positive obligations, the concept of implied rights and limitations, the principle of non-discrimination, the principle of legality, the rule of law and procedural fairness,[9] or the doctrine of "living together."

---

bodies, manifested in the determination of the content of legal norms, leads to the inclusion of new concepts and ideas in the process; and, thirdly, as a consequence of the first two factors, due to the lack of a comprehensive and uniform theory of the interpretative process in the doctrine of international human rights law. One cannot, of course, overlook the numerous publications, often of considerable impact, on the issue of interpretation of the ECHR. See: Youtaka Arai-Takahashi, *The margin of appreciation doctrine and the principle of proportionality in the jurisprudence of the ECHR* (Antwerp: Intersentia, 2002); Eirik Bjorge, *The Evolutionary Interpretation of Treaties,* (Oxford University Press, 2014); Andrew Legg, *The Margin of Appreciation in International Human Rights Law: Deference and Proportionality,* (Oxford University Press, 2012); and Letsas, *A Theory of Interpretation.* However, none of these publications aspired to represent a comprehensive theoretical overview of the interpretation process. See also: Adam Wiśniewski, "Uwagi o teorii interpretacji Europejskiej Konwencji Praw Człowieka." *Między wykładnią a tworzeniem prawa. Refleksje na tle orzecznictwa ETPC,* Cezary Mik, Katarzyna Gałka eds., TNOiK 2011. In the chapter the author critically reviews – in terms of the scope of analysis – the monograph by Letsas, *A Theory of Interpretation,* pointing out that contrary to the title, which seems to suggest comprehensive coverage of the problem of interpretation, the work does not deliver on these assumptions.

4 Following L. Garlicki under the notion "interpretative methods," we understand adjudication techniques/tools developed by decision-making bodies, see Lech Garlicki, "Wprowadzenie." [Introduction], in *Konwencja o ochronie praw człowieka i podstawowych wolności. Komentarz do artykułów 1–18* [Convention on the Protection of Human Rights and Fundamental Freedoms. Commentary on Articles 1–18], ed. Lech Garlicki, (Wydawnictwo C.H. Beck, 2011), 9.

5 Pieter van Dijk, Godefridus J. H. Hoof, *Theory and practice of the European Convention on Human Rights,* (Kluwer Law International, 1998), 71.

6 For example, Arden describes the "living instrument" as a theory. *Cf.* Lady Justice Arden, *An English Judge in Europe*, 11, www.judiciary.uk/wp-content/uploads/JCO/Documents/Speeches/lj-arden-an-english-judge-in-europe.pdf (accessed 11.09.2022).

7 Wiśniewski, "Uwagi o teorii." p. 17.

8 Marek Antoni Nowicki, *Wokół Konwencji Europejskiej* [Around the European Convention], (Wolters Kluwer, 2021), 357–65.

9 Lech Garlicki qualifies the rule of law as one of the five values stemming from the introduction to the Convention, which provides the axiological basis for the Convention. See: Garlicki, "Wprowadzenie." 18.

The ECtHR may, depending on the case in question, employ one or even more interpretative techniques/tools to process the case.

Identification of the interpretative methods or techniques used by the ECtHR in a given case is not sufficient to convey the entirety of the Court's position and argument. The argumentative statements may be based on interpretative tools or be construed with reference to other rhetorical measures. In the book, we attempt to identify the most repetitive patterns or ways of argumentation used by the Court to persuade the addressee of the decision or judgment issued in morally fragile cases. We decided to name them argumentative tools.

A good example of combining interpretation and argumentation, and more precisely of the use of an interpretative instrument for argumentation purposes, is the application of the margin of appreciation in the case of *A., B. and C. v. UK*. The Court referred to it, as in previous abortion cases, but this time pointed out that it no longer relates to the position of States as to whether the foetus is a subject of the right to life, but as to when life begins. The redefinition of the subject of the margin of appreciation allowed the Court to focus its arguments on this issue. This procedure was aimed at convincing the recipients of the correctness of the decision. Thus, the margin of appreciation tool played an argumentative rather than merely interpretative role in this case.

On the other hand, the situation in which there is no connection between interpretive and argumentative tools is visible, *inter alia*, in in the case of *H.S. and Others v. Austria*. Admittedly, the Court has confirmed, by applying a purposive interpretation and within the framework of the concept of "living instrument," the view already established in jurisprudence that Art. 8 of the Convention covers the right to have a child. At the same time, however, in arguing its decision in favour of accepting the limitation of the available methods of artificial procreation, it relied on arguments unrelated to the interpretation made. In particular, it took into account the arguments relating to the need to provide special protection for vulnerable entities: women who may donate genetic material in order to protect them from potential use and children born through *in vitro* fertilisation treatment (hereafter "IVF"), which carries a special risk in the form of maternity split on genetic and biological lines. Arguments of this kind, also repeated in other cases raising significant issues from the moral point of view, were to convince the recipients of the correctness of the issued decision. These are, however, arguments unrelated to interpretive techniques that have their sources elsewhere.

The recurring arguments aim at presenting the Court's position from the perspective desired by that body. Their purpose is to convince the recipient that the decision is appropriate. The fact that they do not aim at merely interpreting the treaty, and that they are intended to achieve the persuasive goals indicated, sets them apart from interpretative methods and tools. However, they are based on these devices on many occasions. In our opinion, the repetitive arguments put forward by the Court pursue the objective defined by it as "maximising the effects of each judgment both in the respondent State and in Council of Europe States generally."[10]

This maximisation occurs in the process of convincing the parties of the rightness of the decision taken – even of its necessity and lack of alternatives. It is therefore a rather strong persuasion, partly because it usually concerns the resolution of conflicts between rights and claims formulated by the claimants as well as the position of the national authorities. This is usually the case when the problem at hand touches upon morally sensitive issues, and where the formulation of judgment requires the adoption of a certain evaluative attitude from the point of view of right and wrong.

Unwilling to formulate this position on morally sensible issues directly, we will argue that the Court uses persuasive argumentative tools referring to three values: external authority, the content of the law or its derivatives, or pragmatic rules of reasoning, inferring the necessity of taking a certain position against possible undesirable consequences of not taking it. It should be noted at the beginning that each of indicated tools is sometimes combined with others to reach the persuasive effect.

When distinguishing argumentative tools, we begin by assuming (following N. MacCormick) that the Court engages in practical argumentation, by which we understand argumentation aimed at achieving the goal of convincing another party to accept a particular solution as opposed to speculative argumentation.

Hence, we assume that courts, including the ECtHR, make use of at least three types of argumentative tools.

The first type refers to authority – the external entity or environment in which the decision is made.

The second category refers to the interpretation of the text of the Convention, seeking to demonstrate that the solution adopted derives from its content and the principles it recites.

The third group involves the consequentialist arguments, such as indicating what consequences the decision will have not only for the parties involved, but more broadly, for the entire audience and community.[11]

Argumentative tools are used by the Court in all adjudicated cases.[12] Their use, however, becomes particularly important in complex cases when it is necessary to balance the rights of the individual and of the public against the background of moral and ethical conflicts.

10 Steven Greer, Luzius Wildhaber, "Revisiting the debate about 'constitutionalising' the European court of human rights." *Human Rights Law Review* 12(4) (2012): 686.

11 Some of the methods classified here are based on the Perelman theory of argumentation and some of them have been mentioned in doctrine, particularly by Daniel Hermann (argument from authority, plasticity of notions – avoidance of incompatibility and technique of restraint). See: Hermann, "Legal Reasoning." 492–5.

12 Janneke Gerards, "Margin of Appreciation and Incrementalism in the Case Law of the European Court of Human Rights." *Human Rights Law Review* 18(3) (2018): 497.

Argumentative tools in cases with ethical and moral considerations: typology

In this book, the analysis will focus only on those tools which the EctHR uses most frequently when delivering rulings on issues pertaining to the end of human life, medically assisted procreation and abortion. Both the ways of reasoning themselves and the consequences of their application will be discussed.

However, the publication does not attempt to interpret and present the substantive moral and legal position of the Court in relation to issues of a sensitive moral and ethical nature in the resolved cases.

We tentatively assume that certain tools – also used in other cases – are applied more frequently in the examined substantive areas. They are also characterised by certain specificity because in its arguments the Court has to take into account the great diversity of national legal regulations and their far-reaching moral and ethical considerations. From a broader perspective, individual argumentative tools used in cases involving the end-of-life, medically assisted procreation or abortion serve the Court to substantiate its position in a pluralistic normative world in cases where the decision is extremely difficult to be justified because of its nature.

Following the analysis of the judicial rulings issued in relation to the issues under consideration, a number of the most frequently used argumentative tools were identified. They were classified into three groups:

Arguments referring to authority

a Arguments referring to external (beyond the ECHR) law sources
b Arguments referring to the margin of appreciation
c Arguments relying on epistemic authority

Deontological argumentation

a Arguments based on incrementalism
b Arguments based on proceduralisation
c Arguments based on plasticity and assimilation of concepts

Teleological argumentation

a Arguments based on examination and assessment of secondary effects

It is crucial to make the preliminary reservation that the argumentative tools identified in the analysed areas are used by the Court in individual judgments in parallel. Furthermore, their scopes often overlap. This stems from the fact that certain legal institutions or interpretative measures, like the topics (commonplaces) we have already identified, underpin particular arguments and constitute an element of not just one, but several argumentative tools. Such is the nature the notion of vulnerable groups, or the concept of pursuing "best interest."

Some of the argumentative tools indicated by us, like proceduralisation, incrementalism, margin of appreciation or the concept of vulnerable groups included in the tool of secondary effects have already been addressed in relevant literature from various angles, which is why some of them are already well-known and outlined.[13] However, the approach we propose consisting of treating them as recurring patterns of argumentation makes it necessary to present the assumptions we formulated for each of them in the course of the study.

A general overview of the tools we identified is presented in the following sections. The use of particular tools in the thematic areas under study will be presented in Chapters 3 (issues of medically assisted procreation), 4 (issues of abortion) and 5 (issues relating to the end-of-life).

Argumentative tools – overview

Argumentation referring to authority

The first group of argumentative tools used in the studied areas consists of appealing to an argument *ad auctoritatem*, meaning to an authority or knowledge external to the court or tribunal. By doing so, the judicial body places the decision in the hands of other actors to whom it gives such authority, as it recognises their authority as proper and outside the subject of consideration and discussion. The definition of authority focuses precisely on this issue. It is a quality that elicits obedience of the subject of the decision without the need for either coercion or additional persuasion. According to Finnis, subjects treat an opinion, plan, or order as authoritative when they believe that this position alone provides sufficient reason to trust it or act upon it. This does not depend on the fact that the subject sees no other justification for a given belief or a given course of action. That the subject recognises that this position, according to Raz, constitutes an exclusive rationale (a rationale for making certain choices, taking certain actions and disregarding other motivations, which would justify a different course of action in the absence thereof).[14] In the argumentation used by the courts, this type of method can even allow for complete avoidance of expressing one's own autonomously developed position – especially with regards to assessments of a moral nature.[15] Authority may be based either on recognised power (including the right to decide certain matters independently) or on knowledge deemed necessary by the authority to reach a certain decision. Another feature of authority is that it is marked by

13 Detailed reference to the literature are provided for in the next chapters.

14 John Finnis, *Natural Law and Natural Rights*, (Oxford University Press, 2011), 234.

15 Raz, "Why Interpret." 6.

"absolute recognition by those from whom obedience is demanded; neither coercion nor persuasion is needed."[16]

According to our understanding, the authority to which the EctHR refers in its argumentation is primarily the will and at times knowledge expressed by an entity other than the Court itself. This authority facilitates referring to it as the exclusive rationale, inducing obedience towards this decision, without resorting to any further persuasion. This kind of argumentation, however, does not come in pure form in the case of the EctHR. In fact, it would be contradictory and incomprehensible given the complexity of the functions the Court performs. However, such argumentative tools can be found in judgments quite regularly – although they are never the only nor the definitive ones, that is those determining the outcome.

A number of types of argumentations fall into the category of methods using reference to external authority. Against the background of cases involving sensitive moral and ethical issues, we have identified three of them as the most common.

Arguments relying on external (beyond the ECHR) sources of law

Although the concept of authority is a complex one and the term has multiple meanings,[17] there is no doubt that the established law will almost always have a weight of authority for the judicial body, construed in accordance with the indication adopted by Finnis. In the case of the ECtHR, it means that the Court refers first and foremost to the content and shape of domestic law in its reasoning, constituting the expression of the will of the domestic legislature, but also to international provisions, like regulations adopted at the

16 According to the definition proposed by H. Arendt, "*power* corresponds to the human capacity to act, but not just to act, but to act in unison. Power is never owned by the individual, it belongs to the group, and exists as long as the group sticks together. When we say that someone is in power, we are actually referring to the fact that a number of people have authorised him to act on their behalf. " H. Arendt postulates to keep the concept of *force* only for the "forces of nature" or the pressure of circumstances, that is factors or attributes which are completely independent from human will. *Violence*, on the other hand, is instrumental in nature, and it relies solely on its tools. According to H. Arendt, power and violence are not two attributes of the same phenomenon – the phenomenon of domination. On the contrary, they are two different phenomena, although they usually occur together. Ultimately, however, violence destroys power, which is clearly visible in situations where the power (government), wishing to save its weakening position, resorts to violence. "*Replacing power with violence can bring victory, but a very high price is paid for it, for the cost is not only borne by the defeated – the victor pays for it with his own power, especially when he enjoys the conquest of a constitutional government in his own country*," writes H. Arendt, quoting the words of H. S. Commager: "*if we overthrow and demolish the prevailing order and peace in the world, we thereby inevitably overthrow and demolish above all our own political institutions*." (H. S. Commager, Can We Limit Presidential Power, *The New Republic*, 6 April 1968, [after:] Arendt, *On Violence*, (Harcourt, Brace & World, 1970, 53).

17 John Randolph Lucas, *The Principles of Politics*, (Oxford University Press, 1966), 16.

supranational level that are thematically relevant to the subject matter in question. The concept of international law includes both hard law and soft law instruments. It is worth emphasising that in its judgments the ECtHR often presents legal arguments from a comparative perspective. In this respect, it does not solely concentrate on the regulations adopted in the defendant State, but reviews domestic legislation as well as instruments of an international nature. International regulations, including soft law as a manifestation of a trend in international law, play an especially important role in this regard, as their existence may be an argument for limiting the margin of appreciation attributable to States.[18]

In this context it will be vital to examine to what extent the authority of law and non-binding regulations (international and domestic) is referred to by the Court as an element of its argumentation and if it is, what is the role of these arguments in the judicial reasoning.

Arguments relying on the margin of appreciation

In relevant literature, the margin of appreciation is usually classified as an interpretative tool reserving a certain sphere of autonomy for States to decide how to implement their obligations under the Convention in a manner that best corresponds to the specifics of local conditions.[19] When Protocol No. 15 came into force, this tool found its place in the preamble of the Convention as one of the two interpretative directives, alongside the principle of subsidiarity.[20] It is a well-known and frequently analysed instrument.[21]

18 Christoph Grabenwarter, "The European Convention on Human Rights: Inherent constitutional tendencies and the role of the European Court of Human Rights." *Constitutional Crisis in the European Constitutional Area, Theory, Law and Politics in Hungary and Romania*, ed. Armin von Bogdandy and Pal Sonnevend, (Hart Publishing, 2014), 114.

19 Garlicki, "Wprowadzenie." 5. On the margin of appreciation, see generally: Legg, *The Margin of Appreciation*; George Letsas, "Two Concepts of the Margin of Appreciation." *Oxford Journal of Legal Studies* 26(4) (2006); Howard Ch. Yourow, *The Margin of Appreciation Doctrine in the Dynamics of European Human Rights Jurisprudence*, (Martinus Nijhoff Publishers, 1996), 192; Gerards, "Margin of Appreciation." 498.

20 The introduction of these two interpretative tools in the Preamble to the Convention is construed as strengthening the role of the national perspective. Cf. Joaquin Cayon, "The widening of the national margin of appreciation allowed by the strasbourg court: A backward step for reproductive rights in Europe?" in *The Role of Courts in Contemporary Legal Orders*, ed. Martin Belov, (Eleven International Publishing, 2019), 402.

21 The margin of appreciation tool is classically defined as "The latitude of deference or error which the Strasbourg organs will allow the national legislative, executive, administrative, and judicial bodies before it is prepared to declare a national derogation from the Convention, or restriction or limitation upon a right guaranteed by the Convention, to constitute a violation of one of the Convention's substantive guarantees. It has been defined as the line at which international supervision should give way to a State Party's discretion in enacting or enforcing its laws." See: Yourow, *The Margin of Appreciation*. See also: Jeffrey A. Brauch, "The dangerous search for and elusive consensus: What the supreme court should learn from the European court of human rights." *Howard Law Journal* 52(2) (2009): 279.

Theorists of law tend to look upon the concept of margin of appreciation as a means of reconciling conflicting legal or cultural traditions.[22] At the same time, however, the Court's starting point in applying this concept is to ensure that the definition of fundamental human rights is the same for all individuals within the jurisdiction of the Member States of the Council of Europe, while potential differentiation takes place with regard to the assessment of the restrictions introduced.[23] As such, the margin of appreciation provides States with a twofold perspective. On the one hand, it gives them space to seek their own determinations. On the other hand, it allows the ECtHR to retain its legitimacy as an authority acting within the limits of the principle of subsidiarity and allows it to avoid handling cases in a way that would risk causing States to disagree with the outcome on grounds of established and socially accepted attitudes and norms. This very premise is the reason for the Court's extensive use of the concept of margin of appreciation in cases concerning the end-of-life, medically assisted procreation or abortion, areas the regulation of which is heavily conditioned – even if only in appearance – by deeply rooted values and traditions.[24]

Several criticisms have been directed at the concept of margin of appreciation. It concerns, in particular, the effect of applying the margin consisting in "nationalisation" of rights,[25] weakness of the methodology of judicial argumentation[26] or the fact that it is used by the Court as a substitute for thorough

22 Patric Glenn, *Legal Traditions of the World,* (Oxford University Press, 2010, 4th ed.), 380; Janneke Gerards, "Pluralism, deference and the margin of appreciation doctrine." *European Law Journal* 17(1) (2011): 80 and 86; Marisa Iglesias Vila, "Subsidiarity, margin of appreciation and international adjudication within a cooperative conception of human rights." *International Journal of Constitutional Law* 15(2) (2017): 407; Janneke Gerards, "Judicial deliberations in the European court of human rights." *Judicial Deliberations in the European Court of Human Rights. The Legitimacy Of Highest Courts' Rulings*, eds. N. Huls, M. Adams and Jacco Bomhoff, (T.M.C. Asser Institute, 2008), 5, https://ssrn.com/abstract=1114906.

23 Gerards, "Margin of Appreciation." 498.

24 It should be noted, however, that, for example, surrogacy agreements are permitted in countries such as Ukraine and Russia, whose authorities are often eager to seek legitimacy for their decisions in the alliance with the Orthodox Church. No such regulations exist in Poland, which is traditionally perceived as ultra-Catholic; meanwhile, such agreements are explicitly forbidden in secular France.

25 Cayon, "The Widening." 397.

26 Cayon, "The Widening." 401. Also, according to Thomas A. O'Donnell, "The margin of appreciation doctrine: Standards in the jurisprudence of the European court of human rights." *Human Rights Quarterly* 4 (1982): 474–96 and 475: "A central problem is to determine a principled basis on which this distinction [between a wide and a narrow margin] can be made so that the Convention may be enforced without infringing upon legitimate activities of governments." Also critical, Letsas, "Two Concepts." 705–32; Thomas W. Stone, "Margin of appreciation gone awry: The European court of human rights' implicit use of the precautionary principle in: Frette v. France to backtrack on protection from discrimination on the basis of sexual orientation." *Connecticut Public Interest Law Journal* 3(1) (2003–2004): 218–36. For a comprehensive overview of the evolution of the doctrine, see: Yourow, *The Margin of Appreciation.*

argumentation.[27] In the context of the latter charge in particular, it is alleged that the application of the doctrine of the margin of appreciation makes it possible to avoid reaching a decision on the substantive level by considering a decision taken by national authorities as legitimate within the permissible margin of appreciation. It is thus possible to bypass a substantive analysis of the measures taken by the State and an in-depth consideration of the scope of the right being decided. The most vocal criticism of the margin of appreciation was summed up by Gerards, when she stated that it had become a "substantively rather empty rhetorical device."[28]

This criticism directed towards the placement of the margin of appreciation as an interpretative tool of the ECHR allows us to classify this concept as one of the argumentative tools used by the EctHR. It is largely centred around the acceptance of the correctness of the domestic legal framework, which encompasses not only the form in which a certain regulation was adopted (such as an act or a document of lower order), but also the direction of political and social policies reflected in it. In its argumentation, the Court points to the legitimacy of States to take certain decisions and thus shapes the content of the decision by the use of this argument. Thereby, the margin of appreciation is given a dimension of argumentative tool. Abortion cases are particularly good examples of how the subject of the margin of appreciation changes, and thus that it is used as an instrument of persuasion.

In cases relating to issues provoking moral and ethical debate, the Court has identified the emergence of a European consensus as one of the factors justifying a wider margin for States. It is understood as a common position of States balancing conflicting interests or their protection.[29] This notion is

27 See all controversies and discrepancies of using this instrument: Gerards, "Margin of Appreciation." 500–6.

28 Gerards, "Margin of Appreciation." 497, 500 et seq.

29 Consensus is classified very differently in the literature. As a doctrine (John L. Murray, see John L. Murray, Consensus: Concordance, Or Hegemony Of The Majority?, Dialogue between judges, Proceedings of the Seminar 25 January 2008, Strasbourg 2008, 17, www.echr.coe.int/documents/dialogue_2008_eng.pdf accessed 11.09.2022), as an interpretative tool alongside other tools of this type, such as the margin of appreciation (Dzehtsiarou), and as an interpretative technique used in the dynamic interpretation of the Convention (Bureš). There are also different evaluations of it, both expressed by judges and in the literature, particularly given the lack of consistency in the Court's application of the concept (John L. Murray, 17). The literature emphasises that it is difficult to draw clear conclusions from the judicial decisions as to how to assess the existence of a common approach. The problem is that the parameters for measuring it are unknown. It may seem that this is a legislative trend (Sheffield and Horsham v. United Kingdom, 1998, appl. no. 31–32/1997/815–816/1018–1019 [ECtHR Judgment 30 July 1998]), but in other cases the Court seems to refer to consensus as a social trend as well (Frette v. France, 2002, appl. no. 36515/97 [ECtHR Judgment 26 February 2002]). Moreover, the Court has not specified what percentage of Member States should recognise a right to assume that a certain consensus status exists (compare Cayon, "The Widening." 409). A comprehensive conception of the consensus tool was presented by Dzehtsiarou, who, on the one hand, defines the tool as a trend in the regulation of a particular

all the more relevant in the context of the analysis of the argumentative tools used by the Court, as it is undoubtedly one of them that allows the legitimacy of this body and its jurisprudence to be reinforced by appealing to the unquestioned standard in most countries (consensus, after all, ties the Court's decision very closely to domestic law and practice), that is, to external authority. In this sense, consensus can curb excessive judicial activism.[30] It constitutes a certain premise – a foundation for adjudication – since it makes it possible to establish not only a regulatory framework, both at a national and international level, but a socially accepted norm outlining the standard and content of law.[31]

In the context of the argumentative method of the margin of appreciation, it will be vital to examine to what extent the Court providing arguments for the validity of a particular decision justifies its decisions with an essentially wide margin of appreciation used by the States in the areas under consideration, as well as what functions the margin method ultimately plays in the Court's argumentation. We need to address the question as to whether the wide discretion granted to States is subject to certain limitations resulting from the validity of other arguments that have been invoked (within the framework of other argumentative methods); whether the lack of common legislative solutions in the areas under consideration results in a de facto absence of European consensus, a factor which, when confronted with an individual's claims, will always prevail to his or her disadvantage; and, finally, what the subject of the margin of appreciation granted to the States is, whether this subject has evolved over time, and what methodology or guidelines the Court uses to define it.

Arguments relying on epistemic authority

The authority to which the courts or tribunals refer sometimes relates not to will (usually expressed in the form of legal regulations or implemented

---

substantive issue (p. 12), but on the other hand emphasises its relative nature by stating that it is "a presumption that favours the solution to a human rights issue which is adopted by the majority of the Contracting Parties. This presumption can be rebutted if the Contracting Party in question offers a compelling justification. Such a conceptualisation implies that European consensus has a strong persuasive effect and its rebuttal should be supported by convincing and lucid reasons. " Cf. Kanstantsin Dzehtsiarou, *European Consensus and the Legitimacy of the European Court of Human Rights*, (Cambridge University Press, 2015), 9 and 17. This author presents the idea that consensus is one of the interpretative tools – alongside the dynamic interpretation of the Convention, the margin of appreciation, autonomous concepts and the principle of proportionality – used by the Court. In the literature, one can also find statements that "consensus" is an "interpretative technique," as it is used by the Court for the dynamic interpretation of the Convention. At the same time, it is "defined" as: "It is not a term the Court would fill with content through its jurisprudential activity. To the contrary, European consensus is more a shortcut to describe a certain use of argumentation or argumentative elements being based on the comparative method," cf. Pavel Bureš, "The dialogue between judges leading to a consensus? On a mute and a silent dialogue before ECtHR." *European Journal of Public Matters* (1) (2017): 68–9.

30 This thesis is presented by Dzehtsiarou, *European Consensus*, 1–6.

31 Ibidem, p. 9.

policies), but to knowledge. It is associated with a certain class (group) of statements that require specific competence, regarding which the decision-making body is not able to take a stand on its own. This argument also makes it possible to entrust the decision to an entity other than the court, and in fact aims at demonstrating the competence of this very decision-maker, which can be described as ***argumentum ad verecundiam*** ("appeal to timidity"), producing, however, the same effect as ***argumentum ad auctoritatem***. This time, however, the authority is not based on a sovereign decision of the subject entitled to it in the light of the accepted rules of system and competence, but on its knowledge. Accordingly, to a certain extent, the courts resign from their own judgment of the situation and entrust it to persons who hold qualifications (competences) allowing for authoritative and thus legitimate determinations in this respect.

In the cases described in our book there are quite a few such areas, as these cases are related to medical procedures and determination of the condition of the patient or the person to whom the procedure applies. The feature of epistemic authority is therefore bestowed on those who have the knowledge and experience necessary to define and justify certain procedures and the underlying condition of the patient.

Resorting to the authority of knowledge[32] is a common and traditional method used by the courts and is well-established in all procedures. It involves seeking an expert's opinion in a situation where adjudication requires specialised knowledge that is unavailable to the court due to lack of appropriate qualifications. Then, a situation arises in which the court entrusts experts with the formulation of statements on a certain state of affairs and, on this basis, after accepting the expert's opinion as being authoritative and drawn up according to verifiable knowledge and rules of art, it renders a decision.

What is important to decide, however, is whether it is an exclusive reason or simply evidence assessed and verified by the court within the limits of its discretion.

Yet this doubt is overshadowed by others that arise when epistemic authority is invoked because, in the justifications of the ECtHR, this appeal to the authority of knowledge is of a somewhat different nature.

32 According to Zagzebski, an epistemic authority is meant as someone who possesses a "normative epistemic power which gives me a reason to take a belief pre-emptively on the grounds that the other person believes it." In her opinion, there are four conditions identified as constitutive of epistemic authority: 1) Content-Independence, which means that an authority figure does not make its position dependent on the object; 2) Pre-emption Thesis for Epistemic Authority (an authority figure's position on a certain statement dictates that it be recognised even against – and not alongside – another); 3) Dependency Thesis (an authority statement is formulated in a way that deserves to be accepted); and 4) Justification Thesis, which is the belief that authority allows me to avoid my own false statement and at the same time formulate a true one. See: Linda Zagzebski, "A defense of epistemic authority." *Research Philosophica* 90(2) (2013): 296, 297–9. See further: Sofia E. Bokros, "A deference model of epistemic authority." *Synthese* 198 (2021), https://doi.org/10.1007/s11229-020-02849-z.

First of all, it is related to the different role of the Court. It does not adjudicate on a specific case and does not have to directly assess the facts and seek expertise at this point. Rather, the Court must assess whether the actions of the domestic courts and authorities aimed at reaching such a judgment were correct and did not violate the rights guaranteed by the Convention. Consequently, the ECtHR's recognition of epistemic authority is of a general character, proceeding somewhat on a meta-level. As such, it is more far-reaching and influential. The Court does not state "it is x because the experts declare it as so," but rather that "the court has recognised that x is legitimate because the experts declare it as so." Or, in other words, that "whenever the experts state x, the ruling based on such 'x' statement will be legitimate." It is very clearly visible in the reasoning concerning the withdrawal of life-sustaining treatment (such as in *Lambert v. France*), when the Court bases its ruling on the correctness of making a domestic decision not only on the quality of law, but also on consulting medical and ethical experts in the decision-making process.

The appeal to epistemic authority to such an extent does not consist solely in entrusting the function of determination by means of opinions and statements. In the previously mentioned *Lambert v. France* case, it also applies to the recommendatory opinions and defining the position of the Court as to how the boundary situation should be resolved. Application of this kind of argument in the cases described in our work concerns, above all, the determination of limits and the contents of the right to live. Against this background, the practice of abuse of authority, consisting in widening the scope of competence, can also be easily observed. The Court assumes that authority no longer only concerns fact findings, but also the formulation of directives, even though these already belong to the sphere of judgments not subject to restrictive limitations due to a lack of adequate knowledge. This happens either due to the delegation of competence explicitly to doctors and medical personnel (in end-of-life matters) or through the use of the broad and fluid category of "best interest of patient." This concept is discussed within the method of plasticity of concepts.

Deontological argumentation

MacCormick describes a category of deontological arguments which involve providing grounds for the adopted solutions based on the following scheme: this decision is correct and finds its source in the rules, principles and values that the law provides for that type of situation.[33] As such, the arguments from this group refer to the content of the law directly or, more rarely, indirectly. Their task is to lead, on the basis of norms and previous case law, to the deciding authority's indication of the scope of the right in order to justify the decision taken as compliant with the limits of binding regulations. In doing

33 MacCormick, "Argumentation and interpretation." 16–29.

so, the body uses deontology of clearly defined imperatives and prohibitions, overriding and developed through careful reasoning.

Arguments based on incrementalism

Both in the universal plane and in relation to the ECHR, there is an evident trend that new individual interests are constantly recognised as elements of fundamental rights. Gradual widening of scope is conditioned by a number of factors and is frequently the principal source of criticism directed at the adjudicating authorities.[34]

Ethically and morally sensitive cases, and above all those falling precisely within the examined areas, are a relatively new and difficult challenge for the Court. These cases make it particularly easy to witness the gradual case-by-case "immersion" of the Court in the merits of the problems under consideration. What is exceptionally evident here is that the reactions of the States to the rulings are checked and arguments are selected in such a way as to ensure that far-reaching solutions, which are a manifestation of judicial activism, are not made too quickly.[35] The need to balance the individual case with the presentation of an overall view of the issue under examination has contributed to the development of an argumentation whereby, in each successive decision concerning a particular subject-matter, the Court has identified and described a new issue, or a new area, which clarifies and generally extends the scope of the protection guaranteed by a given substantive provision of the Convention.

This way of judicial reasoning, described most adequately by Gerards as incrementalism, is understood as a delimitation of the content of the law underlying the decision by means of the Court extracting new elements composing this law.[36] And this meaning is what we will analyse in the book.[37]

The compilation of the Court's statements in successive cases gives a real picture of the scope of guarantees provided for by the Convention. In many cases, such a compilation is included in the judgments issued by the Grand Chamber. The gradual construction of the content of a right or a freedom allows the Court to monitor the reactions of the addressees of the ruling and to adapt the content of subsequent decisions accordingly, while maintaining a fairly open approach to the problematic issues raised by the applicants.

Incrementalism strives to specify and often to redefine the scope of substantive provisions of the ECHR. Its inclusion in the overall argumentation may

34 Gerards, "The prism of fundamental rights." 179 et seq.

35 Gerards, "Margin of Appreciation." 507 and seq.

36 Gerards, "Margin of Appreciation." 508. The author shows, among others, on the example of judgments concerning the issue of abortion, that despite the fact that the Court has not identified the "right to abortion" on the basis of the Convention, it has extracted from Articles 3 and 8 further obligations on States in terms of guaranteeing women access to abortion.

37 Incrementalism is a concept used in logic and computer science, where it is understood as adding one value to an existing value; it is about gradually increasing a value by one.

therefore have profound consequences for the determination of the scope of protected rights and freedoms, hence we will be interested in the intensity of its application and the correlation with other frequently used tools. Its relation to proceduralisation will be of particular interest. On the one hand, incrementalism, understood as indicated here, may aim to limit the possibility of using proceduralisation in a given case. On the other hand, as the examples of decisions we have analysed will illustrate, in assessing the circumstances of a case through the procedural prism, the Court often defines new obligations and requirements directed at public authorities, and thus develops the standard of guarantees owed to individuals. In the latter case, incrementalism and proceduralisation will function as two sides of the same coin.

In the following chapters, we will attempt to demonstrate how the ECtHR developed the content of various substantive provisions of the Convention through incrementalism in relation to the examined issues. We will limit ourselves to highlighting only those statements of the Court which were innovative in their given sphere. Basically, we will not take into account statements contributing to the content of a given right but expressed in the Court's rulings concerning other spheres and implemented to the area of interest to us.

In the context of the ECtHR's case law, incrementalism, that is, the gradual broadening of the scope of a given right or freedom, is of particular significance in the scope of making binding interpretations of the Convention by this body for future reference, and not only in the context of an individual case. After all, the principles and standards developed by the Court in its judicial decisions are treated as *res interpretata*.[38] However, at the same time, as is already apparent from a preliminary analysis of the case law, the Court's conclusions according to which a particular provision of the Convention covers a particular entitlement – even if such a statement meets the interests of the plaintiffs – does not always automatically lead to identification of a violation in the specific circumstances of the case.

However, incrementalism cannot only be treated as an interpretative tool enabling the determination of the scope of individual provisions of the ECHR. Its meaning is much wider. This is particularly evident in cases where the Court, using incrementalism, broadly defined the content of a given right but did not find that in the circumstances of the case there had been a violation of the applicant's rights. In such cases, incrementalism cannot be treated only as a tool for interpreting the Convention, but also as an instrument preparing "the ground" for subsequent decisions, announcing them and justifying self-restraint rulings. How it is used in the selection of arguments justifying the Court's decision will be the subject of our examination.

38 Adam Bodnar, "*Res Interpretata*: Legal effect of the European Court of Human Rights' Judgments for other states than those which were party to the proceedings." *Human Rights and Civil Liberties in the 21st Century*, eds. Yves Haeck and Eva Brems, (Springer, 2014), 223.

Arguments based on proceduralisation

A "procedural turn," recently traced by the number of scholars in the jurisprudence of the ECtHR, is strongly present in cases under consideration.[39] We assume that, among various aspects of proceduralisation, the Court concentrates itself on cases concerning morally sensible matters on two of its modes: procedural requirements and integrated procedural review.[40] Procedural requirements mean continued reading of explicit procedural requirements from the Convention, which took the form of self-standing procedural rights. This kind of States' obligations have become part of the scope of the right in question. There are no doubts that the identification and scope of procedural obligations are in most cases "designed to optimise protection of substantive

39 For example: *Procedural Review in European Fundamental Rights Cases*, eds. Janneke Gerards, Eva Brems (Cambridge University Press, 2017); Patricia Popelier, Catherine Van de Heyning, "Subsidiarity Post-Brighton: Procedural Rationality as Answer?" (2017) 30 Leiden Journal of International Law, 5; Janneke Gerards, "Procedural review by the ECtHR: A typology." *Procedural Review in European Fundamental Rights Cases*, eds. Janneke Gerards, Eva Brems (Cambridge University Press, 2017). This author seeks to categorise the various elements while recognising that the proposed typology will require further development in the future. For the literature on different elements of "proceduralisation," see: C. Van de Heyning, "No Place like Home: Discretionary space for the domestic protection of fundamental rights." *Human rights protection in the European legal order: The interaction between the European and the national courts*, eds. Patricia Popelier, Catherine Van de Heyning and Piet Van Nuffel, (Intersentia, 2011); Patricia Popelier, "The court as regulatory watchdog: The procedural approach in the judicial decisions of the European court of human rights." *The Role of Constitutional Courts in Multilevel Governance*, eds. Patricia Popelier, Armen Mazmanyan, Werner Vandenbruwaene, (Intersentia 2012); Patricia Popelier, Catherine Van de Heyning, "Procedural rationality: Giving teeth to the proportionality analysis." *European Constitutional Law Review* 9(2) (2013): 230; Eva Brems, Laurens Lavrysen, "Procedural justice in human rights adjudication: The European court of human rights." *Human Rights Quarterly* 35 (2013): 176; Eva Brems, "Procedural protection – an examination of procedural safeguards read into substantive Convention rights." *Shaping Rights in the ECHR – The Role of the European Court of Human Rights in Determining the Scope of Human Rights*, eds. Janneke Gerards and Eva Brems (Cambridge University Press, 2013); Jon Petter Rui, "The Interlaken, Izmir and Brighton Declarations: Towards a paradigm shift in the strasbourg court's interpretation of the european convention of human rights?" *Nordic Journal of Human Rights* 31(1) (2013): 28; Aileen Kavanagh, "Proportionality and parliamentary debates: Exploring some forbidden territory." *Oxford Journal of Legal Studies* 34 (2014): 443; Janneke Gerards, "The European court of human rights and the national courts – giving shape to the notion of 'shared responsibility." *Implementation of the European Convention on Human Rights and of the judgments of the ECtHR in national case law. A comparative analysis*, eds. Janneke Gerards and Joseph W.A. Fleuren, (Intersentia, 2014); Matthew Saul, "The European Court of Human Rights' Margin of Appreciation and the Processes of National Parliaments." *Human Rights Law Review* 15(4) (2015).

40 Terminology used after Kleinlein. Thomas Kleinlein, "The procedural approach of the European Court of Human Rights: between subsidiarity and dynamic evolution." *International & Comparative Law Quarterly* 68 (2019): 91–110, 93.

rights."[41] In the integrated procedural review, the Court concentrates on the quality of domestic decision-making processes which refer to domestic judicial, administrative and law-making procedures (analysis based mainly on the quality of the law and the processes leading to its adoption).

The idea of proceduralisation is captured by Gerards and Brems, who state that the essence of the "procedural turn" is in the idea that instead of only reviewing the substantive reasonableness of the interference with a fundamental right or freedom, the ECtHR might also take into account the quality of procedure that led to the alleged violation.[42]

The idea of proceduralisation is highly controversial, primarily due to the shortcomings in its precise definition, the failure to distinguish the types of procedural review and its inconsistent application by the Court. Thus, its effects are difficult to determine.[43] The exact contours of the proceduralisation trend are not defined, and different authors concentrated on different elements of the concept.[44]

However, its basic premise that the supra-national judicial authority should focus on assessing procedural issues not only alongside, but sometimes even instead of substantive issues, is widely used in arguing morally sensitive cases. This happens because the judicial authority often prefers to refrain from formulating clear positions on the merits in such cases. Concentration on examining procedural elements, sometimes perceived as formal, such as transparency, accountability, participation and fact-finding, results in the audit body not being perceived as intervening in a matter where national bodies (legislative, judicial or administrative) certainly have more knowledge and experience, and where it is up to them to make the ultimate choices of appropriate policies.[45] Procedural review can be conducted on more objective and neutral grounds and may therefore be less debatable from the perspective of the role of a European court. Moreover, it seems to mainly be the substantive assessment of reasonableness that causes national criticism of the Court's judgments.[46]

41 Eva Brems, "The 'logics' of procedural-type review by the European court of human rights." *Procedural Review in European Fundamental Rights Cases*, eds. Janneke Gerards, Eva Brems, (Cambridge University Press, 2017), 19.

42 Janneke Gerards, Eva Brems, "Procedural Review in European Fundamental Rights Cases: Introduction." *Procedural Review in European Fundamental Rights Cases,* (Cambridge University Press, 2017), 2.

43 This view is shared, among others, by Gerards, who proposes a typology of procedural review. Gerards, "Procedural Review." 129.

44 Oddný Mjöll Arnardóttir, "Organized Retreat? The Move from 'Substantive' to 'Procedural' Review in the ECtHR's Case Law on the Margin of Appreciation, European Society Of International Law." *Conference Paper Series* Conference Paper No. 4/2015, *2015 Annual Conference, Oslo, 10–12 September 2015,* 7 et seq.

45 Gerards, Brems, "Procedural review." 4.

46 Gerards, "The prism of fundamental rights." 199.

The notion of proceduralisation has not yet become part of the conceptual grid used by the Court. It is, in fact, an external term for a mental construct used in judicial argumentation. The concept thus appears in parallel and frequently draws on concepts from legal theory pertaining to the distinction between negative and positive obligations of States under particular substantive provisions of the Convention. Here, it should be noted that the general assumption of the ECtHR is that the choice of the perspective of assessing the State's compliance with its Convention obligations, such as the distinction between positive (procedural perspective) and negative obligations, is not of key importance. In its opinion, the boundaries between positive and negative obligations cannot always be precisely defined, and the rules applicable in the evaluation process are the same. In both situations, the need to maintain a fair balance between the interests of the individual and society as a whole must be taken into account, and in both cases the State enjoys a certain margin of appreciation.[47]

It seems that the origins of the proceduralisation trend are undoubtedly related to the assessment of the State's fulfilment of its positive obligations, especially when it comes to the development of positive procedural requirements or assessment of the shape of legislation. The extension of the scope of proceduralisation to include the assessment of the decision-making process itself leads to the conclusion that this type of argumentation may be applied both to positive and negative obligations of the State.

The notion of proceduralisation and the understanding of it presented here may suggest a lack of reference in the supranational court's examination to the material scope of the right that has been allegedly infringed. However, this is not a convincing interpretation for at least two reasons. First, proceduralisation in its broadest sense includes procedural obligations of States, which become part of the scope of the right in question as already highlighted.

Secondly, the Court has derived a whole series of procedural requirements for the conduct of judicial, administrative or legislative procedures, "the disobedience of which may give rise to the finding of a Convention violation of its own."[48] For this reason, we include the proceduralisation among deontological ways of argumentation. We intend to examine the extent to which it is used by the ECtHR and the results it produces. We intend to examine whether the proceduralisation influenced strictness of the Court's review in conducting its own assessment *in concreto* (by including into assessment new factors) or whether it lead to replacement of the Court's own assessment with the "complete deference to the national authorities in the form of abandoning *in concreto* proportionality review for *in abstracto* review of the decision making process."[49] And, finally, what are the aims of applying proceduralisation

47 Evans, par. 59–60 of the Chamber judgment.
48 Gerards, "Procedural Review." 158.
49 Arnardóttir, "Organized Retreat." 16.

from the point of view of the Court's desire to persuade the audience to the rightness and legitimacy of its decision.

Arguments based on plasticity and assimilation of concepts used to describe and qualify behaviour

Another argumentative tool that facilitates adjudication and justification in cases with strong ethical overtones is that of specific identification and description of acts and conduct that are subject to adjudication, as well as focus on the creation of new categories of concepts that become keys to current and subsequent adjudications.

Such concepts have long been well-known and widely used in judicial decisions. Suffice to mention the chilling effect – the concept meaning an usually undesirable discouraging effect or influence on the behaviour of an individual or group which can be effectuated by vague provisions of law allowing for too broad of an interpretation.[50] This phrasing has been extremely successful. It has evolved from being a metaphor borrowed from American jurisprudence into a key word for adjudicating cases where there is even a potential obstruction of human rights relating to free speech.[51] As our analysis shows, it has also

50 The term was used in American jurisprudence in the 1950s (in 1952 in Wieman v. Updegraff, 344 US 183, 195 (1952), literally in 1963 in Gibson v. Florida Legislative Investigation Committee. See further: "The Chilling Effect in Constitutional Law." *Columbia Law Review* 69(5) (1969): 808–42 (accessed July 14, 2021).

51 Judith Townend, "Freedom of expression and the chilling effect." in *Routledge Companion to Media and Human Rights*, eds. Howard Tumber and Silvio Waisbord, (Routledge, 2017), 73–82. Frederik Schauer found that the concept of the chilling effect had "grown from an emotive argument into a major substantive component of first amendment adjudication" and that its use "accounts for some very significant advances in free speech theory, and, in fact, the chilling effect doctrine underlies the resolution of many cases in which it is neither expressed nor clearly implied." See: Frederic Schauer, "Fear, Risk and the First Amendment: Unraveling the Chilling Effect." *Boston University Law Review* 58 (5) (1978): 685–732, 685. The metaphor regularly appears in a variety of legal contexts, connected by the theme of freedom of expression, but quite different in nature from those early cases concerning freedom of political expression and association and made a big time in ECtHR jurisprudence, starting with the case of *Donnelly and Others v. UK*, 5 April 1973 to Navalny v. Russia, 15 November 2018 (freedom of association); Korostelev v. Russia, application no. 29290/10, 12 May 2020, par. 64 (prisoners' rights). See further: Townend, "Freedom." 75. Cf. Trine Baumbach, "Chilling Effect as a European Court of Human Rights Concept in Media Law Cases." *Bergen Journal of Criminal Law & Criminal Justice* 6(1) (2018): 98 et seq; Laurent Pech, *The concept of chilling effect. Its untapped potential to better protect democracy, the rule of law, and fundamental rights in the EU.* Open Society European Policy Institute 2021, www.opensocietyfoundations.org/publications/the-concept-of-chilling-effect (accessed 15.09.2022). Recently, the chilling effect concept is also used regarding the rule of law principle, especially in the context of the activities of the CJEU and the European Commission towards Poland and Hungary. An example of the succession and versatility of the use of the term "chilling effect" has already been commented on quite extensively in the literature, and its use is still – as can be assumed – expected to develop. For the sake of precision of the argument it is worth adding that the notion of chilling effect in our classification would rather constitute an argument and an element

been employed by the ECtHR, not only in the framework of the guarantees of the freedom of speech.

In our view, such phrases also occur in the sphere of the issues we are studying in the book, although finding them and reconstructing their meaning and persuasive potential may not be so obvious. These include, above all, the concept of "best interest" (described in the book as one of commonplaces in judicial rhetoric). It came into existence in a field completely different from the one under examination and has since been successfully implemented and used in new contexts – interestingly enough, also in pursuing different persuasive directions.

Another issue in the field of persuasion by means of the language of "phrases" is the use of certain terms to describe facts and, consequently, the qualification of the presented and adjudicated situations in the direction in which these phrases are supposed to incline the recipient (reader) towards certain states and events. Such a troublesome state is, for instance, artificial nutrition and hydration (ANH). Classifying this procedure as medical or non-medical gives rise to considerable controversy, but once it is done, it allows the argumentation to be carried out in the direction chosen by the communicator (the Court). Thus, the way certain behaviours are defined makes it relatively easy to make an *implicite* moral assessment of them.

The argument based on plasticity and assimilation of concepts falls into the deontological category, although it does not directly concern the content of the rules of law. Yet it is founded on an argument that takes the following form: the law orders us to assess this situation or state in a certain way and to formulate directives concerning these situations (states). Therefore, terms in the description of the situation or state must appear that enable or facilitate the application of a specific norm or its interpretation. The Court thus turns to the description of the situation with the aid of phrases and concepts that allow easier qualification and assessment, also made at an ethical and emotional level. The decision will therefore be legitimate and justified if the situation to be resolved is established by means of certain statements, classifications and judgments in accordance with the rules that are provided for in the law regarding such situations. This involves reference to certain concepts or categories whose meaning is predetermined. The use of umbrella terms constitutes the key to further justification and allows for their excellent adaptation in subsequent decisions. They become part of judicial decisions, thus entering the jurisprudence. At the same time, this tool makes it possible to avoid or minimise inferences based on moral judgments. Instead, certain situations – and their

of teleological methods, as it concerns the anticipated (negative) effects of a certain legislative or judicial action. This is primarily because it is an extremely catchy and apt metaphor, and the connotation of the phrase in the audience is unequivocally negative and immediate. It is a kind of keyword, the use of which in an appropriate context (even hitherto completely unused) evokes association and conviction in the accuracy of an argument built on the threat of invoking the chilling effect.

outcomes – are strictly defined and placed in categories where no other decision can be taken by the Court.

Teleological argumentation

The phrase *teleological argument* has historically been associated with arguments concerning the proof of God's existence and the effects of divine action.[52] There is a certain analogy with our argument: teleological argument is an argument of design. It turns in theology to the effects of divine action, thus proving God's existence. In our perspective, it turns to outcomes of a particular solution to justify its acceptance or, more often, rejection.

Teleological tools, in our understanding, and also adopted by MacCormick who indicated them as a separate category of practical argumentation, address the purpose or the outcome of the adjudication. In this case, the court does not refer in its reasoning to the underlying legal and axiological order, that is, the system of rules, principles and values, or their factual sources. Nor does it seek to demonstrate equity by reference to that order. Instead, it develops argumentation using consequences, events or phenomena that may occur as long as the decision has a specific content. Thus, it is about the outcome (intended or not) of a given decision or failure to reach it in a particular shape. Unlike deontological methods, teleological ones are largely non-legal in character, and concern, above all, the recognition of social consequences of a decision, including, in particular, the shaping of certain attitudes towards the content of the law, especially the formation of a habitual acceptance of certain categories of behaviour (acts) and ultimately also the content of rights and social relations.

Arguments based on examination and assessment of secondary effects

As Legarre and Mitchell point out, secondary effects are general, indirect societal harms resulting from a pattern of activity. They are not to be confused with the apparently similar notion of "side effects." The secondary effects are certain, specific consequences of an individual action.[53] These involve actions by individuals or taken in relation to individuals which may produce negative repercussions for entire social groups or societies. Thus, the courts refer to the undesirable effects, even dangerous from the point of view of the community of citizens, that could be brought about by a decision permitting a certain action, which – and this is crucial – in the light of other methods of

52 The argument derives in this form from St. Thomas Aquinas, developed, among others by William Derham (XVIIIth century) and then William Paley (1802 *Natural Theology or Evidences of the Existence and Attributes of the Deity*) published a full presentation of this argument, using the phrase "argument from design" for the first time.

53 Santiago Legarre, Gregory J. Mitchell, "Secondary Effects and Public Morality." *Harvard Journal of Law and Public Policy* 40 (2017): 325.

interpretation would be permissible. So, the judges refer to the future, to a hypothesis built on the basis of concerns about the impact of a potential decision, relying on empirical data (with the reservations about its completeness and reliability) and an image of the undesirable social effect. Such argumentation, in its premise, is as far away from moral judgments as possible, but Legarre and Mitchell argue that already choosing which secondary effects are harmful involves moral reasoning of the same kind as that which underpins public morality, the very doctrine secondary effects appeared designed to avoid.[54] Sociological data and its elaboration, on the other hand, are simply meant to replace them; to make them operational in order to persuade and indicate not just the desired purpose of law and jurisprudence, but of policy in a broader sense. Nevertheless, as the previously quoted authors point out, "secondary effects and public morality often come down to the same thing," regardless of whether a reference to morality or any indication of right and wrong in the judgment is expressed. Secondary effects thus lead to the discovery of morals hidden beneath the indication of undesirable social effects, for this undesirable feature represents the discovery of the moral justification for such a decision.[55]

Although the use of such an appeal to the undesirable consequences of certain decisions in the future carries with it a hidden (and not very deep) moral assessment, it does not yield the concerns of moral majoritarianism, ideological threats or others, which are closely connected to moral reasoning. On the other hand, it allows for conviction-persuasion regarding the decisions made, done in a way that appeals to the common sense, persuasion through potential threats faced by the community and attempts to prevent them, rather than by pointing to an arbitrary (inherently) moral choice.

In the ruling we have studied involving issues entailing strong moral considerations, the Court argues in favour of the solution adopted by analysing the social disadvantages that may occur as a consequence of allowing the individuals concerned to enjoy, or preventing them from enjoying, certain rights or freedoms in the manner they desire. Potential adverse outcomes are identified by singling out groups of individuals in need of special protection whose interests may be violated as a consequence of acknowledging the applicants' claims. Therefore, the argumentation consists in balancing the actual claims of the plaintiffs against the need to extend special protection to hypothetical groups of persons whose rights must, in the Court's view, be taken into account in determining the scope of the rights which the applicants may enjoy.

This construct differs from the Court's approach to ensuring respect for the rights and freedoms of specific individuals or groups by treating them as members of the so-called vulnerable groups. The method of avoiding negative future repercussions by creating a notion of protection for abstract groups in

54 Ibidem, p. 321.
55 Ibidem, pp. 350–1.

need of special protection was accomplished by reference to the "best interests" concept.

The teleological argumentation is of a beyond-logic character and certainly non-syllogistic nature. It does not directly concern the content of law and is not supported by any authoritative force other than law. It refers to practical effects and consequences of a possible decision, but these effects remain outside the area of resolving a particular case. This kind of argumentation must be exceptionally well-founded on the persuasive level. Moreover, it requires empirical support demonstrating the risk of certain consequences, social attitudes or undesired phenomena. One must admit that judges usually have difficulty with this kind of pronouncement. They choose their arguments rhetorically, and thus have to confine themselves to making hypotheses about future cases and circumstances, and refer to them in their interpretation of the case at hand and norms. In essence, they refer to the state of affairs beyond the adjudication of a particular case, regarding extrapolation of adjudication, transfer to other situations and point out the risks of hypothetically extending precedent onto other decisions and social attitudes more broadly. This is a very risky and inconvenient tool to employ. But it is precisely argumentation by secondary effects that allows us to rationalise moral choices and judgments – or at least to point out their rational reasons to the public.

Conclusions

The argumentative tools that we have identified are used by the Court with varying frequency, and they interrelate and overlap. We initially assume that the choice of a particular way of reasoning is made to pursue the different objectives desired and intended by that body. It will have an impact on defining the scope of rights and freedoms guaranteed by the ECHR, but it will also play a role in terms of the possibility of learning the position of the Court in relation to morally sensitive matters.

Accordingly, we will focus our examination on whether the ECtHR combines certain argumentative tools and uses them together more often than not and, if so, what effect is achieved by doing so. We will also study whether certain of them are used more frequently than others in particular substantive areas, and whether in such situations they prove to be of a decisive nature. We will also be interested in examining the effects of particular tools on the scope of individual rights and freedoms. Where appropriate, we will try to extrapolate the positions that the ECtHR has taken with regards to particular moral issues. However, we do not define our role as aiming to present the Court's overall position in this regard.

In our opinion, a closer inspection of the identified tools paves the way for a discussion not only on the evolution of the ECtHR jurisprudence, but also that of domestic courts in particularly difficult cases, such as end-of-life situations, assisted procreation and abortion. It also provides a fresh perspective on the rhetorical tools used in judicial argumentation. Thus far, the relationship between interpretative techniques and argumentative tools in ECtHR judicial decisions has received little attention, as has the relatively scarce literature on rhetoric and the rhetorical function in its reasoning. Meanwhile, this is a fascinating and extremely significant issue, both if we look at the role of ECtHR judgments not only as decisions which are to set limits or milestones in the development of the scope and content of human rights protected by the Convention, but also as an instrument of persuasion concerning the rightness of the decision taken, persuasion concerning not only the scope of rights, but sometimes the most sensitive and deepest layers of a person's sense of being human with a guaranteed sphere of self-determination about their life.

The analysis of the argumentative tools used by the ECtHR also makes it possible to raise questions and hypotheses about the shape of public morality declared in a camouflaged but decipherable way. This blurred shape of moral life – what is allowed and what is not allowed in communities – is nevertheless vague and at times changing, and flickers on the horizon of some of the arguments used in the judgments discussed herein. We will attempt to indicate these contours in some sections. However, it should be noted at the outset that we do not assume any moral standpoint that there is one correct (right) ruling. Instead, we follow the ways legal discourse (the content of justifications) relates to the choice of one of these perspectives and the methods of argumentation used in external justification.

Bibliography

Arai-Takahashi, Youtaka. *The Margin of Appreciation Doctrine and the Principle of Proportionality in the Jurisprudence of the ECHR*. Intersentia, 2002.

Arden, Lady Justice. *An English Judge in Europe*. www.judiciary.uk/wp-content/uploads/JCO/Documents/Speeches/lj-arden-an-english-judge-in-europe.pdf

Arendt, Hannah. *On Violence*. Brace & World, 1970.

Arnardóttir, Oddný Mjöll. "Organized retreat? The move from 'substantive' to 'procedural' review in the ECtHR's case law on the margin of appreciation." *European Society of International Law*. (ESIL) *Conference Paper Series*, vol. 5 iss 4 (2015).

Baumbach, Trine. "Chilling effect as a European Court of Human Rights concept in media law cases." *Bergen Journal of Criminal Law & Criminal Justice* 6(1) (2018): 92–114.

Bjorge, Eirik. *The Evolutionary Interpretation of Treaties*. Oxford University Press, 2014.

Bodnar, Adam. "Res interpretata: Legal effect of the European Court of Human Rights' judgments for other states than those which were party to the proceedings." In *Human Rights and Civil Liberties in the 21st Century*, edited by Yves Haeck and Eva Brems, 223–262. Springer, 2014.

Bokros, Sofia E. "A deference model of epistemic authority." *Synthese* 198 (2021): 12041–12069.

Brauch, Jeffrey A. "The dangerous search for and elusive consensus: What the supreme court should learn from the European Court of Human Rights." *Howard Law Journal* 52(2) (2009): 277–318.

Brems, Eva. "Procedural protection – An examination of procedural safeguards read into substantive convention rights." In *Shaping Rights in the ECHR – The Role of the European Court of Human Rights in Determining the Scope of Human Rights*, edited by Janneke Gerards and Eva Brems, 137–161. Cambridge University Press, 2013.

Brems, Eva. "The 'logics' of procedural-type review by the European Court of Human Rights." In *Procedural Review in European Fundamental Rights Cases*, edited by Janneke Gerards and Eva Brems, 17–39. Cambridge University Press, 2017.

Brems, Eva and Laurens Lavrysen. "Procedural justice in human rights adjudication: The European Court of Human Rights." *Human Rights Quarterly* 35 (2013): 177–200.

Bureš, Pavel. "The dialogue between judges leading to a consensus? On a mute and a silent dialogue before ECtHR." *European Journal of Public Matters* 1 (2017): 63–74.

Cayon, Joaquin. "The widening of the national margin of appreciation allowed by the strasbourg court: A backward step for reproductive rights in Europe?" In *The Role of Courts in Contemporary Legal Orders*, edited by Martin Belov, 397–413. Eleven International Publishing, 2019.

Commager, Henry Steele. "Can we limit presidential power." In: *The Defeat of America: Presidential Power and the National Character*, Works of Henry Steele Commager, Simon and Schuster, 1974 (digital: ACLS Humanities E-Book 2011), first published in: *The New Republic*, 6 April, 1968.

Dijk, Pieter van and Godefridus J. H. Hoof. *Theory and Practice of the European Convention on Human Rights.* Kluwer Law International, 1998.

Dzehtsiarou, Kanstantsin. *European Consensus and the Legitimacy of the European Court of Human Rights.* Cambridge University Press, 2015.

Finnis, John. *Natural Law and Natural Rights.* Oxford University Press, 2011.

Garlicki, Lech. "Wprowadzenie." [Introduction] In *Konwencja o ochronie praw człowieka i podstawowych wolności. Komentarz do artykułów 1–18* [Convention on the Protection of Human Rights and Fundamental Freedoms. Commentary on Articles 1–18], edited by Lech Garlicki, 3–12. Wydawnictwo C.H. Beck, 2011.

Gerards, Janneke. "Judicial deliberations in the European Court of Human Rights." In *Judicial Deliberations in the European Court of Human Rights. The Legitimacy of Highest Courts' Rulings*, edited by Huls N., Adams M. and Jacco Bomhoff, 1–25. T.M.C. Asser Institute, 2008, https://ssrn.com/abstract=1114906.

Gerards, Janneke. "Margin of appreciation and incrementalism in the case law of the European Court of Human Rights." *Human Rights Law Review* 18(3) (2018): 495–515.

Gerards, Janneke. "Pluralism, deference and the margin of appreciation doctrine." *European Law Journal* 17(1) (2011): 80–120.

Gerards, Janneke. "Procedural review by the ECtHR: A typology." In *Procedural Review in European Fundamental Rights Cases*, edited by Janneke Gerards and Eva Brems, 127–160. Cambridge University Press, 2017.

Gerards, Janneke. "The European Court of Human Rights and the National Courts – Giving shape to the notion of 'shared responsibility." In *Implementation of the European Convention on Human Rights and of the Judgments of the ECtHR in National Case Law. A Comparative Analysis*, edited by Janneke Gerards and Joseph W.A. Fleuren, 13–94. Intersentia, 2014.

Gerards, Janneke. "The prism of fundamental rights." *European Constitutional Law Review* 8 (2012): 173–202.

Gerards, Janneke and Eva Brems. "Procedural review in European fundamental rights cases: Introduction." In *Procedural Review in European Fundamental Rights Cases*, edited by Janneke Gerards and Eva Brems, 1–13. Cambridge University Press, 2017.

Glenn, Patric. *Legal Traditions of the World* (4th ed.). Oxford University Press, 2010.

Grabenwarter, Christoph. "The European convention on human rights: Inherent constitutional tendencies and the role of the European Court of Human Rights." In *Constitutional Crisis in the European Constitutional Area, Theory, Law and Politics in Hungary and Romania*, edited by Armin von Bogdandy and Pal Sonnevend, 101–115. Hart Publishing, 2014.

Greer, Steven and Luzius Wildhaber. "Revisiting the debate about 'constitutionalising' the European Court of Human Rights." *Human Rights Law Review* 12(4) (2012): 655–687.

Hermann, Donald H. "Legal reasoning as argumentation." *Northern Kentucky Law Review* 12(3) (1985): 467–510.

Heyning, Catherine Van de. "No place like home: Discretionary space for the domestic protection of fundamental rights." In *Human Rights Protection in the European Legal Order: The Interaction between the European and the National Courts*, edited by Patricia Popelier, Catherine Van de Heyning and Piet Van Nuffel, 65–96. Intersentia, 2011.

Janneke, Gerardsand and Eva Brems. *Procedural Review in European Fundamental Rights Cases*, 230–262. Cambridge University Press, 2017.

Kavanagh, Aileen. "Proportionality and parliamentary debates: Exploring some forbidden territory." *Oxford Journal of Legal Studies* 34 (2014): 443–479.

Kleinlein, Thomas. "The procedural approach of the European Court of Human Rights: Between subsidiarity and dynamic evolution." *International & Comparative Law Quarterly* 68 (2019): 91–110.

Legarre, Santiago and Gregory J. Mitchell. "Secondary effects and public morality." *Harvard Journal of Law and Public Policy* 40 (2017): 320–358.

Legg, Andrew. *The Margin of Appreciation in International Human Rights Law: Deference and Proportionality*. Oxford University Press, 2012.

Letsas, George. *A Theory of Interpretation of the European Convention on Human Rights*. Oxford University Press, 2009.

Letsas, George. "Two concepts of the margin of appreciation." *Oxford Journal of Legal Studies* 26(4) (2006): 705–732.

Lucas, John Randolph. *The Principles of Politics*. Oxford University Press, 1966.

MacCormick, Neil. "Argumentation and interpretation in law." *Ratio Juris* 6(1) (1993): 16–29.

Mik, Cezary. "Metodologia interpretacji traktatów z dziedziny praw człowieka." [Methodology of the interpretation of human rights treates] *Toruński Rocznik Praw Człowieka i Pokoju* (1) (1992–1993): 11–36.

Murray, John L. "Consensus: Concordance, or hegemony of the majority?" *Dialogue between judges, Proceedings of the Seminar*, 25 January, 17, www.echr.coe.int/documents/dialogue_2008_eng.pdf

Note. "The chilling effect in constitutional law." *Columbia Law Review* 69(5) (1969): 808–842.

Nowicki, Marek Antoni. *Wokół Konwencji Europejskiej* [Around the European Convention] Wolters Kluwer, 2021.

O'Donnell, Thomas A. "The margin of appreciation doctrine: Standards in the jurisprudence of the European Court of Human Rights." *Human Rights Quarterly* 4 (1982): 474–496.

Pech, Laurent. "The concept of chilling effect. Its untapped potential to better protect democracy, the rule of law, and fundamental rights in the EU." *Open Society European Policy Institute*, 2021, www.opensocietyfoundations.org/publications/the-concept-of-chilling-effect

Popelier, Patricia. "The court as regulatory watchdog: The procedural approach in the judicial decisions of the European Court of Human Rights." In *The Role of Constitutional Courts in Multilevel Governance*, edited by Patricia Popelier, Armen Mazmanyan and Werner Vandenbruwaene, 249–268. Intersentia, 2012.

Popelier, Patricia and Catherine Van de Heyning. "Procedural rationality: Giving teeth to the proportionality analysis." *European Constitutional Law Review* 9(2) (2013): 230–262.

Popelier, Patricia and Catherine Van de Heyning. "Subsidiarity Post-Brighton: Procedural rationality as answer?" *Leiden Journal of International Law* 30 (2017): 5–23.

Raz, Joseph. "Why interpret." *Ratio Juris* 9(4) (1996): 349–363.

Rui, Jon Petter. "The interlaken, Izmir and Brighton declarations: Towards a paradigm shift in the strasbourg court's interpretation of the European convention of human rights?" *Nordic Journal of Human Rights* 31(1) (2013): 28–54.

Saul, Matthew. "The European Court of Human Rights' margin of appreciation and the processes of national parliaments." *Human Rights Law Review* 15(4) (2015): 745–774.

Schauer, Frederic. "Fear, risk and the first amendment: Unraveling the chilling effect." *Boston University Law Review* 58 (5) (1978): 685–732.

Stone, Thomas W. "Margin of appreciation gone away: The European Court of Human Rights' implicit use of the precautionary principle in: Frette v. France to backtrack on protection from discrimination on the basis of sexual orientation." *Connecticut Public Interest Law Journal* 3(1) (2003–2004): 218–236.

Townend, Judith. "Freedom of expression and the chilling effect." In *Routledge Companion to Media and Human Rights*, edited by Howard Tumber and Silvio Waisbord, 73–82. Routledge, 2017.

Vila, Marisa Iglesias. "Subsidiarity, margin of appreciation and international adjudication within a cooperative conception of human rights." *International Journal of Constitutional Law* 15(2) (2017): 393–413.

Wiśniewski, Adam. "Uwagi o teorii interpretacji Europejskiej Konwencji Praw Człowieka." In *Między wykładnią a tworzeniem prawa. Refleksje na tle orzecznictwa ETPC*, edited by Cezary Mik and Katarzyna Gałka, 15–41. TNOiK, 2011.

Yourow, Howard Ch. *The Margin of Appreciation Doctrine in the Dynamics of European Human Rights Jurisprudence*. Martinus Nijhoff Publishers, 1996.

Zagzebski, Linda. "A defense of epistemic authority." *Research Philosophica* 90(2) (2013): 293–306.

3 Ways of reasoning in medically assisted procreation and surrogacy cases

Introduction

The matters that seem problematic from a moral point of view in the area of medically assisted procreation, including the issues of surrogate motherhood and the use of genetic material, have evolved along with the advancement of medicine.[1] They cover a very broad catalogue of concerns, ranging from the general objections to the technicalisation of the intimate sphere of conception and childbirth to the question of defining the scope of the individual's autonomy in deciding on his or her genetic material. Furthermore, the unauthorised commercialisation of genetic material, the creation of gametes and embryos for scientific research, and the potential risks and dangers of misuse as a result of the commercialisation of reproduction, the manipulation of genetic material in order to conceive an embryo with specific traits, and even reproductive cloning and the creation of human-animal embryos. The existence of a genetic link between the intended parents and the child and separating the biological (genetic) parenthood from the legal one are also highly problematic and carry strong moral and social connotations.[2]

1 Medically assisted procreation (MAP) refers to the situation in which conception occurs by means other than physical intercourse between a man and a woman. This term covers a wide range of medical interventions. Depending on the place where fertilisation takes place, MAP methods can be divided into extracorporeal (*in vitro*) and intracorporeal (*in vivo*). In the former case, the fertilisation process takes place outside the woman's body (in a test tube), while in the latter it takes place inside the patient's reproductive system (artificial insemination). In both types of methods, a distinction is made between homologous procedures (where the donors are spouses) and heterologous procedures (where gametes from donor/donors are used). The circumstances in which individual techniques are used also make it possible to differentiate between surrogate motherhood or surrogacy (understood as a situation in which a woman takes an *in vitro* fertilised ovum of another woman into her uterus and after giving birth to the child gives it to the so-called intended parents) and *post mortem* procreation.

2 Rebecca J. Cook, Bernard M. Dickens, Mahmoud F. Fathalla, *Reproductive Health and Human Rights: Integrating Medicine, Ethics and Law*, (Oxford University Press, 2003); David J. Walsh, Mary L. Ma, Eric S. Sills, "The evolution of health policy guidelines for assisted reproduction in the Republic of Ireland, 2004–2009." *Health Research Policy and Systems* 9(28) (2011); Guillem Cano Palomares. "Right to family life and access to medically assisted procreation in the

DOI: 10.4324/9781003375999-4

There are no universally binding international regulations concerning medically assisted procreation, neither on a universal nor European level. In Europe, however, a number of documents have been adopted by the Council of Europe and the EU aimed at developing standards in the area of carrying out individual procedures.[3] Only some of the developed solutions are binding; moreover, not all European countries ratified them. Consequently, domestic provisions often differ from one another and fail to regulate all contentious issues.

The ECtHR examined cases concerning medically assisted procreation, including both *in vivo* and *in vitro* fertilisation, surrogacy and the possibility of using one's own genetic material, including the legal status of embryos. Judgments in the following cases were selected as being representative for the examination of the Court's practice in terms of analysing the arguments used.

In the case *Evans v. UK*, the applicant, who was suffering from ovarian cancer, underwent *in vitro* fertilisation treatment with her then partner before having her ovaries removed. Six embryos were created and placed in storage. When the couple's relationship ended, her ex-partner withdrew his consent for the embryos to be used, not wanting to be the genetic parent of the applicant's child. National law consequently required that the ova be destroyed. The applicant complained that domestic law permitted her former partner to effectively withdraw his consent to store and use the embryos created jointly by both of them, preventing her from ever having a child to whom she would be genetically related. The Court stated no violation of Articles 2, 8 and 14 of the Convention.[4]

In *Dickson v. UK*, the applicant, a convict serving a minimum sentence of 15 years of imprisonment for murder was denied access to artificial insemination facilities that would allow him to have a child with his wife, who would have little chance of conceiving a child after his release. The Court concluded that there had been a violation of Article 8 of the Convention.[5]

In *S.H. and Others v. Austria*, the applicants, two married Austrian couples, wished to avail themselves of medically assisted procreation techniques which were not permitted under Austrian law. One couple needed sperm from a donor and the other needed ova. The Austrian Artificial Procreation Act prohibits the use of donor sperm for *in vitro* fertilisation and ovum donation in general. At the same time, the Act allows for other assisted procreation techniques, in particular IVF with ova and sperm from the spouses or cohabitees themselves and, under exceptional circumstances, the donation of sperm when

case law of the European Court of Human Rights." *The Right to Family Life in the European*, eds. Maribel G. Pascual and Aida T. Pérez, (Routledge, 2017).

3 For a compilation of legal instruments of a binding nature and other documents adopted within the Council of Europe in relation to bioethical issues, including medically assisted procreation, visit: www.coe.int/t/dg3/healthbioethic/texts_and_documents/.

4 *Evans v. UK*, appl. no. 6339/05, judgment of 7.3.2006 (C), 10.4.2007 (GC).

5 *Dickson v. UK*, appl. no. 44362/04, judgment of 4.12.2007.

it is inserted into the woman's reproductive organs. The applicants argued that the prohibition on the donation of sperm and ova for the purpose of *in vitro* fertilisation violated their right to respect for family life under Article 8 of the Convention and that the difference in treatment compared with couples who wished to use medically assisted procreation techniques but did not have to use ova and sperm donation for *in vitro* fertilisation constituted discriminatory treatment which violated Article 14 of the Convention. The Court found no violation of Article 8 of the Convention and no violation of Article 8 in conjunction with Article 14.[6]

The case of *Mennesson v. France* concerned a French heterosexual couple and their children born in California from gestational surrogacy. The embryos were conceived through *in vitro* fertilisation using the couple's husband's gametes and donor ova. Since the procedure is legal in California, the relevant US courts ruled prenatally that the applicants were to be recognised as parents once the children were born. The children were then issued US birth certificates, as ordered by the courts. The children's birth certificates were entered into the French central register of births, marriages and deaths, but the prosecutor requested that this entry be invalidated. The French courts ruled that giving effect to the surrogacy agreement by registering the American birth certificates contravened French public policy. The applicants objected that the welfare of the children had been harmed by the failure to recognise the legal parent-child relationship. The Court drew a distinction between the applicants' right to respect for their family life and the applicants' children's right to respect for their private life and, as regards their family life, found no violation of Article 8. However, Article 8 was found to have been violated as regards the children's right to respect for their private life.[7]

In *Parrillo v. Italy*, the applicant resorted to *in vitro* fertilisation with her partner in 2002. A total of five embryos resulting from that procedure were cryopreserved. Her partner died in 2003. The applicant did not wish to proceed with the pregnancy and requested the release of the embryos so that she could donate them to stem cell research, but the clinic refused to release them on the basis of the applicable regulations. The embryos remained in the cryogenic storage bank. The applicant's main complaint was brought under Article 8 of the Convention and Article 1 of Protocol No. 1 against the statutory prohibition. As far as the first complaint was concerned, the Court found no violation and the second complaint was declared incompatible *ratione materiae* because human embryos could not be reduced to "possessions" within the meaning of that provision.[8]

6 S.H. and Others v. Austria, appl. no. 57813/00, judgment of 11.3.2010, judgment of 3.11.2011. (GC).

7 Mennesson v. France, appl. no. 65192/11, judgment of 26.6.2014.

8 Parrillo v. Italy, appl. no. 46470/11, judgment of 27.8.2015.

In *Paradiso and Campanelli v. Italy*, the applicants, an Italian couple, entered into a surrogacy arrangement in Russia. The child born as a result thereof was purportedly biologically related to the husband (the applicant). Under Russian law, the applicants were registered as the child's parents. However, upon their return to Italy, criminal proceedings were brought against them because they had allegedly brought the child to Italy in violation of the law prohibiting medically assisted procreation and had allegedly violated the conditions set out in their previous adoption permit. The child, aged nine months, was taken from the applicants and placed in a children's home. The applicants were ordered not to contact the child. The applicants alleged a violation of Article 8 of the Convention, claiming that the refusal to recognise the legal parent-child relationship, the removal of the child and its placement in foster care infringed their right to respect for their private and family life. In the end, the Grand Chamber found no violation of Article 8 of the Convention.[9]

Arguments referring to authority

Arguments based on the authority of the codified law – intense search for an applicable standard

Comparative law reasoning and reasoning relating to international law may provide the basis for the formulation of certain separate arguments strongly oriented towards supporting the direction of Court's decision-making activities. At the same time, argumentation that is based on the search for consensus between national regulations, on the search for prevailing trends, or referring to the existing or emerging international regulations as the basis for supporting the Court's ruling is basically one element to be taken into consideration when applying the margin of appreciation concept.

Given the absence of any universally binding provisions of international law in this area, the ECtHR is not in a position to provide sufficiently persuasive and conclusive arguments solely on the basis of standards stemming from international regulations other than the ECHR. The existing legal instruments of soft and hard law character are, however, always thoroughly discussed in the judgments.[10] Moreover, the judgments always contain an extensive amount of comparative material.[11]

When presenting the regulations contained in both non-binding and binding international instruments, the Court primarily seeks to answer the question of whether there is a standard that could be applied to a given case. Already at the outset, it can be said that internationally adopted acts fail to provide any

9 Paradiso and Campanelli v. Italy, appl. no. 25358/12, judgment of 24.1.2017.

10 Such as Paradiso and Campanelli v. Italy, par. 75–80; Parrillo v. Italy, par. 54–68.

11 Such as Evans v. UK, par. 39–49; Paradiso and Campanelli v. Italy, par. 81; Parrillo v. Italy, par. 69–75.

clear guidance on any of the legal issues to be decided by the Court, either at the level of binding or non-binding regulations.

In *Dickson v. UK*, the Court made reference to the International Covenant on Civil and Political Rights (ICCPR) – Article 10 (3) and to two documents of a non-binding nature, that is the United Nations Standard Minimum Rules for the Treatment of Prisoners (1957) and the European Prison Rules 1987 and 2006. These documents were presented in such a way that the ECtHR could use them to conclude that, irrespective of the repressive and preventive objectives that imprisonment must pursue, all detention shall be managed so as to facilitate the reintegration into free society of persons who have been deprived of their liberty and that steps should be taken to guarantee that conditions inside prison are as similar to normal life as possible.[12] The conclusions reached in the light of these documents were then used by the Court to make a negative assessment of the domestic decision-making process, the result of which was that the applicant could not have availed himself of medically assisted procreation procedures.

Again, in *Evans v. UK*, the reference made to international instruments in the form of the Council of Europe Convention on Human Rights and Biomedicine and Universal Declaration on Bioethics and Human Rights served the purpose of indicating the arguments supporting the proposition that a person participating in a medical procedure can express consent as well as withdraw it at any time and for any reason without disadvantage or prejudice.[13] The store and use of embryos were then treated as medical procedure on a parent, which facilitated the reasoning about their rights, referring to wording from the Oviedo Convention.

In turn, in the case of *S.H. and Others v. Austria*, there was a rather selective reference to international instruments. Here, the Court resorted to Principle 11 of the principles adopted in 1989 by the Ad Hoc Committee of Experts on Progress in the Biomedical Sciences (CAHBI), which states that "In principle, *in vitro* fertilisation shall be effected using gametes of the members of the couple." In addition, it referred to the 2002 Additional Protocol to the Convention on Human Rights and Biomedicine concerning Transplantation of Organs and Tissues of Human Origin, which promotes organ donation but explicitly excludes reproductive organs and tissues from this scope, and to one of the EU Directives[14] which contains a provision asserting that it should not interfere with decisions made by States concerning the use or non-use of any specific type of human cells, including germ cells and embryonic stem cells. Recourse to the shape of international regulations has made it possible

12 Dickson v. UK, par. 29–36.

13 Evans v. UK, par. 50–2.

14 Directive 2004/23/EC of the European Parliament and of the Council of 31 March 2004 on the setting of standards of quality and safety for the donation, procurement, testing, processing, preservation, storage and distribution of human tissues and cells.

to indicate that it is preferable for medically assisted procreation to be carried out using the genetic material of the partners, and that the final decision as to whether it is possible to use genetic material from the donor rests in the hands of the State.

The point of referring to multiple internationally binding regulations in the *Paradiso and Campanelli v. Italy* case was primarily to look at State action through the prism of regulations concerning the status of children, particularly with regards to the recognition of parentage. In turn, citing Article 3 of the Convention on the Rights of the Child enabled the concept of "best interests," which should be the paramount consideration in all actions concerning children undertaken by either public or private bodies, to be introduced into the conceptual grid of the ECtHR judgment.

In *Parrillo v. Italy*, the Court referred to the numerous binding and non-binding instruments of the Council of Europe, the European Union as well as the United Nations. One of the documents referred to was the resolution of the PACE,[15] in which the Assembly clearly identified the need for adopting proper legislation to regulate the use of embryos while drawing attention to the ethical concerns that needed to be addressed:

> [T]he Assembly holds that more concerted ethical consideration should be given – at national, supraregional and global levels – to the goals and purposes pursued by science and technology, to the instruments and methods they employ, to their possible consequences and side effects, and to the overall system of rules and behaviour within which they operate.

The ECtHR also highlighted the opinion of one of the advisory bodies of the European Commission, according to which research on human embryos should not be excluded *a priori*, as this issue "is the object of different ethical choices in different countries."[16] Reference to a wide range of documents issued by international bodies served to reinforce the point that the legal status of the embryo and foetus has not been defined by law up to this point and also to indicate that the use of embryos for research purposes must have limits.

In contrast, a modest reference to international law in the *Mennesson* case in the form of the Principles of the Council of Europe Ad Hoc Committee of Experts on Progress in the Biomedical Sciences (CAHBI) (especially Principle 15, on "Surrogate Motherhood"), with regard to the admissibility of surrogacy arrangements, allowed for the presentation of conclusions about the

15 Resolution 1934 (2013) of the Parliamentary Assembly of the Council of Europe on ethics in science and technology.

16 European Group on Ethics in Science and New Technologies (EGE) to the European Commission Opinion no. 12: Ethical aspects of research involving the use of human embryo in the context of the 5th Framework Programme, 23 November 1998.

lack of an international standard in this area and the admissibility of various solutions.[17]

At no point in the course of reviewing the cases did the Court find a straightforward answer in the international regulations as to which standard of assessment it should apply in that case. Nevertheless, it was undoubtedly able to draw conclusions from these instruments in the first place, which indirectly constituted the grounds for arguments about the wide discretion available to States to regulate particular issues, thus strengthening the justification in the direction of finding no violation of individual rights.

The second specific external legal authority referred to by the Court in its arguments, in addition to international law, is the content of legal principles found both in the legal system of the respondent State as well as in other States.

In its judgment delivered in *S.H. v. Austria*, the Court attached particular importance to the fact that the provisions of Austrian law gave effect to one of the underlying principles of civil law, namely *mater semper certa est*. Both the reasoning set out in the judgment of the Austrian Constitutional Court which examined the applicants' constitutional complaint and the reasoning put forward by the Austrian Government, accompanied by the Italian (one of the most restrictive legislations which strictly prohibits the donation of genetic material) and German governments acting as third parties in the case, indicated that the risk of "split maternity" and the consequent undermining of the *mater semper certa est* principle constituted one of the key negative aspects associated with medically assisted procreation.[18] The Court accepted this standpoint along with the consequent restrictions on the performance of medically assisted procreation procedures with regard to the option of using donated genetic material. As a result, it granted the Austrian State broad discretion in this case by accepting the solutions introduced to limit the scope of permissible medical procedures.

Having failed to find clear guidelines in internationally accepted regulations concerning the cases pending before it, the ECtHR treats the arguments formulated on the basis of the analysis of these instruments as a certain

17 Mennesson v. France, par. 39.

18 Cf. More in Wannes Hoof, Guido Pennings, "The consequences of S.H. and Others v. Austria for legislation on gamete donation in Europe: An ethical analysis of the European Court of Human Rights judgments." *Reproductive Biomedicine Online* 25 (2012): 667. At the same time, the authors draw attention to the inconsistency of the argumentation used by the Austrian government to justify the introduction of a ban on *in vitro* fertilisation versus the general possibility of sperm donation, essentially solely on practical grounds. They pointed out that *in vitro* fertilisation is a highly specialised technology where the implementation of the ban can be monitored, whereas normal donations, being much simpler, cannot. In view of the fact that such a simplistic justification was put forward, in their opinion it is difficult to regard any other justification, particularly those of a moral and ethical nature, as credible.

framework – a context for present but also future adjudication, reinforcing the direction of the finding.

Besides international law, the Court finds the solutions adopted at the national level to be of great importance. Comparing them and trying to draw a common denominator in the form of a European consensus will be discussed as part of the arguments pertaining to the margin of appreciation.

Argumentation based on the margin of appreciation – what issues should be left to the discretion of the domestic authorities

Since there are no common binding solutions at European level governing the issue of medically assisted procreation in detail, the burden of regulation falls on the States. The Court qualifies complaints concerning medically assisted procreation *a priori* as sensitive social issues, in which the States have a wider margin of appreciation; that is, they are left with a greater degree of discretion whether or not to adopt certain regulations and in shaping their domestic legislation and balancing competing interests.[19]

When deciding cases on this matter, the Court made only perfunctory statements about the moral sensitivity of the issues at stake in order to substantiate that wider margin without identifying the problems that gave rise to that sensitivity. It employed a set of repetitive phrases such as "morally and ethically delicate nature,"[20] "sensitive moral and ethical issues,"[21] "sensitive domain,"[22] "sensitive ethical questions,"[23] "ethically sensitive issues,"[24] and "delicate moral and ethical questions."[25] None of the judgments gave any explanation as to why certain types of issues or medical procedures are "sensitive" from an ethical and moral point of view.

Instead, each case made it necessary for the Court to define the area in which the State would be granted discretion and to indicate its scope by taking into account both restrictive and extenuating factors. Here, special attention should be drawn to the notion of European consensus, the lack of which was the factor which justified the widening of the margin of appreciation and in doing so played the most significant role in Court's deliberations. This notion is perceived as a common approach of States to balance conflicting interests or

19 Evans v. UK, par. 81; Dickson v. UK, par. 81; S.H and Others v. Austria, par. 97; Mennesson v. France, par. 79; Parrillo v. Italy, par. 197; Paradiso and Campanelli v. Italy, par. 184.

20 In Evans v. UK, the ECtHR only laconically concludes that the issue of *in vitro* fertilisation and the legal status and disposal of embryos is undoubtedly of a sensitive moral and ethical nature. Evans, paras. 78 and 81.

21 S.H. and Others v. Austria, par. 97 and 100.

22 S.H. and Others v. Austria, par. 97.

23 Mennesson v. France, par. 79.

24 Paradiso and Campanelli v. Italy, par. 194.

25 Parrillo v. Italy, par. 176.

to protect them, especially when the matter gives rise to morally and ethically sensitive issues.[26]

According to the Court's decision, the margin of appreciation concerns the regulation of conjugal visits in penal institutions.[27] Here, the Court highlighted that the right to become genetic parents is an important facet of an individual's existence or identity and it being at stake could limit the State's freedom to make a decision.[28] Simultaneously, the Grand Chamber failed to explicitly identify the existence of a consensus in that regard, although it noted the evolution in some European States towards consenting to so-called conjugal visits.[29] The lack of consensus observed in respect of the case concerned both the lack of similar regulations and the lack of a shared approach to the problem among the States.

Another subject of the States margin of appreciation identified by the Court was the rules regulating the use of *in vitro* treatment, especially concerning the possibility to withdraw consent to the use of genetic material and the use of heterologous genetic material.[30] In *Evans v. UK*, the Grand Chamber concluded that it could not be argued that there is any consensus as to the stage in IVF treatment when the gamete providers' consent becomes irrevocable[31] and that there was no consensus that the woman's Article 8 rights should have taken precedence over her partner's rights.[32] In conclusion, it was stated that there is a "lack of any European consensus" that could allow a conclusion that the applicant's right to respect for the decision to become a parent in the genetic sense should be accorded greater weight than her former partner's right

26 The Court has not defined the term "consensus" in its jurisprudence, nor has it done so in cases involving medically assisted procreation. As indicated in the literature, this is a deliberate move, allowing for flexibility in applying this device. See: Luzius Wildhaber, Arnaldur. Hjartarson, Stephen Donnelly, "No Consensus on Consensus? The Practice of the European Court of Human Rights." *Human Rights Law Journal* 33 (2013): 248, 249, and also Jeffrey A. Brauch, "The Dangerous Search for an Elusive Consensus: What the Supreme Court Should Learn from the European Court of Human Rights." *Howard Law Journal* 52 (2008–2009): 277, 278. The last author even puts forward the thesis that the ECHR should not clarify the notion of consensus, as it is a device detrimental to the idea of human rights as well as the rule of law. At this point, it must also be pointed out that the Court does not interpret the term "consensus" as unanimity, but as the expression of a particular trend. Alternatively, the Court uses a variety of terms to describe the consensus. See, *Dialogue between Judges, European Court of Human Rights, Council of Europe*, 2008, 14 and Dzehtsiarou, European Consensus, 12.

27 Dickson v. UK, par. 81.

28 Dickson v. UK, par. 72 and 78 and a contrario Paradiso and Campanelli v. Italy, par. 195.

29 Dickson v. UK, par. 81. While noting the argument concerning the European consensus used by the Chamber, the GC referred only to "the evolution observed in several European countries towards conjugal visits" and did not recognise the existence of a consensus.

30 Evans v. UK, par. 82 and S.H. and Others v. Austria, par. 97.

31 Evans v. UK, par. 79.

32 Evans v. UK, par. 80.

to respect for his decision not to have a genetically related child with her.[33] The lack of the consensus was observed both at the highly detailed level of Member States' legislation concerning the moment when donor consent becomes irrevocable and at the level of the general approach to the question of whether the rights of a person who wishes to become a genetic parent should prevail over the rights of a person who does not wish to become one in a particular situation.

In turn, in the case *S.H. and Others v. Austria*, the Court considered the use of heterologous genetic material. The Grand Chamber concluded that there was no European consensus on the donation of gametes for the purpose of *in vitro* fertilisation.[34] Indeed, the absence of this consensus was multilayered. It concerned both Member States' legislation, the general approach of Member States to the issue and the lack of consensus in the views expressed by the public. With regards to the latter, the Court derived an additional quantifier of "social acceptability."[35] Besides the lack of a common approach at an international level, that new concept became an additional premise intended to substantiate the introduction of certain restrictions by the Austrian government. The restriction was aimed at preventing individuals from benefiting from certain medical procedures related to the medically assisted procreation. This concept was referred to when considering whether a total ban on the use of certain artificial insemination techniques was justified. The Court held that although moral considerations and social acceptability ought to play an important role in domestic decision-making in the field of artificial procreation, these factors cannot be regarded as sufficient reasons for imposing a total ban

33 Evans v. UK, par. 90.

34 S.H. and Others v. Austria, par. 96, 97, 106, 113, 117. The Court used as many as four terms to describe the potential consensus: "a clear trend in the legislation of the Contracting States," "an emerging European consensus," "clear common ground among the member States" and "a consensus in society."

35 S.H. and Others v. Austria, par. 54 and 100. The Court went even further and introduced new determinants for the definition of the "European consensus." While it recognised the consensus being "born," it held that it was not based on well-established and long-standing principles established in the law of the State but reflected the degree of development in a particularly dynamic area of law and did not decisively limit the States' margin of discretion (par. 96). Although, it did assess that there is a lack of "common ground" between states, and therefore the margin of discretion granted to the State must be wide and allow for the reconciliation of social reality with the fundamental principles on which the functioning of the state is founded (positions of principle). "Social reality" and the "principles of states" (positions on principle) have thus become values that the judgment gives precedence over the existence of a European consensus, consisting of the existence of similar and reasonably convergent national solutions. Recognising that there is no European consensus because of these two factors has significantly widened the margin of appreciation available to the State, since by doing so new elements were introduced on which the achievement of this consensus was made conditional. The introduction of the new quantifier of consensus was vehemently criticised by the judges who submitted a dissenting opinion to the judgment. Most significantly, the newly developed methodology for establishing consensus has not been applied in subsequent judgments.

on the use of certain artificial fertilisation techniques, such as ova donation. Various legitimate interests need to be taken into account when designing a legal framework to regulate such matters.[36] However, the Court gave no indication as to what other interests were to be taken into account, although it could naturally be assumed that this would include the couple's interest in "conceiving a child" and the opposing public interest, which in this case was construed primarily through the prism of the need to provide protection to potentially disadvantaged women. However, even by the mere reference to social acceptability, the Court showed that it was seeking acceptance of the adopted course of action by a very broad group of addressees, including public opinion across the country. Therefore, one can risk a conclusion that social acceptability, by becoming a substitute for Court's moral views, has at the same time become an argument for convincing the group that expressed such a view to the taken ruling.[37]

Another subject of margin of appreciation was the freedom of States in regulating surrogacy agreements.[38] Here, it indicated that matters concerning the identity of the child, the recognition (in law) of genetic origin[39] and capacity to recognise the legal relationship between child and parent, and in situations where it is not only a question of regulating the relationship with the biological parent but also with the other parent[40] were such particularly

36 S.H. and Others v. Austria, par. 100.

37 While indicating two factors, that is moral considerations and social acceptability, as fundamental constraints to be taken into account by the State when introducing medically assisted procreation solutions, the Court has neither specified what particular moral concerns were at stake nor did it indicate how to interpret the concept of "social acceptability." In fact, the term has appeared in the Court's case law only once, in this very case. These issues are partly explained not so much in the government's argumentation as in the government documents prepared during the introduction phase of each regulation and in the decisions of domestic courts. See S. H. and Others v. Austria, par. 100: The Court considers that concerns based on moral considerations or on social acceptability must be taken seriously in a sensitive domain like artificial procreation. However, they are not in themselves sufficient reasons for a complete ban on a specific artificial procreation technique such as ovum donation. Notwithstanding the wide margin of appreciation afforded to the Contracting States, the legal framework devised for this purpose must be shaped in a coherent manner which allows the different legitimate interests involved to be adequately taken into account.

38 Mennesson v. France, par. 79 (recourse to a surrogacy arrangement).

39 Mennesson v. France, par. 96–7 and a contrario Paradiso and Campanelli v. Italy, par. 195.

40 ECtHR advisory opinion to the Court of Cassation. It was not until the advisory opinion issued in connection with the French Court of Cassation's question that the Court allowed itself to reflect more widely on the determination of the width of the margin of appreciation. It elaborated and presented new elements in the opinion to determine the scope of the margin of appreciation available to the States. On the one hand, it reaffirmed its previous position that, in legal situations in which there is no fairly uniform view between the States, the States are granted a wider margin of appreciation, thus confirming that this is precisely one such case. At the same time, however, it stated that where the case concerned particularly significant aspects of an individual's identity, for example the legal relationship between a child and a parent, that margin would be limited. Importantly, the Court's conclusion referred to the regulation of

important facets of an individual's existence or identity that they limited the States' margin of appreciation. In *Mennesson v. France*, the Court reported a lack of consensus on the legality of surrogacy arrangements (States' policy) and the legal recognition of the relationship between the intended (social) parents and the child thereby born abroad as a result of the fact that these issues raise sensitive ethical questions.[41] As seen by the Court, the fact that there is no consensus reflects the highly problematic ethical nature of surrogacy agreements. The lack of consensus among States thus touches upon fundamental issues: the very assumptions about the legitimacy of this institution and the recognition of its legal effects. However, despite the failure to establish the consensus, the Court considered that since the lack of recognition of the legal effects of the birth of a child from a surrogacy contract in domestic law relates to fundamental aspects of human identity, the lack of the consensus does not preclude the need to limit the States' margin of appreciation.

Yet another scope of the margin of appreciation was identified in the case *Paradiso and Campanelli v. Italy*. Here, it concerned adoption of a child in the context of medically assisted procreation and surrogacy.[42] The Court did not expressly pronounce on whether or not there was a consensus as to the legal issues discussed in the case. It did so rather indirectly by indicating that in cases that involve morally and ethically sensitive/delicate issues about which there is no consensus at a European level, the Court must follow the nuanced approach presented in *S.H. and Others v. Austria* and *Mennesson v. France*.[43]

Finally, the Court embraced by the margin of appreciation the use of genetic material, including the possibility of using embryos for the purposes of scientific research.[44] In the case of *Parrillo v. Italy*, it explicitly stated that the lack of consensus revolves around the possibility of transferring embryos for scientific purposes.[45]

The margin of appreciation attributed to States in medically assisted procreation cases is correspondingly wider.[46] A wide margin of appreciation means

the parental relationship with a person who is not the biological parent. The Court reiterated aspects such as the stability of the environment in which the child grows up and develops and the sustainability of the bond with the person who raises the child. See, Advisory Opinion concerning the recognition in domestic law of a legal parent – child relationship between a child born through a gestational surrogacy arrangement abroad and the intended mother (request no. P16-2018-001), 10.04.2019, par. 44–5.

41 Mennesson v. France, par. 78–9.

42 Paradiso and Campanelli: 184 (issue of heterologous assisted fertilisation, in the context of surrogacy arrangements and the legal recognition of the parent-child relationship between intended parents and the children thus legally conceived abroad, adoption, the taking of a child into care, medically assisted reproduction and surrogate motherhood).

43 Paradiso and Campanelli v. Italy, par. 184.

44 Parrillo v. Italy, par. 197.

45 Parrillo v. Italy, par. 176.

46 Paul Mahoney, Rachael Kondak, "Common ground. A starting point or destination for comparative-law analysis by the European Court of Human Rights?" *Courts and Comparative*

that the Court will not find the law or practice of the Member State to be in breach of the Convention and that "the Court would generally respect the legislature's policy choice unless it is manifestly without reasonable foundation."[47] The ruling in the *Mennesson* case confirms, though, that this is not an automatically applied principle, but merely a presumption which is then reviewed by the Court.

Secondly, when it comes to the area of reproductive rights, the ECtHR's application of the concept of the wide margin often leads to a *de facto domestication/nationalisation* of the scope of protection of rights guaranteed under European law.[48] Yet another conclusion is connected with this observation, namely that the application of an inherently wide margin of assessment in this area results in the consolidation of a number of negative phenomena in legal and social reality, the elimination of which has been indicated as the objective of restrictive State actions. Thus, the literature calls for narrowing the scope of the applied margin of appreciation, including through the development of some common minimum solutions in the disputed area.[49] Accepting far-reaching restrictions introduced by the States in the face of the total diversity of national regulations results in inequality (between citizens of Council of Europe Member States) in access to such medical techniques, leads to such services being offered outside the official medical market (development of a grey market in medical services), particularly to cross-border tourism[50] and *de facto* results in the acceptance of a situation where disadvantaged women, in countries where such practices are available, enter into contracts for the provision of such services.

The fact that countries are formally granted a wide margin of appreciation in the sphere of reproductive rights in a situation in which the national regulations adopted in this sphere are characterised by extensive diversity, *de facto* unprecedented in other areas (it suffices to say that the conclusion of contracts of surrogacy, which is completely legal in one country, is subject to criminal sanctions in another), leads to the situation in which, whilst expressing understanding for the regulations adopted by a given country for a particular protective purpose (protection of children, protection of women and so on), the Court accepts all the negative consequences primarily arising from the cross-border exercise of reproductive rights. Thus, the case law in which the Court refrains from taking a clear position on the legal admissibility of certain procedures by ceding the decision to domestic authorities in the face of such an enormous diversity of national solutions perpetuates a reality in which all

Law, eds. Mads Andenas and Duncan Fairgrieve, (Oxford University Press, 2015, p. 134, Dzehtsiarou, *European Consensus*, 37.

47 Dickson v. the UK, par. 78.

48 Cayon, "The Widening." 397.

49 Cayon, "The Widening." 410.

50 Cayon, "The Widening." 410 and 411.

the negative consequences of resorting to medical interference in the procreative process are manifested.

Thirdly, the above conclusion corresponds perfectly with the views expressed in the doctrine that the manner in which the Court uses this doctrinal concept makes it more of a rhetorical device than a concept with substantive content.[51] Still, there is confusion about the margin's scope. This is due to the lack of uniformity of the criteria applied and the lack of predictability of decisions. This conclusion can also be drawn from the judgments in cases involving medically assisted procreation. This lack of uniformity of the methodology of application and substantive content of the margin of appreciation is evident on a number of levels.

The judges who delivered the dissenting opinion in *Evans v. UK* drew particular attention to the "void meaning" surrounding the margin of appreciation in the substantive layer, stating that:

> The Court should not use the margin of appreciation principle as a merely pragmatic substitute for a thought-out approach to the problem of proper scope of review.

Having read the judgments, one gets the impression that there is no connection between the generic circumstances determining the scope of the margin and the actual margin that was applied. Although the Court indicates that the margin can be limited if the issues to be decided constitute an exceptionally important interest for the applicant, it reached this conclusion only twice in the examined judgments. It has held that the State's margin of appreciation is limited in cases where we are dealing with the right to become genetic parents where a person is deprived of his or her liberty (*Dickson*) and also in regards the question of the child's identity and the recognition of the child's genetic descent through the establishment of a legal bond between parent and child (*Mennesson*). Essentially, the Court failed to present any arguments to justify why, in the other cases, the interests pursued by the applicants had not been given the same weight and had not led to a narrowing of the margin.

Finally, notwithstanding the absence of the European consensus on medically assisted procreation,[52] it can be acknowledged that in terms of deciding the minimum moral standard that the ECtHR formulates in relation to particular issues, this European consensus is the absolute lowest starting point. The presence of such a standard implies that States accept a certain minimum

51 Gerards, "Margin of Appreciation." 500 et seq.

52 In the consequence of the determination that no consensus existed in the reviewed judgments, the Court established that States had complied with all of their obligations under the Convention. This conclusion with regard to the situation of lack of consensus was also indicated in "The Role of Consensus in the System of the European Convention on Human Rights." *Dialogue between Judges*, European Court of Human Rights, Council of Europe, 2008, p. 12.

level of common solutions, which the Court refers to when arguing a case and seeking understanding for the decision taken. Despite the fact that the Court has not identified the existence of the European consensus in cases involving medically assisted procreation, it has used its case law to partially initiate the formation of such a consensus. Its foundation will primarily consist of innovative pronouncements of the Court identified within the framework of teleological argumentation, which will be discussed later in this chapter.[53] What is more, implementation of this concept made it possible to strengthen the principle of subsidiarity by substantiating the decision taken by the Court based on arguments developed by the State. The absence of a finding of the consensus resulted in the States being granted a wide margin of appreciation in respect of the policies pursued and the regulations adopted. In only one case did the Court consider at the stage of assessing the proportionality of interference, despite the absence of a consensus, that the restrictions imposed did not ensure a balance between the protection of individual and public interests (*Mennesson v. France*).[54]

Although the ECtHR did not expect unanimity but sought consensus among the majority, in the *S.H. and Others* judgment it introduced additional quantifiers for understanding the consensus: firstly, its peculiar consolidation and reliance on the principles of states, and, secondly, its conditioning of the consent to the introduction of certain new solutions on the position of public opinion in a given State. Both of these quantifiers essentially made it more difficult to ascertain the existence of consensus at the European level. However, their introduction was undoubtedly of a persuasive nature, and constituted an element of argumentation aimed at effectively convincing the audience of the rationale presented by the Court.

As far as the case law on medically assisted procreation is concerned, the concept of margin of appreciation is of persuasive and argumentative significance, and does not serve as an interpretative tool which allows for the delineation of clear principles which should guide the States in regulating substantive

53 "to what extent is the Court able through its case-law to lay the foundations for the creation of a future consensus? Where the Court adopts a novel approach without the basis of an existing consensus, this question is of particular importance. This is in contrast to those cases where the Court's case-law can sometimes be considered to be merely illustrative of an international consensus on a given question rather than breaking new ground in relation to the level of human rights protection in Europe." Cf. Dialogue between judges, p. 11.

54 It should be stressed that the need to find a "way out" of the situation and to provide protection to the two underage applicants was met not by recourse to the concept of "autonomous concepts" but precisely by the proportionality test. Cf. J. Gerards, "Judicial Deliberations." The manner in which the cases under consideration were decided fits perfectly into the approach proposed by Mahoney and Kondak, according to which all the cases under consideration can be placed in Group III (cases where there is no European consensus and the Court finds no violation as such) and the Mennesson case in Group IV (cases where the Court finds no consensus but nevertheless finds a violation of the Convention). Cf. Mahoney, Kondak, "Common Ground." 128–34.

issues. As illustrated by the previous examples, the margin of appreciation treated as a argumentative tool is addressed primarily to the States and societies whose approval is sought by the Court upon reaching certain decisions. It is an argumentation that gives less consideration to the perspective of individuals and gives more weight to the general public interest.

Deontological arguments

The second group of arguments consists of those which the Court uses when giving reasons for its standpoint by interpreting the substantive provisions of the Convention and outlining their scope. Contrary to the deontological tools identified in the area of abortion cases and end-of-life situations, in the field of medically assisted procreation, the Court does not argue with the tool of plasticity and assimilation of notions.

Incrementalism – right to become parents and what an embryo is not

One of the key techniques used by the ECtHR in its argumentation is the delineation of the content of the right examined by picking out/extracting the elements which comprise it. Without prejudging the conclusion of the subsequent analysis, it can be hinted that this is one of the most significant ways in which a judicial body substantiates its decision regarding medically assisted procreation. It allows the Court to present its position on the scope of the guaranteed rights, even if in the circumstances of the case in question it did not state any violation of law.

Incrementalism was used in this area to define and *de facto* extend the limits of the right to respect for private and family life under Article 8 of the ECHR.

Only once has the Court referred to the right to life of embryo under Article 2 (*Evans v. the United Kingdom*). Both the Court's Chamber[55] and the Grand Chamber held that the embryo enjoyed no independent rights and interests and could not have claimed (nor could it be claimed on its behalf) respect for the right to life under Article 2 of the Convention.[56]

The second major pronunciation in the *Evans* case was the Chamber's acknowledgement that Article 8 covers the right to become or not to become parents,[57] which was further clarified by the Grand Chamber as the right to respect for the decision to become a parent in the genetic sense.[58]

The right to respect for the decision to become a parent in the genetic sense and consequently also for the decision not to procreate derived in the *Evans* case from Article 8 of the Convention was subsequently reaffirmed in *Dickson*

55 Evans v. UK (Chamber), par. 46.
56 Evans v. UK (GC), par. 46, 56.
57 Evans v. UK (Chamber), par. 57.
58 Evans v. UK (GC), par. 72.

v. UK. The Court held there that Article 8 would apply because the refusal to allow artificial insemination concerned the applicants' right to private and family life, the concepts encompassing the right to respect for the decision to become a genetic parent.[59]

In the *S. H. and Others v. Austria* case, the ECtHR first held that the couple's right to respect for the decision to conceive together with the couple's right to use medically assisted procreation as an expression of their right to private and family life fell within the scope governed by Article 8.[60] The Court's conclusion needs to be interpreted as a development of the standpoint previously articulated in *Evans v. UK* and *Dickson v. UK*. After all, in *Evans v. UK*, the Court held that Article 8 includes the right to respect for the decision to have a child or not to have one.

In turn, from *Mennesson v. France* one can indirectly derive a right under Article 8 of the Convention to acquire recognition of one's genetic descent from a biological parent.[61] The Court decided to take such a position in spite of having accepted that the impossibility of recognising the parent-child relationship under French law was a consequence of the French authorities' explicit refusal to recognise surrogacy based on arguments of a moral and ethical nature.[62] Subsequently, the Court also embraced with Article 8 the right to recognition of a legal parent-child relationship with the intended mother, indicated on a birth certificate legally issued abroad as "legal mother."[63] In that

59 Dickson v. UK, par. 66.

60 S.H. and Others v. Austria, par. 82.

61 Mennesson v. France, par. 100. This opinion was clearly formulated in the judgment in *Paradiso and Campanelli v. Italy*, par. 195.

62 Mennesson v. France, par. 83.

63 Foulon and Buvet v. France (appl. No. 9063/14), judgment of 21.07.2017, par. 58, Laborie v. France, judgment of 19.01.2017, par. 32, D. v. France, judgment of 16.07.2020, par. 50–54. The Court confirmed in the judgments that the manner of recognising the bond was left to the discretion of the State. The Mennesson and Labassee judgments made it clear that, in the Court's view, it was unacceptable not to be able to confirm or establish a link between a biological father and children under French law. In the meantime, there was a change in French jurisprudence. Since 2017, the Court of Cassation began to allow partial transcription of birth certificates in relation to the biological father, while still recognising that transcription is not possible in relation to the mother because, under French law, the mother is the woman who gave birth to the child. Consequently, the Court of Cassation asked the ECtHR, in the form of a request for an advisory opinion, to determine the legal position of the intended mother. Whether, while exercising the rights of the biological father and recognising under French law the link between him and the child/children through the entry in the civil-status registers of the data on the birth record issued abroad, it is admissible to refuse to enter the data on the mother or it is necessary to establish such a link with the mother, who is indicated as "legal mother" in the foreign documents. In addition, the French court asked whether a distinction should be made between the situation of a woman who was the donor of genetic material and a woman who was not, and in what form, if any, the confirmation of the existence of a legal bond between the potential/intended mother who was the legal mother – according to the foreign documents – and the child. See, Advisory opinion, request no. P16–2018–001, par. 46 and 52.

way, it expressed its unequivocal position in favour and gave greater importance of the legalisation of the child's legal status over the ethical concerns underlying the State's decision.

The argumentation based on the development of a new principle, that is defining a new meaning of the right in question, although without identifying a violation in the circumstances of the particular case, was also applied in *Paradiso and Campanelli v. Italy*. Here, the Court redefined the elements that had to coincide in order for the situation to be assessed from the point of view of the right to respect for family life in the context of the relationship between a child and its carers.[64]

The application of incrementalism in the *Parrillo v. Italy* judgment led the Court to innovatory statements that strongly substantiated its position about non-violation of the applicant's rights. So, although it held that the right to respect for private life under Article 8 of the ECHR would cover issues relating to the disposal of embryos obtained by *in vitro* fertilisation and not intended for implantation,[65] at the same time it went on to collect arguments for justifying as legitimate the ban introduced by the State. One of these arguments was the clarification about the legal standing of embryo. In this regard, the Court stated that the "protection of the embryo's potential for life" may be linked to the aim of protecting morals and the rights and freedoms of others, and it is within that legitimate aim. The clarification was not complete because it failed to conclude whether the word "others" encompasses human embryos.[66] Further, to substantiate the position taken, the Court went on to state that the possibility of donating embryos for scientific purposes does not constitute a fundamental right protected under Article 8 of the Convention and does not represent a particularly important aspect of the existence and identity of an individual.[67] Here, the Court also backed its line of argumentation with the lack of European consensus in the field of the donation of non-implantable

64 From that judgment on, these are: the existence of a biological link between at least one of the future parents and the child; an appropriate length of time for which they had taken care of the child, which is assessed as necessary to create close personal ties; and compliance with the law of actions aimed at establishment of relationship with the child in order to ensure the validity of the bond from a legal perspective, par. 151. The Court's new approach to defining the scope of the right to respect for family life has been noted in the literature. Cf. Marianna Iliadou, "Surrogacy and the ECtHR: Reflections on Paradiso and Campanelli v. Italy. Commentary." *Medical Law Review* 27, no. 1: 148. The author underlined that the introduction of the condition of legality of the established parental relationship represented a step back – in relation to previous case law (Marcx v. Belgium) – due to the introduction of the division into "legal" and "illegal" families.

65 The assumption for further considerations of the Court was that the notion of "private life" could not be defined by means of an exhaustive definition and that it included, inter alia, the right to self-determination (para. 153). In turn, it decided that the possibility of making a conscious choice, preceded by careful consideration concerning the fate of embryos, touches upon intimate aspects of personal life and thus constitutes an element of this right (par. 159).

66 Parrillo v. Italy, par. 167.

67 Parrillo v. Italy, par. 174.

embryos for research.[68] The final crowning argument was the distinction of a principle that embryos cannot be regarded as property within the meaning of Article 1 of Protocol No. 1 to the Convention, as the legal situation of human embryos could not be reduced to the concept of "property." If the Court were to make a different assessment in this area, the whole reasoning would have to go the other direction.

Incrementalism served the Court in the *Parrillo* case by achieving at least two goals. First, determining the status of the embryo by applying the combination of three factors: recognition of the embryo's potential for life, recognition that the embryo is not property and resorting to national legislation which endows the embryo with rights and protections in certain areas.[69] Secondly, by determining in that particular form the status of embryos, the Court was able to justify its conclusion as to non-violation of the applicant's right. This case is somewhat at odds with the up-to-date position of the Court avoiding the sensitive and controversial question concerning the beginning of human life. Thus, by recognising the embryo's potential for life, not only did the Court address ethical questions – defining the embryo as a subject potentially protected under the Convention – but also the scope of the possible conduct of scientific research.[70]

The considerations described here prove that incrementalism is one of the most intriguing ways of arguing cases. In some cases, like *Evans* and *S.H. and Others*, the Court significantly strengthened the applicant's legal position by explicitly assigning them specific rights. However, at the same time, it did not come to the conclusion about the violations of their rights. In other cases, like *Mennesson*, the strengthening of the applicant's position resulted in assessment about non-fulfilment of the States obligations. In still other cases, such as *Paradiso and Campanelli* and *Parrillo*, incrementalism helped the Court to develop argumentation arguing to the disadvantage of the applicant. In the light of these conclusions, it is therefore difficult to agree with the objections raised against incrementalism alleging that through this mode of argumentation the Court leads to a constant – unjustified or excessive – expansion of the scope of the rights guaranteed under the Convention.[71] Certainly, it is not the case in medically assisted procreation. Undoubtedly, however, when precisely

68 Parrillo v. Italy, par. 176.

69 Margaret Eder, "Parillo v. Italy. ECHR Allows States to Interfere with Individuals' Admittedly Private Lives." *Tulane Journal of International and Comparative Law* 24 (2) (2014–2015): 389.

70 Such as Eder, "Parillo v. Italy." 389. The opposing view, according to which the Court's failure to pronounce on the legal distinctiveness of the embryo and to view its "fate" in the light of the guarantee of the right to respect for the private life of the woman (under Article 8), would lead to the conclusion that the "rights" of the embryo are covered and subordinated to those of the applicant. Such an understanding of the Court's conclusions was presented by some of the judges in their dissenting opinion. See par. 7 of the judgment.

71 The critical stance is taken, for example, by Gerards, "The prism of fundamental rights." 184.

defining the scope of individual rights, the Court provides States with clear guidelines of how similar cases may be decided in the future.

In the case of *S.H. and Others v. Austria*, the Court supplemented the incremental argumentation with an additional observation on the developmental nature of the issue by indicating that contrary to the recommendations of the Austrian Constitutional Court, the Austrian legislator had not taken measures to adapt the legislation to current medical knowledge and progress in this field. The ECtHR stressed that in the area of the complaint, scientific developments necessitate constant amendments to the law. Therefore, States should monitor the situation and, as can be presumed, reflect current medical knowledge by amending existing regulations.[72] It is suggested that the Court's conclusion has to be read in the context of establishment of a possible future common European approach to the issue.[73] However, more important is that by using the argument about the developmental nature of the issue, the Court seems to indicate the future direction of its case law, thus preparing States for more progressive rulings. This reflects yet another function of the discussed argumentative tool.

Proceduralisation – how to avoid substantive review

Proceduralisation takes on various forms in decisions concerning medically assisted procreation, and this diversity is certainly illustrative of the thesis that the Court refers to elements of procedure in different ways and to different effects.[74]

In *Evans v. UK*, the Court (both the Chamber and the Grand Chamber[75]) chose to analyse the case from the point of view of the discharge of positive obligations having in mind that the State adopted provisions enabling persons not capable of doing so naturally to conceive a child through the use of medically assisted techniques. Adoption of that perspective has determined the course of further deliberations.

The Court's examination focused on assessing whether the legislation adopted by the parliament had correctly pursued the general interest, which

72 *S.H. and Others v. Austria*, par. 118.

73 Cf. e.g. David Kete, "Case of S.H. and Others v. Austria: Practical Concern over Individual Rights." Boston College International & Comparative Law Review 36 (E. Supp) (2013): 50.

74 Cf. J. Gerards, "Procedural Review." 127 and subs. Among the cases we have analysed, there were those in which the Court adjudicated the case by assessing the fulfilment of negative obligations. For example, in the *Mannesson v. France* case, the refusal of the French authorities to legally recognise the family tie between the applicants was qualified as an "interference" in their right to respect for their family life, which raised questions with regard to the negative obligations of the respondent State under Article 8 (Mennesson, par. 48). Similarly in the *Parrillo v. Italy* case the Court stated that the ban on donating to scientific research embryos obtained from an *in vitro* fertilisation and not destined for implantation constitutes an interference with the applicant's right to respect for her private life (Parrillo, par. 161).

75 Evans v. UK, par. 59 (judgment C), par. 75 (judgment GC).

consisted of respect for commonly accepted values like human dignity and free will, and rather more procedural requirements like the need to ensure fairness between persons participating in the IVF procedure, respect for the principle of legal certainty and the need to avoid problems with potential arbitrary and inconsistent decisions in the balancing of interests on a case-by-case basis. It came to the conclusion that the State's choice as to the values deserving protection was legitimate and consistent, and thus it subscribed to the State's assessment.[76] Additionally, the Court assessed in the positive way the quality of procedures leading up to the adoption of the contested measures and underlined that they were the result of "exceptionally detailed examination of the social, ethical and legal implications of developments in the field of human fertilisation and embryology."[77]

The Court's conclusion as to the non-violation of the applicant's rights followed from the acknowledgement that it was the national authorities which, through the correct conduct of the legislative process, had fulfilled their positive obligations as regards the shaping of the legislation in such a way as to give effect to the substantive values guaranteeing the protection of the right contained in Article 8 of the ECHR.

The procedural approach undertaken by the Court in the case limited the scope of the examination to the analysis of the regulations adopted by the Parliament *in abstracto*. There was no in-depth analysis *in concreto*, detached from the form of the legislation and taking into account the exceptional circumstances of the case.[78] The adoption of the perspective of assessing the State's compliance with its obligation to enact legislation that adequately balances the conflicting individual interest and the public interest led to a shift in the focus of the inquiry from the individual circumstances of the case to questions of the legitimacy of the general policy.[79] The Court felt absolved of having to balance the goods on its own.

76 Evans v. UK (GC), par. 89 and 90.

77 Evans v. UK (GC), par. 86.

78 Jacco Bomhoff, Lorenzo Zucca, "Evans v. UK: European Court of Human Rights." *European Constitutional Law Review* 2(3) (2006): 429.

79 When reflecting on the rationale that led the Court to follow this line of argument, one can refer to the position expressed by Lady Arden in the judgment handed down in this case by the England and Wales Court of Appeal. She made it clear that the balancing of conflicting goods must be performed at an abstract level by the national legislature because the judge does not have the tools to make the necessary choices: "As this is a sensitive area of ethical judgment, the balance to be struck between the parties must primarily be a matter for Parliament. . . . The personal circumstances of the parties are different from what they are at the outset of the treatment, and it would be difficult for a court to judge whether the effect of Mr Johnston's withdrawal of his consent on Ms Evans is greater that the effect that the invalidation of that withdrawal of consent would have on Mr Johnston. The court has no point of reference by which to make that sort of evaluation." (par. 110). Evans v. Amicus Healthcare Ltd.& Ors, England and Wales Court of Appeal (Civil Division), 25.6.2004, (2004) 78 BMLR 181.

It should be emphasised that a general procedural requirement resulting from the case law is that there should always be a room for individualised (judicial or administrative) decision-making.[80] Nevertheless, exceptions to this presumption are visible in many cases, including where moral issues are at stake. In *Evans*, the Court accepted that the legislation in question served a number of wider public interests in upholding the principle of the primacy of consent and promoting legal clarity and certainty.[81] The same procedural approach was applied in *S.H. and Others v. Austria*. Thus, in cases where the general measures were diligently prepared by the Parliament, the Court does not always requires individualisation, especially due to the need to assure legal certainty.[82] In this case, the Court did so in order to avoid favouring one justice (that of the applicant's) over another.[83] The confinement of the scrutiny to a narrow procedural analysis and failing to weigh the competing goods independently proved our thesis that the choice of the perspective of positive obligations was of considerable importance for the final decision, for it determined the scope of the Court's examination and consequently the scope of protection of the applicant's rights in the individual circumstances of the case.[84]

The Court adopted a perspective of examination similar to that used in *Evans* in *Dickson v. UK*. However, it went even further in failing to distinguish between positive and negative obligations, finding that it was not necessary to define an evaluative perspective, but that attention should be focused on the way in which the competing public and private interests were weighed in the decision-making process that had been put in place as a result of the applicant's request to undergo the artificial insemination procedure.

Lack of a deep national parliamentary debate that would result in adoption of an act of a statutory character[85] as well as lack of procedural safeguards in the decision-making process based on a document having only the character of guidelines for the prison authorities (a document issued by the secretary of state dated 28 May 2003 and referred in the ruling as "the Policy") was assessed by the Court as a situation that did not guarantee a sufficient balancing

80 Philip Sale, B. Hopper, "Proportionality and the Form of Law." *Law Quarterly Review* 19 (2003): 426–54, 429.

81 Evans v. UK (GC), par. 74.

82 Gerards, "Procedural Review." 135.

83 Angelika Nussberger, "Procedural review by the ECHR: View from the Court." in *Procedural Review in European Fundamental Rights Cases*, eds. Janneke Gerards and Eva Brems, (Cambridge University Press, 2017), 170.

84 Further argumentation supporting the view for the need to apply substantive review is provided in the dissenting opinion of judge Turman and other judges that was submitted to the GC's judgment. See the joint dissenting opinion of judges Türmen, Tsatsa-Nikolovska, Spielmann and Ziemele, par. 7. The judges who filed the dissenting opinion had had no doubt that balancing the interests of the applicant and the former partner would have led to different results than the final conclusion of the ECtHR.

85 Dickson v. UK, par. 83–4.

of the interests of the individual against the general interest.[86] However, here the Court's conclusion about the insufficient quality of the general regulations influenced the assessment of the individual situation of the applicant. The Court stated that the shape of regulations "prevented the required assessment of the proportionality of a restriction, in any individual case." Thus, the negative procedural review prompted the Court to make its own evaluation.

By contrast, in *S.H and Others v. Austria*, the Court classified the outcome of the statutory provisions prohibiting the recourse to techniques of artificial procreation as State's interference with the rights of individuals, which triggered scrutiny from the perspective of the State's compliance with negative obligations, that is, the absence of arbitrary interference.[87] Despite adopting such a perspective, the Court evaluated – as far as the potential violation of the applicants' rights were concerned – the shape of the regulation and the way it balanced the public interest with private interests. The Court's line of argumentation was thus consistent with that used in previous cases, like *Evans v. UK*, in which it however adopted an entirely different perspective, though that of the fulfilment of positive obligations. The Court applied procedural reasoning in those cases with respect to the examination of the reasonableness and proportionality of the legislative measures at stake. Such action by the Court demonstrates the flexibility of the Court's approach to the perspective in assessing cases. It thus confirms the position taken by the Court itself that, for the final conclusion of the judgment, the adoption of the perspective of examining the fulfilment of positive or negative obligations by the State is not of fundamental importance.

In its judgment in *H.S. and Others*, the Court concentrated entirely on the assessment of the applicable provisions *in abstracto*. This is clearly reflected in the Court's statement that in terms of Article 8 of the Convention, the central question is not whether a different solution might have been adopted by the legislature that would arguably have struck a fairer balance (*more fair to the applicants – AM*), but whether the Austrian legislature exceeded the margin of appreciation afforded to it under that Article when striking the balance at the point at which it did.[88] The Court stated that the fact that the margin of appreciation afforded to States is a wide one does not mean

> that the solutions reached by the legislature are beyond the scrutiny of the Court. It falls to the Court to examine carefully the arguments taken into consideration during the legislative process and leading to the choices that have been made by the legislature and to determine whether a fair balance has been struck between the competing interests of the State and those directly affected by those legislative choices.[89]

86 Dickson v. UK, par. 85.
87 S.H. and Others v. Austria, par. 88.
88 S.H. and Others v. Austria, par. 106.
89 S.H. and Others v. Austria, par. 97.

The fact that the Court indicated that the situation of persons directly affected by those legislative choices should be considered was not followed by an in-depth analysis of the situations in which the applicants found themselves. Additional argument reinforcing the arguments *ad abstractum* was the Court's reference "to the fact that . . . there is no sufficiently established European consensus as to whether ovum donation for *in vitro* fertilisation should be allowed."[90] The sole reference to the individual situation of the complainants was to indicate that there were no contraindications to carrying out the treatment they sought in another country, so as to encourage procreative tourism.[91]

A similar approach of examining the case from the perspective of the State's interference (here, in the form of adopting a legislation introducing a ban on donating to scientific research embryos obtained from an *in vitro* fertilisation and not destined for implantation) and of assessing the arguments from the *abstracto* perspective can be found in *Parrillo v. Italy*.[92]

The case *Paradiso and Campanelli v. Italy* was again considered from the perspective of the State's interference with the applicants private life, here by issuing judicial decisions which resulted in the child's removal and being placed in the care of the social services with a view to adoption.[93] While deciding about the legitimacy of the intervention, the Court applied another mode of proceduralisation, namely the mode of assessment resembling the "responsible courts doctrine."[94] Although the Court did not refer to its classic approach that national authorities are a "better place" to balance individual interests and did not use the formulation that "the Court would require strong reasons to substitute its view for that of the domestic courts,"[95] it entirely confined its assessment to the analysis of the rulings of domestic courts. Instead of interpreting the norms to the facts of the case, it deferred the task of performing its own proportionality assessment *in concreto*. When conducting the procedural review of the Italian courts' decisions, the Court underlined that they struck a fair balance between the various interests involved,[96] were compatible with the 1961 Hague Convention[97] and that the application of a set of certain provisions of Italian law was foreseeable.[98] The Court had no

90 S.H. and Others v. Austria, par. 106.
91 S.H. and Others v. Austria, par. 114.
92 Parrillo v. Italy, par. 183.
93 Paradiso and Campanelli v. Italy, par. 166.
94 Basak Cali, "From Flexible to Variable Standards of Judicial Review: The Responsible Domestic Courts Doctrine at the European Court of Human Rights." *Shifting Centres of Gravity in Human Rights Protection: Rethinking relations between the ECHR, EU and national legal orders*, eds. Oddný Mjöll Arnardóttir and Antoine Buyse. Basingstoke: Routledge, 2016, 144 and subs.
95 Such as Axel Spriner AG v. Germany, appl. no. 39954/08, judgment of 7 Feb. 2012, para. 88.
96 Paradiso and Campanelli v. Italy, par. 215.
97 Paradiso and Campanelli v. Italy, par. 170.
98 Paradiso and Campanelli v. Italy, par. 173.

doubt that the reasons advanced by the domestic courts are relevant,[99] sufficient[100] and proportional.[101] The fact that the Court focused its reasoning on reference to the reasons and arguments used by the domestic authorities was underlined by dissenting judges.[102]

In cases where the verdict was that there had been no violation of individual rights (*Evans*, *S.H. and Others*, *Paradiso* and *Campanelli*), the tool of proceduralisation, particularly in the form of integrated procedural review (referring to both procedural review of legislation as well as procedural review of national judicial decision-making), had the effect that the Court concentrated on the assessment of the case *in abstracto* without carrying out its own assessment *in concreto*. Viewing the case through the prism of the "fairness" of the domestic regulations or decisions taken by the judicial authorities provided the Court with an opportunity to "avoid" having to take a clear position on the case by balancing the public interest against the private interest independently. The general acceptance of the shape of the national legislation allowed the Court to limit its statements on moral and ethical issues to the necessary minimum. It simply restrained its statements to acceptance of values secured by national legislation protections.

However, it is worth stressing that the procedural reasoning was applied irrespective of whether the case was examined from the point of view of the State's compliance with negative obligations or positive obligations.

Teleological argumentation

Argumentation based on examination and assessment of secondary effects – a new concept of groups deserving special protection

In the case law of the ECtHR, one can discern at least two perspectives for assessing potential (also negative) effects of the decisions taken regarding the applicant. In the temporal dimension, the consequences can be assessed in the short and long term.[103] In the personal perspective, the consequences may concern the applicant him/herself and this is the typical situation and *ratio* of individual complaints. They may also concern individuals whose interests directly conflict with those of the applicants[104] and also other groups of people.

99 Paradiso and Campanelli v. Italy, par. 197.
100 Paradiso and Campanelli v. Italy, par. 199.
101 Paradiso and Campanelli v. Italy, par. 215.
102 Joint dissenting opinion of Judges Lazarova Trajkovska, Bianku, Laffranque, Lemmens and Grozev, par. 11, Concurring opinion of judge Dedov.
103 Compare the analysis of the negative consequences suffered or to be suffered in the future by the underage applicants in *Mennesson v. France* due to the lack of recognition in the French legal system of their legal bond with their guardians, cf. Mennesson v. France, par. 96–9.
104 Cf. the situation in *Evans v. UK* and the balancing of the applicant's rights against those of her former partner.

The latter situation occurs rather rarely in the jurisprudence of the ECtHR and cases concerning medically assisted procreation are good examples of it. Here, the Court argues to convince the audience to the adopted solution by analysing socially unfavourable phenomena which may occur as a consequence of enabling the applicants to exercise certain rights or freedoms. The phenomena that may potentially appear are identified by the Court by way of distinguishing hypothetical groups of individuals that deserve special attention in securing their rights. Therefore, the argumentation consists in balancing the actual claims of the applicants with the necessity to provide protection to certain abstractly distinguished groups of persons whose rights, in the Court's view, must be taken into account when determining the scope of the rights and freedoms the applicants may enjoy.

Given the lack of application by the Court of the legitimate aim of morals in cases involving medically assisted procreation, while simultaneously resorting to the premise of "rights and freedoms of others" as a basis for justification of interference with the rights of the applicants, the Court's key line of argument is to balance the interests of individual applicants against the rights of "others." The interests of these entities are treated as the designator of the legitimate public interest; it is a kind of personalisation of public interest.[105]

The applicants, being persons applying for the possibility of access to medically assisted procreation procedures or for the legalisation of certain legal statuses resulting from such procedures, do not fall within one of the so-called vulnerable groups and are not subject to any special preferential treatment on that account.[106] As we have already mentioned in Chapter 1, the Court has introduced a group-based approach on vulnerability by distinguishing particular groups, which are "labelled" as vulnerable because of certain reasons: their weakness and susceptibility to harm or structural discrimination and historical, systematic violations of their rights. Any interference with their rights requires not only due, but even special diligence on the part of the State. On

105 It should be pointed out that although in *S.H. and Others v. Austria* the Court indicated public morality as the grounds for restricting rights and freedoms in addition to the legitimate aim of the rights and freedoms of others, the entire reasoning of the judgment refers to both premises.

106 The ECtHR's construct that we named "groups deserving special protection" is distinct from the concept of "vulnerable groups," also taking into account the characteristics of the latter concept identified in the literature, that is their: 1. relationality (vulnerability concerns a group, not individuals, and is conditioned by social, historical and institutional elements); 2. particularity/uniqueness (vulnerability presumably concerns every individual, but members of particular communities are particularly vulnerable) and the harm suffered. Distinguishing features of the concept of "vulnerable groups" after Peroni and Timmer, "Vulnerable Groups." 1064–65. This theme is further developed in Chapter 2. The two groups of protected persons may be identical, especially in cases concerning end-of-life situations. However, these groups are not synonymous, and the distinct way in which they have been identified results in a different scope of obligations for States and the corresponding rights of individuals.

the other hand, in the area under discussion the applicants did not fall into the category of vulnerable and simultaneously the Court identified certain groups whose interest – potentially contrary to the applicant's interests – appeared to be decisive by deserving special protection in weighing the public interest against that of the applicants. The Court focused on the need to provide special protection to two groups of persons: a group of potentially disadvantaged women who need to be protected from the possible donation of genetic material or surrogacy arrangements under economic pressure as well as a group of potential children born through medically assisted procreation. As already mentioned in previous chapters, for the purposes of this monograph they will be referred to as "groups deserving special attention." In some circumstances those groups will be equivalent with vulnerable groups (like in the euthanasia cases), however in others not. And this is exactly the case of applications concerning medically assisted procreation.

When it comes to the protection of women's interests, the Court first accepts the governments' argument that restrictions on the available methods of artificial procreation can be motivated by the need to protect women who decide to donate genetic material (ova). In this regard, the primary concern is to prevent the exploitation of women who are in a vulnerable situation, mainly in economic terms, and to limit potential risks to the donor's health. These considerations also extend to women who, when deciding on a procedure leading to the production of more ova, donate some of them to finance their own treatment. Such an argument was raised by the Austrian Government in *S.H. and Others v. Austria* and was not contested by the Court.[107]

In addition, the Court accepted the government's argument in *Mennesson v. France* regarding the fact that the human body (female) could not become a commercial instrument.[108] Furthermore, the French government pointed out that the basis for the interference with the applicants' rights was "health protection," and the Court accepted this.[109] When we ask the legitimate question of whose health is at stake, we should probably get the answer that it is the health of surrogate mothers. However, this conclusion is not obvious.

By contrast, in the *Paradiso and Campanelli v. Italy* case, the Court accepted the government's argument that the prohibition of surrogacy agreements was intended to protect women and children who could potentially be adversely affected by such practices as a valid public interest. It is worth noting that the public interest aimed at protecting women and children was so important to the Italian government that it decided to introduce very restrictive legislation aimed at discouraging potentially interested parties from pursuing their intentions abroad.[110] This point was singled out and emphasised by the

107 S.H. and Others v. Austria, par. 66, 101, 104, 105 and 113.
108 S.H. and Others v. Austria, par. 60.
109 S.H. and Others v. Austria, par. 60, 62.
110 S.H. and Others v. Austria, par. 203.

Court. This is different from the approach taken, for example, by the Austrian authorities in *H.S. and Others v. Austria*. They explicitly demonstrated that by prohibiting certain procedures in their own country the authorities allowed their nationals to undergo such procedures abroad and did not exclude the possibility of legalising the new legal situations thus created. It can be inferred that the authorities have therefore accepted circumstances where the rights of economically disadvantaged women are potentially violated by the fact that other countries do not implement policies that protect women and permit certain medical procedures.[111]

The second group whose interests draw the Court's special attention in cases involving medically assisted procreation are children.

In its rulings on medically assisted procreation, the concept of protecting the interests of children – not in a specific, but in a broad/general context – has been extensively applied through the Court's use of the concept of "best interest of a child/children" as the interest that dictates the weight of the public interest.

In the analysed judgments, the ECtHR did not explain the substance of the concept of "best interest" it uses. This situation may generate confusion as to how to interpret the scope of protection that, in the Court's view, should be afforded to this group (and not to individuals – in contrast to the concept of protecting individuals belonging to vulnerable groups) under the Convention, due to the reasons stated in the following.

The concept of best interest is employed in cases involving medically assisted procreation in a dual sense. First of all, it applies to scenarios where the situation of the child is directly at stake and, consequently, the best interest of the individual child is of paramount importance.[112] However, in this case, the child is a participant or otherwise a subject of the proceedings before the Court. In such a situation, the applicability of the concept is beyond any doubt.

However, the Court does not limit itself to articulating the need to extend special protection to children whose rights and obligations are the subject of the ruling. By referring to the premise of the limitation of rights and freedoms due to the need to protect the rights of "others," it places children who may

111 Judge Dedov expressed an explicitly negative view of private adoptions and surrogacy arrangements in his concurring opinion to the *Paradiso and Campanelli* case. He shared the view that surrogacy arrangements bring forth the possibility of commercialisation and human trafficking and pose a threat to the well-being of society. By contrast, it is intriguing that judge Dedov expressed satisfaction that the judgment in *Paradiso and Campanelli* is one of those in which the Court ruled more in relation to moral values than taking into account the margin of appreciation, at the same time criticising on this point the judgments in *Lautsi and Others* and *Parrillo v. Italy* case. However, it seems that the judge's opinion is rather a product of his way of interpreting the rather neutral reflections of the Court. The Court neither condemned the surrogacy contracts as strongly as the judge believes, nor did it express itself so clearly about the moral needs of societies.

112 Mennesson v. France, par. 81, 84 and 85.

be born as a result of the use of assisted procreation methods in that category. This group is to receive special attention for a variety of reasons. In this way, the Court defines the scope of the public interest based on the general need to protect children, not yet born (!) from certain risks.

In cases concerning medically assisted procreation, it is the individual interests of the applicants – the people who are unable to procreate naturally – that are the trigger point. Nevertheless, in the process of assessing the proportionality of State action, the abstractly defined interests of children potentially born through the use of medically assisted procreation methods are put at stake. The Court identified a number of specific risks to the welfare of children which, in its view, were associated with medically assisted procreation.

Firstly, it accepted the reasoning set out in the Austrian Constitutional Court's judgment that ova donation poses the risk of a far-reaching "split" of maternity into genetic and biological motherhood, which leads to undesirable and abnormal situations in the child-parent relationship. The Court agreed that the solutions adopted by the Austrian legislature were aimed at avoiding risks to the welfare of the child thus conceived, its health, rights or the circumstances in which it would find itself (the aim was to anticipate potential conflicts between the women involved in the procedure).[113]

Secondly, the Court accepted the French legislator's view that surrogacy entailed the risk that the child would become an object of trade and therefore the French legislator chose to prohibit surrogacy on the grounds of the child's "best interests."[114] The Court did not challenge this argument because it did not question the prohibition of surrogacy, but merely drew attention to the need to be able to establish a legal bond between the genetic parent and the children born of surrogacy. The Court again had the opportunity to assess the impact of surrogacy on the pursuit of the welfare of children by issuing an advisory opinion in relation to the French Court of Cassation's questions. In the advisory opinion, the Court determined the conditions for the fulfilment of the good of the child in a new way. It held that, in the context of surrogacy agreements, the evaluation of the child's good will not be limited to an assessment of the respect for particular aspects of the child's right to private life, but will be influenced primarily by two factors: (a) the need to protect individual members of society from the risk of being exploited in connection with the conclusion of surrogacy agreements and to ensure the possibility of knowing one's origins, and (b) the possibility of creating a legal bond with the person who raises a child and the right to grow in a stable environment – including legally.

Thirdly, the Court accepts that children must be protected from potential selection practices on account of traits desired by prospective parents.[115]

113 S.H. and Others v. Austria, par. 104 i 105.
114 Mennesson v. France, par. 72.
115 S.H. and Others v. Austria, par. 100.

Fourthly, indeed, the Court's entire reasoning in *Paradiso and Campanelli v. Italy* was constructed around the protection of the interests of the child.[116] Paradoxically, this happened even though the Court had refused to extend the protection of the right to family to the applicants in this case, instead ruling that only the right to protection of private life would apply here. By failing to afford the applicants the opportunity to bring an action on behalf of a child born under a surrogacy arrangement and by failing to extend the protection inherent in the right to family life within the meaning of Article 8 of the Convention to their mutual relationship, the Court could not in principle directly refer to the child's welfare as a protected good and address whether the domestic authorities had sufficiently protected the child's good. At the same time, the Court found that the applicants' situation could be covered by the right to protection of private life, understood as the right to respect for the applicants' personal development through the parental role they wished to undertake in relation to the child.[117] As such, the best interests of the child came up repeatedly in the context of considerations on guaranteeing respect for the applicants' right to private life.

In the discussed case, the Court approached the interest of the child both from the perspective of the particular child concerned by the proceedings and from a more general perspective. Interpretation in the specific context was used by the Court to perform a balancing test. On the one side of the scale was the view that separating the child from the applicants would not cause significant harm to the child along with the imperative of respecting the domestic legal order by operating within a certain legal framework, and on the other side was the applicants' desire to develop a relationship with the child that was not genetically related to them and with whom they had stayed for a relatively short time (a few months). According to the majority of the Court's judges, the Italian authorities balanced these values correctly. Whereas from a general perspective, the interests of children were defined as the need to protect children from private adoption and the possible consequences thereof in the context of human trafficking.

The child's best interests thus transpired as a premise for assessing the legitimacy of the interference. The Court accepted the Italian government's submissions in which it reserved competence to "reaffirm its exclusive competence to recognise a legal parent – child relationship – and this solely in the case of a biological tie or lawful adoption – with a view to protecting children."[118] Moreover, protection of children appeared again in the considerations concerning

116 In parallel, the representatives of the legal literature point to a number of shortcomings in the Court's reasoning. On the one hand, the Court referred to the welfare of the child as a legitimate rationale for the interference and, on the other hand, it did not consider a number of factual circumstances, the inclusion of which seemed crucial for the assessment of the proportionality of the Italian authorities' action. Iliadou, "Surrogacy." 9–10.

117 Paradisso and Campanelli v. Italy, par. 163

118 Paradisso and Campanelli v. Italy, par. 177.

the necessity of taking action in a democratic society, and to that extent in the considerations on the width of the margin of appreciation. This is where the ECtHR accepted the necessity to act promptly to prevent violations of public order and the protection of children by establishing parental ties only through a lawfully conducted adoption. Interestingly, the Court indicated that the reasons for which the national authorities intervened were directly related to the pursuit of legitimate aim of preventing a violation of public policy, but also to the protection of children, and not only of one particular child concerned, but of children in general.[119] The protection of children and women was also identified as a legitimate public interest rationale in light of the fact that they may be affected by practices that are highly questionable from a moral standpoint.[120]

The Court's argumentation regarding the need to protect groups that deserve special attention is quite innovative and entails numerous, also legal, consequences. Attributing determinative importance to the interests of those fragile groups – be they children or women – creates imbalance in the weighing of protected goods and insufficient consideration of the need to protect the interests of the intended parents – that is, the applicants. One might view the effect of the cumulative application of this argument in conjunction with other arguments, including those involving the narrow definition of locus standi (as in *Paradiso and Campanelli*), as a kind of Court's "escape" from presenting its position on the scope of protection of the intended parents. This conclusion is exactly opposite to the conclusion on the ECtHR's application of the concept of "vulnerable groups" the application of which strengthens the legal position of the applicants.[121] This state of affairs also reflects a trend that has been observed for a while now, namely a slow transformation of the ECHR's role from that of a guardian of individual rights to that of common values (such as an idea of the ECtHR as a constitutional court).

In the light of the Court's singling out of groups deserving special protection, attention should be drawn to certain relativism expressed by the Court when accepting certain behaviour of States. It refers to scenarios when certain behaviour is prohibited under national law and which triggers a complaint to the ECtHR, yet the Court unreservedly accepts a situation when identical requests can be satisfied by the applicant abroad without any obstacles.

In the *Mennesson* case, the Court was not inclined to express a positive, nor negative, view of the actions of the applicants who had travelled abroad to conclude and perform a surrogacy agreement inadmissible in France, despite the fact that the national court had found that such actions constituted a

119 Paradisso and Campanelli v. Italy, par. 197.

120 Paradisso and Campanelli v. Italy, par. 204.

121 For the consequences of applying the concept of "vulnerable groups," see Peroni, Timmer, "Vulnerable Groups." 1079–80.

circumvention of the law.[122] The Court remained reserved in its consideration in this respect. By contrast, in the case of *S.H. and Others*, it made it evident that the applicants could have travelled abroad for the purpose of having IVF treatment and then legalised their parenthood in Austria.[123] In contrast, the Court's conclusion in *Paradiso and Campanelli* took a very different path. The ECtHR accepted the government's argument emphasising the importance of acting within the limits of the law and held that allowing the applicants to continue to raise their child would legalise the situation they had created in contravention of Italian law.[124]

The Court's diversified approach to the issue of the possible enjoyment of rights beyond the borders of one's own country may, on the one hand, be assessed as introducing the acceptance of double standards of human rights protection, but, on the other hand, it may also be treated as a "safety valve." Such an approach allows the Court to not venture into the area of potential moral conflict while at the same time accepting a minimum level of respect for the moral autonomy of persons who do not share views reflected in the shape of national regulations.[125] As in other categories of cases analysed in this book, the opportunity to exercise the right to privacy in another country is noticed by the Court and treated as the reason for not finding a violation of the Convention.

Another consequence of the Court's application of the argumentation concerning potential secondary effects by distinguishing specific groups subject to protection is *de facto* further expansion of the States' margin of appreciation and reinforcement of the primacy of national regulation. The Court's acknowledgement that the specific good to be protected as part of the public interest is the care offered to certain groups – potentially economically disadvantaged women and the potential children born of medically assisted procreation who will be brought up in non-standard family relationships (the concept introduced by the Austrian legislator) – means that, in the event of conflict with the interests of the applicants, those interests of other people, as

122 Mennesson v. France, par. 90.

123 This moral relativism of the Court in accepting potential travel abroad in order to undergo procedures prohibited by law was particularly evident in the case of *A., B. and C. v. Ireland* concerning the issue of abortion. For a detailed explanation, see Chapter 4.

124 Paradiso and Campanelli, par. 215.

125 A comprehensive concept justifying the latter view was presented by Penning. According to this author, the option of cross-border use of medically assisted procreation (the so-called external tolerance policy) means that certain norms are shaped and applied in a given legal area in accordance with the will of the majority, while at the same time representatives of the minority are able to act in accordance with their views when travelling abroad. When it comes to areas where regulations are extremely deeply morally conditioned, for example medically assisted procreation, abortion and euthanasia, such a policy prevents open confrontation of views. Cf. inter alia Guido Pennings, "Legal harmonization and reproductive tourism in Europe." *Human Reproduction* 19, no. 12 (2004): 2694 and Guido Pennings, "Reproductive tourism as moral pluralism in motion." *Journal of Medical Ethics* 28 (2002): 341.

specially protected, may outweigh the interests of individual applicants. And again, this is a completely opposite conclusion to the one drawn with regard to the Court's approach in distinguishing "vulnerable groups" where the "recognition" of an applicant as a member of a "vulnerable group" results in a narrowing of the State's margin of appreciation (albeit not automatically).[126]

When analysing the Court's considerations regarding the negative social effects that a judgment may have on particular individuals or groups, it is essential to point out the specificity of the *Parrillo v. Italy* case. In all the judgments under review, it is fairly clear what interests of a public nature or of an individual nature were subject to balancing versus the interests of the applicants. In the *Parrillo* case, the "embryo's potential for life" was weighed against the applicant's interests. Such an outcome does not allow this case to be assigned either to the group of cases in which the interests of other individual entities are of key importance (such as in *Evans*, with the applicant's former partner) or to the one in which the public interest is determined by the prism of the needs of groups deserving special attention (such as *H.S. v. Austria, Mennesson v. France, Paradiso and Campanelli v. Italy*) unless the embryos are treated as requiring protection under the provisions of the ECHR. If this is true, the use of the discussed argumentative tool led to an extremely important Court's statement on this morally sensitive issue, namely that embryos are protected under the Convention.

Summary

For the purpose of our study, we began with the observation that in the three areas under analysis the ECtHR does not generally legitimise interference with the rights and freedoms of individuals by referring to the premise of public morality. As follows from the current chapter in the field of medically assisted procreation, it uses several different approaches: in certain cases, it chooses not to express an opinion on whether the case should be examined from the point of view of the State's compliance with its negative or positive obligation;[127] in some cases it rules by reference to the fulfilment of positive obligations;[128] in other cases it makes an auxiliary reference to the premise of morality, but cites other considerations as being decisive;[129] and in the remaining cases, it assesses the appropriateness of the interference in the light of other recurring

126 Peroni, Timmer, "Vulnerable Groups." 1080. Cf. judgment: Kiyutin v. Russia, appl. no. 2700/10, par. 63 and 74, Alajos Kiss v. Hungary, appl. no. 38832/06, par. 42.

127 Dickson v. UK, par. 71.

128 Evans v. UK, par. 58 (Chamber).

129 In *S. H. and Others v. Austria*, the Court observed that the parties had no doubt that the State had acted with the aim of "protecting health and morals" and "the rights and freedoms of others" when taking regulatory measures in the field of medically assisted procreation, par. 90.

requirements laid down by the general clause of Article 8 ECHR, excluding the rationale of public morality.[130]

The Court's avoidance of pointing to the premise of morality as the basis for interference with the rights of individuals in the sphere of medically assisted procreation and its reasoning based on the other premises contained in Article 8 ECHR (health, rights and freedoms of others, public policy) can even at the outset be interpreted on multiple levels.

First of all, this line of argumentation confirms that the Court is not inclined to simply accept the moralistic preferences of the majority as being synonymous with "public morals." This approach contrasts with the one taken in cases in which restrictions on the rights and freedoms of individuals have been authorised precisely in the name of this legitimate aim.[131] Reference to the premise of morality, interpreted as the medium carrying certain traditions and values specific to a given State, would position the judgment as protective of the public interest to the extent asserted by a State pursuing certain social policies. Since the Court does not apply the premise of morality, therefore, its pronouncements on the moral aspects of the issues under consideration cannot be reduced to simply approving the position of governments insofar as they invoked public morality.

On the other hand, due to the sparse reasoning, the rare cases in which a reference to the legitimate aim of morality can be found do not allow for an initial determination of the extent to which the Court accepts the moral arguments put forward in support of the State's sovereign actions. It is our

130 *Mennesson v. France* – in the shared opinion of the government and the Court, the premises justifying the interference were "protection of health" and "rights and freedoms of others." However, the premise of the need to preserve public order was not taken into account, paras. 60, 73, 77, 79, 83. In *Paradiso and Campanelli v. Italy* – protection of health, protection of the rights and freedoms of others, with particular emphasis on the rights of children and the need to prevent crime (public order protection), paras. 177, 184 and 194. In *Parrillo v. Italy* – the rationale for the interference was "protection of morals" and "rights and freedoms of others" in the context of "protection of the embryo's potential for life," par. 123, 163 and 165.

131 Cf. Letsas, *A Theory of Interpretation,* 121. When referring to cases in which the Court ruled to limit an individual's rights specifically on the basis of morality, the author writes as follows: "All these instances involve the moralistic preferences of the majority, i.e. its external preference that some people should not enjoy some liberty on the basis that their plan of life is inferior. People who enjoy books with sexual advice or erotic art should be deprived of this liberty because pornography or erotic art is considered degrading by the majority. People who are atheists or believe in unpopular religions should not have the right to express themselves or advertise their religious views because their views offend the religious beliefs of the majority. People who have a sex operation should not be granted legal recognition of their new gender because change of sex offends the institution of marriage. People who are in a homosexual relationship and wish to adopt should not be allowed this liberty because the majority despises homosexual families and the adopted children will suffer from this prejudice. It is clear moreover that in these cases the Court takes the moralistic preferences of the majority as being synonymous with 'public morals' and thus constituting a legitimate aim."

intention to draw conclusions in this regard in the final chapter (Conclusion) of the book.

While the Court refrains from assessing the moral reasons behind interference in individual rights, it shifts the examination of the issues to the level of argumentation related to balancing the public interest (especially the rights of others) with the interests of the individuals concerned. In the context of medically assisted procreation, the legitimacy of balancing the rights of the persons concerned with an abstractly defined group of women who agree to enter into surrogacy arrangements for financial reasons, a group of children born as a result of medically assisted procreation or the protection of the embryo's potential for life are used very often but at the same time can be quite problematic.

Consequently, the ECtHR's justification of interference on grounds other than morality leads to a situation in which the Court has the opportunity to avoid presenting its moral view of the issue under examination in a straightforward manner. Through the analysis of selected argumentative tools, we attempted to demonstrate that it justifies its decision in other ways than by accepting certain moral views and that, after all, from some of these statements – especially those framed in incrementalism and protection of groups deserving special attention – one can read its position on moral issues.

Bibliography

Bomhoff, Jacco and Lorenzo Zucca. "Evans v. UK: European Court of Human Rights." *European Constitutional Law Review* 2(3) (2006): 424–442.

Brauch, Jeffrey A. "The dangerous search for an elusive consensus: What the supreme court should learn from the European Court of Human Rights." *Howard Law Journal* 52 (2008–2009): 277–318.

Cali, Basak. "From flexible to variable standards of judicial review: The responsible domestic courts doctrine at the European Court of Human Rights." In *Shifting Centres of Gravity in Human Rights Protection: Rethinking Relations between the ECHR, EU and National Legal Orders*, edited by Oddný Mjöll Arnardóttir and Antoine Buyse, 144–161. Routledge, 2016.

Cayon, Joaquin. "The widening of the national margin of appreciation allowed by the strasbourg court: A backward step for reproductive rights in Europe?" In *The Role of Courts in Contemporary Legal Orders*, edited by Martin Belov, 397–413. Eleven International Publishing, 2019.

Cook, Rebecca J., Bernard M. Dickens and Mahmoud F. Fathalla. *Reproductive Health and Human Rights: Integrating Medicine, Ethics and Law*. Oxford University Press, 2003.

David, Kete. "Case of S.H. and Others v. Austria: Practical concern over individual rights." *Boston College International & Comparative Law Review* 36(E. Supp) (2013).

Dialogue between Judges, European Court of Human Rights, Council of Europe, 2008.

Dzehtsiarou, Kanstantsin. *European Consensus and the Legitimacy of the European Court of Human Rights*. Cambridge University Press, 2015.

Eder, Margaret. "Parillo v. Italy. ECHR allows states to interfere with individuals' admittedly private lives." *Tulane Journal of International and Comparative Law* 24(2) (2014–2015): 371–390.

Gerards, Janneke. "Judicial deliberations in the European Court of Human Rights." In *Judicial Deliberations in the European Court of Human Rights. The Legitimacy of Highest Courts' Rulings*, edited by N Huls, M Adams and Jacco Bomhoff, 1–25. T.M.C. Asser Institute, 2008, https://ssrn.com/abstract=1114906.

Gerards, Janneke. "Margin of appreciation and incrementalism in the case law of the European Court of Human Rights." *Human Rights Law Review* 18(3) (2018): 495–515.

Gerards, Janneke. "Procedural review by the ECtHR: A typology." In *Procedural Review in European Fundamental Rights Cases*, edited by Janneke Gerards and Eva Brems, 127–160. Cambridge University Press, 2017.

Gerards, Janneke. "The prism of fundamental rights." *European Constitutional Law Review* 8 (2012): 173–202.

Hoof, Wannes and Guido Pennings, "The consequences of S.H. and Others v. Austria for legislation on gamete donation in Europe: An ethical analysis of the European Court of Human Rights judgments." *Reproductive Biomedicine Online* 25 (2012): 665–669.

Iliadou, Marianna "Surrogacy and the ECtHR: Reflections on paradiso and campanelli v Italy. Commentary." *Medical Law Review* 27(1): 144–154.

Letsas, George. *A Theory of Interpretation of the European Convention on Human Rights*. Oxford University Press, 2009.

Mahoney, Paul and Rachael Kondak. "Common ground. A starting point or destination for comparative-law analysis by the European Court of Human Rights?" In *Courts and Comparative Law*, edited by Mads Andenas and Duncan Fairgrieve, 118–140. Oxford University Press, 2015.

Nussberger, Angelika. "Procedural review by the ECHR: View from the court." In *Procedural Review in European Fundamental Rights Cases*, edited by Janneke Gerards and Eva Brems, 161–176. Cambridge University Press, 2017.

Palomares, Guillem Cano. "Right to family life and access to medically assisted procreation in the case law of the European court of human rights." In *The Right to Family Life in the European*, edited by Maribel G. Pascual and Aida T. Pérez, 99–114. Routledge, 2017.

Pennings, Guido. "Legal harmonization and reproductive tourism in Europe." *Human Reproduction* 19(12) (2004): 689–2694.

Pennings, Guido. "Reproductive tourism as moral pluralism in motion." *Journal of Medical Ethics* 28 (2002): 337–341.

Peroni, Peroni, Lourdes and Alexandra Timmer. "Vulnerable groups: The promise of an emerging concept in European human rights convention law." *International Journal of Constitutional Law* 11 (2013): 1056–1085.

Sale, Philip and Hopper B. "Proportionality and the form of law." *Law Quarterly Review* 19 (2003): 426–454.

"The role of consensus in the system of the European convention on human rights." Discussion paper prepared by the Organising Committee, composed of Anatoly Kovler, Vladimiro Zagrebelsky, Lech Garlicki, Dean Spielmann, Renate Jaeger and Roderick Liddell. In *Dialogue between Judges*. European Court of Human Rights, Council of Europe, 2008.

Walsh, David J., Mary L. Ma and Eric S. Sills. "The evolution of health policy guidelines for assisted reproduction in the republic of Ireland, 2004–2009." *Health Research Policy and Systems* 9(28) (2011): 1–5.

Wildhaber, Luzius, Arnaldur Hjartarson and Stephen Donnelly. "No consensus on consensus? The practice of the European Court of Human Rights." *Human Rights Law Journal* 33 (2013): 248–263.

4 Ways of reasoning in abortion cases

Introduction

The problem to give effect to the right to life and right to privacy in relation to the beginning or ending of human life emerged first in the cases involving termination of pregnancy. Abortion is a relatively simple medical procedure, performed practically since the dawn of civilisation. At the same time, its legality has always been a source of considerable controversy and has remained outside the scope of law for a long time. The regulations on legalising the termination of pregnancy were only introduced in the 20th century, establishing the conditions under which it can be performed. Considerable liberalisation of national laws began to take place in the European countries in the late 1960s,[1] although this did not reduce the social and ideological controversy concerning the admissibility of abortion. On the contrary, it emphasised the differences in the perception of the act of termination of pregnancy as either the deprivation of life of the unborn child or an act pertaining to private and sexual life and belonging to the sphere protected by Article 8 of the Convention.

The evolution of arguments presented in cases concerning abortion is extensive, as is the use of specific tools of argumentation. Even though the Court tries to avoid making a definitive decision on the legality of abortion within the framework of the Convention, it does, however, reach fundamental

1 Great Britain made abortion legal in 1968, a major reform and relaxation of the law on criminalisation of abortion took place in Germany in 1976, in Italy in 1978, in Finland in 1970, in France the act of 1975 (Veil law) allows for IVG – voluntary interruption of pregnancy at the mother's request up to the twelfth week of pregnancy – and IMG – medical termination of pregnancy at any stage of pregnancy in certain situations (threat to mother's life, deformity of the foetus). In Sweden, abortion was legalised in 1974, while in Belgium it was not until 1990 that a law was passed legalising abortion at patient's request. In Portugal, considering specific factors led to legalisation in 1984. It was a completely different situation in the communist states – abortion had been legal there since the 1950s, while the regaining of independence by the eastern bloc countries resulted in stricter rules on the permissibility of abortion in several of them. The most drastic example is Poland, where the CT ruled in 2020 that abortion on embryopathological grounds was incompatible with the constitutional principle of protection of life.

DOI: 10.4324/9781003375999-5

conclusions as to the admissibility of its prohibition, having pursued the line of argumentation in this sphere[2] elaborately and very cautiously for nearly 50 years. To begin with, it is appropriate to present the most important decisions in the cases that will be discussed later in this chapter.[3]

Attempts to make the laws on the permissibility of abortion more liberal led to the first case, which was decided by the European Commission of Human Rights in 1977 in the case *Brüggemann and Scheuten v. Germany*.[4] The application concerned the shape of criminal provisions on the termination of pregnancy in the Federal Republic of Germany. It resulted from the fact that the Fifth Criminal Law Reform Act of 1974 causing the liberalisation of those provisions was declared unconstitutional by the Federal Constitutional Court in its judgment of 25 February 1975.[5] After the Court's decision, the 15th Criminal Law Reform Act 1976 was introduced, maintaining that abortion is a criminal offence, yet providing very strict exceptions. Applicants submitted that the last Act interfered with their right to private life under Article 8 and that this interference was not justified on any of the grounds enumerated in paragraph 2 of that Article and also constituted violation of Articles 9 and 12 of the Convention.[6] The Commission considered that the right to respect for private life was the relevant standard of review for this case, yet it found that Article 8 of the Convention could not have been interpreted to mean that pregnancy and its termination were, in principle, solely a matter of mother's private life. In consequence, the Commission unanimously concluded that the case did not constitute a breach of Art. 8 of the Convention.

2 Chiara Cosentino, "Safe and Legal Abortion: An Emerging Human Right: The Long-Lasting Dispute with Sovereignty in ECHR Jurisprudence." *Human Rights Law Review* 15(3) (2015): 569–90, pp. 570, 589. See also: W. Nigel Irvine, "A Time to Regulate: Possible Implications of European Human Rights Law on Abortion in Northern Ireland." *Medical Law International* 5(2) (2001): 127–40, 132.

3 The cases listed and described here do not constitute the entirety of the case law of the Commission and the Court in abortion cases. In addition, it may be pointed out that initially the Commission refused to examine *in abstracto* the compatibility of abortion laws with Article 2 of the Convention (see X v. Norway, no. 867/60, Commission decision of 29 May 1961, Collection of Decisions, vol. 6, p. 34, and X v. Austria, no. 7045/75, Commission decision of 10 December 1976, DR 7, p. 87. The Court ruled on abortion while examining the case of Open Doors and Dublin Well Women v. Ireland [appl. no. 14234/88], judgment of 29 October 1992), in which the allegation concerned violation of Article 10 by prohibiting information about abortion options outside the country. At the same time the Court did not consider it relevant to determine "whether a right to abortion is guaranteed under the Convention or whether the fetus is encompassed by the right to life as contained in Article 2" (p. 28, par. 66).

4 Brüggemann and Scheuten v. Germany, appl. no. 6959/75, decision of 12.7.1977.

5 Judgment of Feb. 25, 1975, BVerfGe (W. Ger.), 39 BVerfGE 1.

6 For more on the circumstances and implications of the judgment, see: Thomas Richard Sealy II., "Abortion Law Reform in Europe: The European Commission on Human Rights Upholds German Restrictions on Abortion–Bruggemann and Scheuten v. Federal Republic of Germany." *Texas International Law Journal* 15(1) (1980): 162–86.

The ruling made in the case *Vo v. France*[7] decided in 2004 was particularly significant considering the legal status of the foetus. The case did not concern the permissibility of abortion, quite the contrary. The applicant alleged that the French authorities had violated Article 2 of the Convention through the lack of protection for her unborn child under French criminal law. The applicant had mistakenly received treatment that she should not have received while being pregnant. As a result, the applicant was obliged to undergo a therapeutic abortion of a healthy foetus of 21–22 weeks. She lodged a criminal complaint for unintentional homicide against her unborn child. The Court found no violation of Article 2, assessing the positive obligations incumbent on the French authorities and concluding that they protect life sufficiently. It is worth noting that the conclusion in the judgment was highly controversial, with two separate opinions and two dissenting opinions filed in the case.

The Court also adjudicated in several cases in which the applicant was the partner of a woman who underwent abortion against his will.

In the first case in this category, application *X v. United Kingdom*,[8] the applicant alleged violations of Article 2 of the Convention by permitting abortion in general, and of Articles 6, 8 and 9 of the Convention by denying the father of the child the right to be informed about and to object to the planned abortion. In *H. R. v. Norway*[9] the man claimed, inter alia, violations of Articles 2 and 3 of the Convention by taking the life of the unborn child and causing suffering, and Articles 8 and 9 of the Convention by failing to provide instruments under domestic law to prevent his partner from proceeding with an abortion against his will and convictions. The Commission found both complaints to be inadmissible.

Also, in the case *Boso v. Italy*[10], decided by the Court, the applicant complained under Articles 2 and 8 that the law enabled women to make decisions regarding abortions on their own and did not take into account the presumed father's opinion. Following the footsteps of the Commission in previous such cases, having acknowledged the extent to which the applicant had been affected by his partner's termination of pregnancy, the Court recognised his status as a victim. However, the Court declared the application inadmissible, finding that in a situation where the mother intended to have an abortion, any interpretation of the potential father's rights should first and foremost take into account her rights, as she was the person primarily affected by the pregnancy and its continuation or termination, and declared the application clearly unfounded.

7 Vo v. France, app. 53924/00, judgment of 8.7.2004.
8 X v. the United Kingdom, appl. no. 8416/78, Commission dec.13.5.1980.
9 H. v. Norway, appl. no. 17004/90, Commission dec. 19.5.1992.
10 Boso v. Italy, appl. no. 50490/99, ECtHR dec. 5.9.2002.

In the case *D. v. Ireland*,[11] the applicant, who was pregnant with twins, decided to terminate her pregnancy after learning that one foetus had died and the other had developed a fatal anomaly. Given that abortion is a criminal offence in Ireland, excluding cases where the pregnancy poses a threat to the woman's life, she was forced to travel to the UK to undergo the procedure legally. She claimed that Ireland's ban on abortion, particularly in cases of foetal impairment, as well as restrictions on doctors' ability to advise patients on abortion and to provide full referrals to legal services abroad, violated Articles 3, 8 and 10 of the European Convention on Human Rights. The Court declared the case inadmissible on the ground that the applicant had failed to exhaust available domestic legal remedies.

The first case in which the Court stated a violation of the Article 8 right in the context of lack of access to abortion was *Tysiąc v. Poland*.[12] The applicant was a severely visually impaired Polish woman who in fact (despite the formal legal possibility of termination of pregnancy in such circumstances) was refused an abortion to protect her physical health; she had to carry the pregnancy. The Court found that domestic law did not contain any effective mechanism to determine whether the conditions for obtaining a legal abortion were met. The Polish State thus failed to comply with its positive obligations to protect the applicant's right to respect for her private life.

Three years later, when adjudicating in *A., B. and C. v. Ireland*,[13] the Court (Grand Chamber) addressed the claims of three women living in Ireland who had become pregnant unintentionally and complained of their inability to legally undergo abortion in Ireland on the grounds of well-being, health risks and threat to life, respectively. It should be added that all three applicants had undergone abortions in the United Kingdom. The Court identified a violation of Article 8 only in relation to applicant C., who was suffering from cancer and whose life was in danger. In relation to the other two applicants, the Court found no violation of Article 8.

In another case which concerned the permissibility of abortion in Poland, *R. R. v. Poland*,[14] a complaint was lodged by a pregnant woman who was deliberately denied timely genetic testing and whose child was presumed to be suffering from a serious genetic anomaly. Ultimately, the test results were delivered too late for her to make an informed decision about whether to continue with the pregnancy or seek a legal abortion instead. Her daughter was subsequently born with a severe genetic defect. The Court acknowledged violation of Article 3 as well as Article 8 of the Convention in that the Polish law (in general: permitting abortion in such cases of fatal foetal anomaly) did not contain any effective mechanisms that would have enabled the applicant to

11 D. v. Ireland, appl. no. 26499/02, ECtHR dec. 28.6.2006.
12 Tysiąc v. Poland, appl. no. 5410/03, ECtHR judgment of 20.03.2007.
13 A., B. and C. v. Ireland, appl. no. 25579/05, judgment of 16.12.2010.
14 R. R. v. Poland, appl. no. 27617/04, judgment of 26.05.2011.

access any available diagnostic services and to make, in the light of the results, an informed decision as to whether to seek an abortion or not.

Similarly, in the next, and last (for the time being) of the adjudicated cases in this category, *P. and S. v. Poland*,[15] the Court found that there had been a violation of Articles 3 and 8 and of Article 5 § 1 of the Convention. This case concerned the difficulties faced by a teenage girl (and her mother), who became pregnant following rape, in gaining access to abortion, mainly due to the lack of a clear legal framework and the dilatory attitude of medical staff, as well as her harassment during medical and legal proceedings.

It is no coincidence that all the abortion cases in recent years in which breaches of the law have been confirmed have so far concerned two countries: Poland and Ireland. In this context, it is appropriate to briefly present the legal order of these countries in terms of access to abortion, especially as it is undergoing dynamic changes.

Abortion in Ireland has been a crime punishable by life imprisonment since 1861 under the Offences Against the Person Act, and contraception was completely illegal until 1978.[16] The referendum regarding access to abortion was held in Ireland several times in the late 20th century. One such referendum from 1983 saw the adoption of the Eighth Amendment to the Constitution, which recognised the right of the unborn to life and the absence of grounds to justify abortion (Article 40.3). In 1992, a proposal to amend the Constitution to provide for lawful abortion where there would otherwise be a real and substantial risk to the mother's life, except a risk of suicide, was rejected. However, the second proposal was accepted and subsequently became the Thirteenth Amendment to the Constitution to ensure that a woman could not be prevented from leaving the country to undergo an abortion abroad. The third proposal allowing people in Ireland to be informed about abortion services abroad was also passed and became the Fourteenth Amendment (both were added to Article 40.3.3). In March 2002, another referendum on abortion was held, again rejecting a proposal to legalise abortion in cases where the mother's life was in danger.[17]

Case law of domestic courts and the ECtHR has had an impact on changes in attitudes towards abortion, particularly the cases recognising the right of

15 P. and S. v. Poland, appl. no. 57375/08, judgment of 30.10.2012.

16 On detailed description of evolution and history of Irish abortion law, see: W. Nigel Irvine, "A Time to Regulate: Possible Implications of European Human Rights Law on Abortion in Northern Ireland." *Medical Law International* 5(2) (2001): 127–40; also (contemporary law): Brenda Daly, "Access to Abortion Services: The Impact of the European Convention on Human Rights in Ireland." *Medicine and Law* 30(2) (2011): 267–78.

17 More on the subject: Morgan A. Rhinehart, "Abortions in Ireland: Reconciling a History of Restrictive Abortion Practices with the European Court of Human Rights' Ruling in A., B. and C. v. Ireland." *Penn State Law Review* 117(3) (2013): 959–78. 960–72.

raped teenagers to legally terminate their pregnancies in the face of the risk of suicide (X case 1992[18]).

The second decade of the 21st century has been marked by significant liberalisation of constitutional and statutory provisions. Under the Protection of Life During Pregnancy Act 2013, abortion was illegal unless it was the result of a medical intervention carried out to save the woman's life. In May 2018, another referendum was held on the 36th Constitutional Amendment, which replaced the 8th Amendment with the clause allowing the Oireachtas (Parliament) to legislate for the termination of pregnancy. Abortion in Ireland is currently regulated by the Health Act 2018 (Regulation of Termination of Pregnancy). It is currently permitted in Ireland during the first 12 weeks of pregnancy, and afterwards in cases where the life or health of the pregnant woman is at risk, or in the case of a fatal foetal anomaly.

The evolution of Polish regulation is moving in quite a different direction. At the time of accession to the Council of Europe and the ECHR, the Act adopted in 1956 was in force that allowed abortion due to medical indications, as a result of a criminal offence and due to adverse living conditions of the pregnant woman. The abortion law began to change in the 1990s. The Law on the Protection of the Human Foetus and the Conditions for Permitting the Termination of Pregnancy (still in force), enacted by Parliament in 1993, provided at the time (Article 4[a]) for the permissibility of abortion as long as it is carried out exclusively by a physician and when:

1 Pregnancy endangers the mother's life or health.
2 Prenatal tests or other medical findings indicate a high risk that the foetus will be severely and irreversibly damaged or suffer from an incurable life-threatening ailment.
3 There are strong grounds for believing that the pregnancy is the result of a criminal act.

In 1996, the Parliament passed an amendment to that law and added the admissibility of abortion due to adverse living conditions or a woman's personal situation. However, this provision was found by the Constitutional Tribunal to be unconstitutional in the judgment of 28 May 1997 as infringing the rule of law principle.

In October 2020, the Constitutional Tribunal issued a ruling on the constitutionality of the provision allowing for abortion in case of fatal foetal abnormality of the foetus (judgment K 1/20). It stated that the challenged provision is inconsistent with the legally defined protection of life. Thus, abortion on fatal foetal abnormality grounds has been prohibited in Poland. Poland has become one of the five European countries (the group also includes Andorra, Malta, San Marino and Liechtenstein) in which abortion is not permitted in

18 Attorney General v. X and Others, [1992] 1 I.R. 1 (S.C.).

the event of severe foetal abnormality, while in only six it is not permitted due to social circumstances.[19]

After such an abrupt exacerbation of the conditions under which abortion is permissible, over 1,000 similar Polish applications have been received by the Court in which the applicants complain that they are potential victims of a breach of the Convention.[20] All were given priority and the Court communicated the applications to the Polish government and addressed questions to the parties, paying particular attention to Article 8 (right to respect for private and family life) and Article 3 (prohibition of inhuman or degrading treatment) of the Convention on account of the restrictions imposed by the Constitutional Tribunal's judgment with respect to legal abortion on the ground of foetal defects.

Arguments referring to authority

In cases related to abortion, the question of the limits of a woman's autonomy is connected particularly strongly with the right to private life and the right to life, and this means the life of a being incapable of independent existence, tied to the life of the woman. Concerns of an ethical nature and fear of making a decision, or even of including statements that are too far-reaching in the justification of the decision, are prominent here. This is probably why the ECtHR's argumentation makes extensive use of external assertions – ones we call *ad auctoritatem*. The instrument of the margin of appreciation occupies a special place among them. Although auxiliary references to the international law are also included, at the same time it must be admitted that this argument is not conclusive and is only used in a supplementary and indirect way; as an explanation, or rather justification for the Court being cautious in the interpretation and application of Article 2 with regard to the life of a human foetus.

Arguments based on the authority of the codified law – pick and choose strategy

Firstly, it should be noted that both the European Commission of Human Rights and the European Court of Human Rights frequently referred to the international legal order and comparatively to the domestic legal orders in cases concerning abortion, even if the regulations referred to had not exactly related to the subject matter being examined. When deciding on the first

19 These are: Andorra, Liechtenstein, Malta, Monaco, Poland and San Marino. https://reproductiverights.org/european-abortion-laws-comparative-overview (access: 12.12.2020).

20 Pending applications include: *K.B. v. Poland* and three other applications (appl. nos. 1819/21, 3682/21, 4957/21 and 6217/21), *K.C. v. Poland* and three other applications (appl. nos. 3639/21, 4188/21, 5876/21 and 6030/21), *A. L. B. v. Poland* and three other applications (appl. nos. 3801/21, 4218/21, 5114/21 and 5390/21) and *M. L. v. Poland* (appl. 40119/21).

application concerning the admissibility of abortion lodged in the *Brüggemann and Scheuten v. Germany* case, the Commission made a reference to the domestic legal orders in the Member States of the Council of Europe (CoE) (albeit very general), including the German civil law system, which recognises the interests of the unborn child as something to be protected. Secondly, the Commission referred to the prohibition of capital punishment for pregnant women, established in the International Covenant on Civil and Political Rights.[21] These references led to the conclusion that, indirectly, both national legislations and the Covenant grant protection to the foetus and thus recognise the value of its life.

The remaining, not very frequent, references to international law beyond the Convention took the opposite direction. In *X v. United Kingdom*, the Commission referred to the American Convention on Human Rights (1969), Article 4 (1), which explicitly grants the right to life to the unborn through the phrase: "*the right to life shall be protected by law and, in general, from the moment of conception*." The absence of such a phrase in the European Convention was seen by the Commission as a deliberate omission and, consequently, the absence of a formulation that would have implied an obligation on States to protect life from conception. This conclusion remains in the sphere of interpretation but serves perfectly well to argue that the possibility of performing an abortion does not constitute a violation of the Convention.

Reasoning regarding external sources of law has a similar character and effect in the *Vo v. France* case, where the Court noted that the international treaties – the Convention for the Protection of Human Rights and Dignity of the Human Being with regard to the Application of Biology and Medicine ("The Oviedo Convention on Human Rights and Biomedicine") and the Additional Protocol on the Prohibition of Cloning Human Beings and the Additional Protocol on Biomedical Research – are careful not to provide any definition of the term "everyone." Thus, in the absence of a unanimous consensus on the definition, it is up to domestic law to provide clarification for the meaning of that notion for the purposes of the application of that Convention. The Court concluded that it was unable to determine the issue of the "beginning" of "everyone's right to life" within the meaning of Article 2 and whether the unborn child is entitled to such a right.[22] This kind of argument, deriving from interpretation, has strengthened the Court's argumentation aimed at refusing to recognise that the foetus is a subject of right guaranteed in Article 2.

In turn, both the Commission and the Court point in their other judgments not to the lack of useful solutions at the international level but to domestic legal orders and their diversity in both legal content and jurisprudence. This argument supports the notion that there is no consensus on the scope of permissibility of abortion among European countries and this consequently leads the

21 Brüggemann and Scheuten v. Germany, par. 60.
22 Vo v. France, par. 75.

Court to resort to the instrument of the margin of appreciation.[23] But this kind of argumentation goes beyond demonstrating a simple lack of consensus among European states to demonstrate various approaches towards extending protection to the unborn. The Commission in the *X v. the UK* decision even referred to the US Supreme Court ruling in *Roe v. Wade*.[24] This kind of argument goes beyond interpretation, which is clearly visible in the selection of the material used for comparisons. For example, significantly, when referring to this argument in another "paternity" case, *H. v. Norway*, the Commission had already made a certain choice of external sources; it first pointed to a decision of the Austrian Court, which denied the unborn child the right to life and only then mentioned the position of the German Constitutional Court, which covered the life of the unborn with the protection of the right to life. It is easy to notice that these sources were cited in order to legitimise the scepticism of the CoE authorities in terms of extending legal protection to the life of the unborn, and therefore to dismiss the allegation of a violation of Article 2 of the Convention.

This kind of argument is also applied in the argumentation concerning the violation of Article 8 of the Convention. In the *Tysiąc v. Poland* case, the Court indicated "Relevant non-Convention material" in the separate part of its justification, including, among others, reports of the Human Rights Committee created under the International Covenant on Civil and Political Rights (ICCPR) indicating very restrictive laws on abortion and limited accessibility to contraceptives and family planning programmes in Poland.[25] It also noted observations of non-governmental organizations,[26] highlighting the negative consequences of the anti-abortion law in force, as well as expert bodies[27] expressing concern over the lack of balance between the right of the woman and the protection of potential human life on the other hand, as well as the impact of prohibition on non-therapeutic abortion or the practical unavailability of abortion on raising the number of abortions undergone in secret.

This kind of reference to, not even the law, but rather the positions of certain bodies creates a context which makes it possible to strengthen the argumentation that the applicant's rights have been violated.

23 In *X v. the United Kingdom*, the Commission adequately referred to Austrian Constitutional Court Decision of 11 October 1974, which refuses to grant the right to life to unborn children, to the German Federal Constitutional Court, interpreting the provision "Everyone has the right to life" in Article 2 (2) of the Basic Law as covering every human individual including unborn human beings (judgment of 25 February 1975), and to the Norwegian Supreme Court which stated that abortion laws must necessarily be based on the compromise between the respect for the unborn life and other essential and worthy considerations. Erk. Slg. (Collection of Decisions) No. 7400, EuGRZ 1975, p. 74.

24 410 U.S., 113. In the justification of the *X v. UK* decision, the Commission also cited the reasoning used by the state of Texas in these proceedings.

25 Document CCPR/C/SR.1779, 1999, Document CCPR/C/SR.2251, 2004.

26 ASTRA Network on Reproductive Health and Rights in Central and Eastern Europe for the European Population Forum, Geneva, 2004.

27 Synthesis Report of the European Union Network of Independent Experts on Fundamental Rights "Conclusions and Recommendations on the Situation of Fundamental Rights in the European Union and its Member States in 2004," 2005.

The same argumentative device was applied by the Court in the case of *R. R. v. Poland*, indicating separate part as "Relevant non-Convention material" derived from international bodies and experts.[28] This exceptionally broad reference to documents and positions serves in the justification of this ruling to demonstrate an unequivocal position and concern for the comfort of a pregnant woman who requires diagnostic tests for foetal abnormalities for medical reasons. This creates a setting for acknowledging the procrastination of the Polish health service – something that is indisputably apparent given the circumstances of the case. Secondly, referring to reports on the policy in force in Poland shows that problems with access to abortion in situations provided for by the law are persistent and systemic. This also supports the argumentation of a violation of the applicant's right, also under Article 3 of the Convention.

In *A., B. and C. v. Ireland* the Court cited another soft law document: PACE Resolution 1607 (2008), entitled "Access to safe and legal abortion in Europe," in which the Assembly "invites" the Member States of the Council of Europe to decriminalise abortion within reasonable gestational limits, guarantee women's effective exercise of their right of access to a safe and legal abortion, allow women freedom of choice and offer the conditions for a free and enlightened choice without specifically promoting abortion and, finally, lift restrictions which hinder, de jure or de facto, access to safe abortion, and, in particular, take the necessary steps to create the appropriate conditions for health, medical and psychological care and offer suitable financial cover.[29]

Consequently, by citing the documents of the Council of Europe and coming from the same legal and international environment, the Court justifies in this judgment the adoption of certain standpoint. The documents call for a specific approach in domestic law, which perfectly forms the context in which the Court adjudicates. At the same time, it is worth noting that despite the existence of documents that more firmly affirm women's right to reproductive self-determination – like the Convention on the Elimination of All Forms of Discrimination Against Women (CEDAW) in its Article 16(1)(e) – the Court did not use these in such a context, as if wishing to maintain an exceedingly toned-down attitude.

28 The Recommendation No. R (90) 13 on prenatal genetic screening, prenatal genetic diagnosis and associated genetic counselling (1990), adopted by the Committee of Ministers of the Council of Europe, the Resolution 1607 (2008) "Access to safe and legal abortion in Europe" adopted by the Parliamentary Assembly of the Council of Europe and the Convention on Human Rights and Biomedicine. It also then referred to the concluding observations of the UN Human Rights Committee on Poland reiterating "its deep concern about restrictive abortion laws in Poland" CCPR/C/POL/2004/5). The Court also mentioned reports of the Committee on the Elimination of Discrimination against Women (CEDAW) of 2007, and the positions of expert bodies, such as the International Federation of Gynaecology and Obstetrics, addressing the need for availability and conditions for carrying out prenatal diagnosis and the CEDAW's 1994 statement on the Ethical Framework for Gynaecologic and Obstetric Care.

29 A., B. and C. v. Ireland, par. 107–8.

Arguments from the margin of appreciation – evolution of deference

In cases concerning abortion, the Court, and before that the Commission, has very often and extensively resorted to the instrument of the margin of appreciation.[30] The attributes of this interpretative instrument fully manifest themselves in these cases. First, it should be remembered that the margin of appreciation is a tool of judicial self-restraint,[31] at the same time, a formula by which the Court addresses and refers to the audience. As we have indicated, this group of recipients, having in mind its broadness, is of special character and requires a special kind of argumentation, or rather persuasion.

Because of this, the Court faces extremely difficult task of, as Sunstein puts it, "making it possible to reach agreement where agreement is necessary and making it unnecessary where agreement is not possible."[32] The margin of appreciation is precisely intended to leave differences where agreement is not necessary. This is particularly evident in abortion-related cases. Here, the margin of appreciation is used specifically as an instrument to show that agreement on the content of Article 8 and Article 2 of the Convention is not absolutely necessary, and differences in their interpretation are accepted. The abortion cases also clearly show that the margin of appreciation, being a well-established and repeatedly analysed interpretative technique used in the ECtHR case law, constitutes, as far as the cases in question are concerned, not so much a way of interpreting and understanding the Convention norms and delimiting their scope, but a certain strategy of arguing for the position adopted in the ruling. Its use is subservient to this purpose, although the object of its use evolves. Let us therefore trace when and for what purpose the Court (formerly the Commission) referred to the concept of margin of appreciation in abortion-related cases and with what aim. We can identify three stages here.

In *Brüggemann and Scheuten v. Germany*, the first abortion-related case, the Commission addressed the question of the discretion of the States in the sphere under consideration ("problem of abortion" as it was pointed out) and included in its decision the sentence crucial to understanding this verdict:

> There is no evidence that it was the intention of the Parties to the Convention to bind themselves in favour of any particular solution under discussion.[33]

30 Cosentino, "Safe and Legal Abortion." 569–90; Daniel Fenwick, "The Modern Abortion Jurisprudence under Article 8 of the European Convention on Human Rights." *Medical Law International* 12(3–4) (2012): 249–76.

31 Dominic McGoldrick, "A Defence of the Margin of Appreciation and an Argument for Its Application by the Human Rights Committee." *International and Comparative Law Quarterly* 65(1) (2016): 23.

32 Cass Sunstein, *Designing Democracy: What Constitutions Do*, (Oxford University Press, 2001), 53.

33 Brüggemann and Scheuten v. Germany, p. 64.

The emerging doctrine of the margin of appreciation thus prompted the Commission to take a very prudent and calculated position, referring to the will of the States which had decided to accede to the Convention a quarter of a century earlier. It decided that the issue of abortion was so undeveloped at the European level, and that there were such considerable differences, that it was difficult to consider that States had the will to endow the Convention norms (in particular, Articles 2 and 8) with a meaning that would prejudge the question of the admissibility of abortion. The Commission has therefore sought to interpret the rights contained in the Convention in the light of States' potential acceptance of their meaning.[34] Initially, therefore, the problem of abortion was entirely covered by the margin of appreciation without indicating its subject. Instead, the Commission indicated only a reason of self-restraint in this matter, which was the lack of an unequivocal and unanimous will of the States in the time of expressing the will to accede the Convention.

This view has been further developed in subsequent decisions, concerning in particular the rights of the partners (fathers) of children-to-be-born to participate in the decision-making or to object to their partner's decision to proceed with the abortion. In the *X. v. the UK* case, the Commission ruled out the interpretation according to which the Convention would confer the right to life on the foetus by extending the protection provided by Article 2.[35] It stated that at the time of ratification of the Convention, abortion for the purpose of saving the life of the mother was permitted in all ("with one possible exception") of the signatory States, with tendency towards further liberalisation, as the Commission added. Thus, the Commission excluded the interpretation according to which the "unborn life" of the foetus would be regarded as being of higher value than the life of pregnant women.[36]

In this case, the Commission signalled the possibility of introducing a new line of argumentation to address the problem of admissibility of abortion.[37] The Commission stated that, in view of the fact that the cause of the abortion was actually the woman's state of health, it was not required to rule on the extent of the protection which the unborn child would be entitled to.[38]

34 In a subsequent judgment in *X. v. UK*, the Commission expressly acknowledged that in its judgment in *Brüggemann and Scheuten v. Germany* it deliberately left open the issue whether the unborn child is covered by Article 2. X. v. UK, par. 5.

35 The Commission considered that "general usage of the term 'everyone' . . . in the Convention . . . and the context in which this term is employed in Art. 2 . . . tend to support the view that it does not include the unborn." Par. 9. Additionally, it stated that in the circumstances of the case it was not called to decide whether Article 2 does not cover the foetus at all or whether it recognises the "right to life" of the foetus with implied limitations. X. v. UK, p. 23.

36 X. v. UK, p. 19, 20.

37 X. v. UK, p. 12.

38 X. v. UK, p. 23. In this respect, the decision in *Boso v. Italy* is analogous. The Court considered therein that it was not required to determine whether the foetus may qualify for protection under the first sentence of Article 2 as interpreted previously.

This concept has been upheld in subsequent cases. In *H. v. Norway*, the Commission noted the disparity in regulation and jurisprudence and in the interpretation of the personal scope of the right to life at national level, referring again to the radically different rulings of the Austrian and German constitutional courts.[39] Against that background, it deemed that there was no consensus on the problem of extending the legal protection of life to the unborn:

> The Commission finds that it does not have to decide whether the fetus may enjoy a certain protection under Article 2 (Art. 2), first sentence as interpreted above, but it will not exclude that in certain circumstances this may be the case notwithstanding that there is in the Contracting States a considerable divergence of views on whether or to what extent Article 2 (Art. 2) protects the unborn life.

However, problems with the permissibility of abortion and the extension of the protection of life to include the unborn had just begun. The liberalisation of abortion laws was slowly becoming a reality in most European countries, and it proved increasingly difficult to use the argument about the will of States to provide the unborn children with protection.

The problem manifested itself with full force in the *Vo v. France* case. The Court explicitly based its decision on the concept of the margin of appreciation, with profound consequences at that. The Court stated for the first time that the issue of when the right to life begins falls under the margin of appreciation, which in the Court's opinion, should generally be enjoyed by States in this particular sphere. Such determination of the object of the margin of appreciation was made by the Court with the proviso that the Convention should be interpreted evolutionarily as a "living instrument which must be interpreted in the light of present-day conditions."[40]

The Solomonic statement regarding the object of margin of appreciation contains two thoughts of key importance from the perspective of resolving cases concerning abortion. Firstly, the margin of appreciation is justified not by the lack of consensus on the interpretation of Article 2 of the Convention, but by the lack of agreement on the point at which human life begins. This is where the second key stage begins to take shape in terms of forming abortion jurisprudence in the context of the argumentation being used. The notion that States are unwilling to be bound by the particular meaning of Article 2 gives way to the notion that there is no consensus on the beginning of life. In *Vo v. France*, the Court thus made a fundamental semantic shift. It held that the margin of appreciation no longer only concerned the limits of States' discretion as to the implementation of the provisions and guarantees of the Convention, but extended to the very definition of life's beginning. It determined

39 Compare footnote 25.
40 Vo v. France, par. 82.

that there is no consensus at a European level on the nature and status of the embryo and foetus.[41] Assuming such a standpoint gives States virtually absolute freedom to set the boundaries of the protection of the life of the unborn and thus the legality of abortion. The issue has been moved to another level of argumentation to make it immune to the charge of violating the right to life of the foetus and the right to autonomy of the pregnant women (as it turned out later in the decision in *A., B. and C. v. Ireland*). This is an extremely controversial argumentative solution, but it allowed the Court to avoid the necessity of interpreting the meaning of Article 2 as well as to avoid a situation that could undermine the enforceability of its judgments due to an elimination of controversies in political, social or religious areas. At the same time, such reasoning did not deprive the Court its responsibility for the interpreting and applying the Convention rights.[42]

Secondly, in the quoted statement, the Court indicates the need for an evolutive interpretation of the Convention, which does not close the way to other interpretations in future decisions and opens the jurisprudence to the application of incrementalism.

The margin of appreciation implemented in this way is a fascinating instrument of argumentation, since it consists of using the well-known interpretative device of the margin of appreciation, which allows the sphere of the boundaries of the realisation of a certain right to be left to the discretion of the State, acknowledging the ambiguity of the concept of the beginning of life. Consequently, it is a way for the ECtHR to refrain from deciding when it is going to protect life or its potential existence, leaving this sphere in uncertainty by indicating that it raises scientific doubts. It is thus a type of appeal to epistemic authority – an argument *ad verecundiam* – out of timidity in the face of the fact deemed to be inconclusive at the judicial level. In consequence, such an appeal is much harder to disagree with.

Such pairing of the sphere of permissible State discretion with taking note of the disagreement on the assessment of the beginning of life allowed the Court to rule on abortion cases without making a firm ruling on the scope of the right to life and the other right at stake, namely the right to privacy.

The Court's approach towards the scope of margin of appreciation taken in the case *Vo v. France* can be found in *A., B. and C. v. Ireland*. When deciding on this case, the Court was already compelled to settle the conflict between the two values – that is, the pregnant woman's right to self-determination and the foetus' right to life – with that very right being guaranteed by the Irish Constitution and legislation. The Court considered that there is indeed a consensus

41 Vo v. France, par. 84.

42 This issue was discussed in the separate opinion by Judge Ress. He indicated that margin of appreciation could not be used for the purposes of interpretation of Article 2 protecting life (p. 8). As he wrote: "it is not possible to restrict the applicability of Article 2 by reference to the margin of appreciation. The question of the interpretation or applicability of Article 2 (an absolute right) cannot depend on the margin of appreciation."

amongst a substantial majority of the Contracting States of the Council of Europe towards allowing abortion on broader grounds than accorded under Irish law.[43] The fact that this consensus existed, did not, however, affect the fact that there has been no agreement as to the beginning of life.

Following the assumption that it was impossible to answer the question of whether the unborn was a person to be protected for the purposes of Article 2, in its judgment against Ireland the Court introduced another interpretation of the margin of appreciation. This time its scope covered balancing the interests of the mother and the unborn child.[44]

The Court recognised that the observation made earlier in *Vo. v. France* is of key importance, in that the question of determining the beginning of life falls within the States' margin of appreciation, since there is no scientific or legal consensus on the issue. At the same time, it concluded that while there is a broad consensus among States on the permissibility of abortion, there is no consensus on the moment from which life is protected. Since the rights of the mother and the unborn child are intertwined, the margin of discretion of States in protecting the unborn is superimposed on the margin as to how to balance these conflicting interests.[45]

In this regard, the Court notes that though it is apparent from the comparison of national laws that the majority of the Contracting Parties could have resolved those conflicting rights and interests in their legislation in favour of greater access to legal abortion, that consensus cannot be a decisive factor in the Court's examination of whether the contested ban on abortion in Ireland on health and well-being grounds struck a fair balance between the conflicting rights and interests, despite the evolving interpretation of the Convention. And, as far as that balancing exercise is concerned, the Court finds that the acute sensitivity of the moral and ethical issues raised by the question of abortion or as to the importance of the public interest at stake call for a broad margin of appreciation, which is to be accorded to the Irish State in determining the question whether a fair balance was struck between the protection of that public interest, notably the protection accorded under Irish law to the right to life of the unborn and the conflicting rights of the applicants to respect for their private lives under Article 8 of the Convention.[46]

43 As the Court has scrupulously pointed out, the first and second applicants could have obtained abortion on request (according to certain criteria including gestational limits) in some 30 such States. The first applicant could receive abortion on health and well-being grounds in approximately 40 Contracting States, and the second applicant could receive abortion on well-being grounds in approximately 35 Contracting States. Only three countries are more restrictive than Ireland on access to abortion services, with a ban on abortion regardless of the risk to the woman's life. In recent years, some countries have expanded the number of grounds under which abortion can be performed. A. B. and C. v. Ireland, par. 235.

44 A., B. and C. v. Ireland, par. 237.

45 A., B. and C. v. Ireland, par. 237.

46 A., B. and C. v. Ireland, par. 233.

Therefore, the margin of appreciation for balancing the interests of the mother and the child is already subject to a different assessment. The Court ultimately takes the view that abortion can be prohibited for well-being and health reasons (like in the situation of A. and B.), but bases that conviction on the procedural rationale referred to in the following. So here, once again, we have a combination of arguments based on the margin of appreciation with deontological arguments, referring to the assessment of the correctness of the legislative steps taken. It is about assessing the extent to which existing regulations have been adopted as part of a broad and democratically conducted public debate, reflecting the deeply rooted views of the Irish people. This criterion is met and therefore the margin is wide and justifies the conclusion that there has been no breach of Article 8.

Understanding the margin of appreciation as one concerning the balancing of the mother's and child's welfare (or public interest, as the Court considers it) was referred to by the ECtHR in *P. and S. v. Poland*. It ruled that in the absence of a common approach regarding the beginning of life, the examination of national legal solutions as applied to the circumstances of individual cases is of particular importance for the assessment of whether a fair balance between individual rights of the mother to be and the public interest – covering the conflicting rights of the foetus – has been maintained.[47] The consensus on balancing the interests of both woman and foetus (public interest) is broad and serves as the criterion used by the Court in recognising the violation of Article 8 in this case. Thus, the lack of a joint position on the beginning of life does not imply complete freedom and discretion for the State. The same reasoning was echoed in *R. R. v. Poland*.[48] Thus, the new subject of the margin of appreciation – balancing the conflicting goods – signalled in *A., B. and C. v. Ireland* and developed into a conclusive argument in *P. and S. v. Poland* and *R. R v. Poland* – came to the fore.

It is also worth noting that in cases against Poland[49] (unlike for applicants A. and B. in *A., B. and C. v. Ireland* and in *D. v. Ireland*), the Court has so far applied a margin of appreciation reasoning relating to the balancing of interests in circumstances where Polish law permitted abortion for the reasons underlying the complaints (women's health, fatal foetal anomalies and crime). Declaring that there had been a violation – and therefore arguing on the basis of the margin of appreciation – concerned only the actual actions of the public bodies (in terms of the shape of the procedure authorising the procedure and determining the decision-making process) which were responsible for negligence in this respect, not the wording of the law itself. This was clearly confirmed by the Court in *R. R. v. Poland*, indicating that while a broad margin of appreciation is accorded to the State as regards the circumstances in which an abortion will be permitted in a State, once that decision is taken, the legal

47 P. and S. v. Poland, par. 97.

48 R. R. v. Poland, par. 186.

49 Similar approach was applied in *Tysiac v. Poland*.

framework devised for this purpose should be "shaped in a coherent manner which allows the different legitimate interests involved to be taken into account adequately and in accordance with the obligations deriving from the Convention".[50] Nevertheless, there is no doubt that the subject matter which the margin of appreciation argument relates to has been changed from its previously stated subject matter relating to the assessment of the beginning of life.

Consequently, there are three stages of the development and three subjects of margin of appreciation in abortion cases. The first one, concerning the will of the States to be bound by an interpretation of the Convention allowing for admissibility of abortion, and in the next stage, also starting to consider the status of a foetus under Article 2. The second, explicitly adopted in *Vo v. France* and used in part to decide the case of *A., B. and C. v. Ireland*, pertains to the assessment of when life actually begins. The third stage, hinted at and considered in *A., B. and C. v. Ireland*, further developed to become the argument underlying the finding of the infringement of Article 8 in *R.R v. Poland* and *P. and S. v. Poland*, concerns the freedom of the State to balance the interests of the mother and child,[51] implicit in the wording of public interest.

This observable evolution indicates submission of the use of the margin of appreciation instrument to rhetorical and argumentative purposes. There is no doubt that the criterion for the use of the margin of appreciation is met. The cases involving abortion and the resolving of the dilemma between the will of the woman and the life of the foetus are morally sensitive like few others. This exposure to worldview and moral issues is, in a way, primary to further findings. The Court refrains from entering into the structure of the moral versus legal conflict that may exist. In doing so, it makes a gradual but visible change in the subject of the margin and a related change in the manner of assessing its limits, and thus the permissible actions – or omissions (in the Polish cases so far) – of the State.

Resorting to the margin of appreciation requires the use of an argument about the lack of consensus – a consensus at the level of the Member States as to the assumptions concerning both the adopted legal solutions and their axiological foundations.[52] The consensus that exists between the States to the Convention as regards the regulations is one of the elements conditioning the granting of the margin of appreciation, and is one of the basic factors determining its scope. Also, it must be pointed out that the Court adopts a very creative approach as to what the subject of this consensus (lack thereof) is. And this, in turn, makes it possible to consider the margin of appreciation as an excellent argumentative – and no longer (at least not only) interpretative – tool. As demonstrated herein, all the various ways in which it is applied are subordinated to the objective of adjudicating a violation of Article 8 of the Convention. In fact, it is no longer an instrument that allows for the

50 Par. 187. Here, the Court referred to the findings of the A., B. and C. v. Ireland, par. 249.

51 Such approach was also alluded in *Tysiac v. Poland* and *Open Door v. Ireland*.

52 Kanstantsin Dzehtsiarou, "European Consensus and the Evolutive Interpretation of the ECHR." *German Law Journal* 12(10) (2011): 1730, McGoldrick, "A Defence." 28–9.

interpretation of Convention norms, but for the justification of the fact that they tend to mean different things in different States.

The argumentation based on the margin of appreciation is complemented by another construction constituting its reverse side: States' acceptance of travelling for services abroad in order to realise certain claimed rights in European states other than the country of origin.[53] "Abortion tourism" is a good example of this, although it is usually discreetly ignored by the Court in abortion cases, as well as other cases discussed in this work. It does, however, lead to a coherent and reproducible concept of the "right to travel" – that is, the acceptance of the practice of allowing for abortion tourism, which proves relevant especially in the context of the Irish cases.[54] This technique of replacing the right to undergo an abortion – a troublesome and difficult right to articulate – with rights associated with the exercise of that entitlement is particularly noteworthy. It is also present in other cases discussed in the book. It is true in the case of end-of-life situations, in which the issue of travelling to a clinic in Switzerland that offers to perform a euthanasic death is raised on several occasions; it is also true in the case of medically assisted procreation, where the issue of travelling abroad in order to undergo procedures is raised, as well as the problem of recognition of foreign birth certificates and the origin of a child conceived or born outside the legal mother's organism. However, these issues – as we have sought to demonstrate – continue to remain on the periphery of the Court's considerations. It does take note of them, but the argumentation concerning this element – testifying, after all, most clearly to the multiplicity of approaches and the paradox of the sometimes radically different scope of implementation of autonomy under Article 8 of the Convention – is sparse.[55]

53 This concept is different from the concept of migration, which means settling in other European countries which protect rights to a greater degree than the home country. This is not addressed in the abortion jurisprudence, although it occurs in other areas which raise margin of appreciation issues, such as LGBT rights.

54 The controversy surrounding migration law is mentioned by Fenwick, "The Modern Abortion Jurisprudence." 272.

55 In abortion cases, this problem had to appear in a slightly different context as well, and was analysed more broadly. An important decision has already been made in the case of *Open Door and Dublin Well Women v. Ireland*, which does not directly concern abortion, but information about the possibility of having an abortion outside Ireland (Open Door and Dublin Well Women v. Ireland, appl. no. 14234/88 and 14235/8, judgment of 29 October 1992). The Irish prohibition on information was found by the Court to be in breach of Art. 10 (2) ECHR. The Court considered that an injunction preventing dissemination of information on abortion to women "regardless of age or state of health or their reasons for seeking counselling on the termination of pregnancy" (para. 73) was disproportionate to the moral damage likely to be caused by non-directive counselling that did not recommend abortion, was not available to the public at large, and non-effective as readily available from foreign sources; the Court also considered that large numbers of women continued to travel despite the constitutional provisions. On the impact of the Open Door case on regulation: Rick Lawson, "The Irish Abortion Cases: European Limits to National Sovereignty." *European Journal of Health Law* 1(2) (1994): 167–86.

In *A., B. and C. v. Ireland*, the applicants alleged that their journey to the United Kingdom for the purpose of having an abortion procedure put them under significant mental and organisational stress and therefore infringed their rights.[56] The Court considered it evident that travelling abroad for an abortion constituted a significant psychological burden on each applicant and constituted a significant source of added anxiety.[57] When reviewing the actions of the Irish authorities and doctors, though, the Court did not find reasons for either such a burden or delays that could have contributed to increasing the distress suffered by the applicants. Instead, it notes that the wording of the Irish law, derived from the lengthy, complex and sensitive debate, prohibits abortion for health and well-being reasons but allows women the option of lawfully travelling to another State to do so.[58] The Thirteenth and Fourteenth Amendments to the Constitution removed any legal impediment to adult women travelling abroad for an abortion and obtaining information in that respect. The complaints were not found meritorious on the ground that the lack of information impeded the performance of the abortion, although the Court noted "the serious impact of the impugned restriction on the applicants" (first and second).[59]

Another argument was also raised here. The applicants alleged that the impugned prohibition on abortion is to a large extent ineffective in protecting the unborn in the sense that a substantial number of women take the option open to them in the law of travelling abroad for an abortion not available in Ireland.[60] The relevant statistics provided to the Court were particularly telling in this regard. The Court, on the other hand, decided to draw a clear line between the prohibition of abortion and the authorisation to travel outside the country in order to perform it. As it stated, such a choice of measure falls within the margin of appreciation[61] and it struck a fair balance between the right of the applicants (first and second) to respect for their private lives and the rights invoked on behalf of the unborn.

56 It needs to be added that the issue of travelling for the purpose of having an abortion had previously been the subject of national judgments – including judgment of the High Court, 9 May 2007 in Case D (A Minor) v. District Judge Brennan, the Health Services Executive, Ireland and the Attorney General. The High Court clarified that the case was "not about abortion or termination of pregnancy. It is about the right to travel, admittedly for the purposes of a pregnancy termination, but that does not convert it into an abortion case." The High Court held that the right to travel guaranteed by the Thirteenth Amendment took precedence over the right of the unborn guaranteed by Article 40.3.3. There was no statutory or constitutional impediment preventing D. from travelling to the United Kingdom for an abortion.

57 A., B. and C. v. Ireland, par. 126.

58 A., B. and C. v. Ireland, par. 239.

59 A., B. and C. v. Ireland, par. 240.

60 This allegation referred to the Court's conclusions in the Open Door case, in which the Court found that the prohibition on information was ineffective to protect the right to life because women travelled abroad anyway (par. 76).

61 A., B. and C. v. Ireland, par. 240.

The option to perform a procedure banned in the country outside its borders has greatly facilitated the adjudication of abortion cases involving Ireland.[62] This situation has enabled the most difficult questions to be avoided.[63] Ultimately, all the abortions in the Irish cases have been performed, and Irish law clearly allows for this travelling practice, or even facilitates it. Things are – and probably will be – completely different in cases concerning abortions filed against Poland, where the language barrier and other organisational obstacles may make such migrations much harder.

Nevertheless, it is noteworthy that the ECtHR exercises self-restraint in yet another dimension. In abortion cases, it treats migration for the purpose of exercising the right completely neutrally, although it acknowledges and approves of it. Undoubtedly, the assessment of the factual and quite straightforward possibility to seek abortion is somewhat of a facilitating factor in leaving the issue of the scope of the right to autonomy itself and the limits of the permissibility of abortion without finding a violation of Article 8 of the Convention. Nor does the Court consider that the abortion law is thereby rendered less effective in the country in which it is in force, leaving the matter within the State's margin of appreciation. From the point of view of the argumentative tools discussed herein, it is difficult to qualify this type of argumentation unequivocally. It is in part the reverse of the State's margin of appreciation, as the Court observes the potential for migration to be used to enforce the right, thus justifying a decision on the broad limits of its discretion as to the content of the right itself. The argument that it is relatively easy to exercise the right to a greater extent outside the State borders (provided that it is done under conditions deemed not to be too onerous) is an additional argument in favour of maintaining the domestic law within the limits set by the State. At the same time, the Court does not share the argument of inefficiency, which could be called an argument based on hypocrisy of the State. Quite the contrary, it draws a clear line between the legitimacy of the State to establish its own boundaries of law and allowing the individual interests to be realised outside its jurisdiction. This line of argumentation, which comes up in the background of the Irish cases, can in turn be qualified as a pragmatic argument. It is an indication of the easily accessible possibility to undergo abortion in a neighbouring State, which can be regarded as equivalent to considering the mitigating circumstances of the abortion prohibition and significantly influences the assessment of the extent to which the rights of pregnant women are respected. The "right to travel" argument therefore reaches back to practical rationality. It refers to the real outcome that the person claiming protection can easily achieve (and usually has achieved), which prejudges the assessment of the degree of severity of national restrictions on the right. In this way, the Court can leave the plea without prejudging the legal limits of abortion in

62 This approach has even been called "the culture of abortion tourism" in: Irvine 2001, p. 136.
63 Cosentino, "Safe and Legal Abortion." 583.

domestic legislation or, even more so, at the European level. In this respect, this argumentative instrument largely replaces recourse to teleological methods not present in cases concerning abortion. The reference to the finally achieved result in the form of a legally performed abortion – albeit on the territory of another state – undoubtedly helps the ECtHR to avoid a categorical statement about the scope of the right to reproductive self-determination in its decisions, for it indicates the results are actually produced or are possible to achieve, which coincides with the demands of the applicants. It thus makes it easier to decide and argue that there is no violation.

Deontological argumentation

All of the remaining argumentation employed by the Court is exhausted at the deontological level. Indeed, the deontological perspective is particularly extensive, especially when it comes to incrementalism, proceduralisation and the plasticity of used notions.

Arguments based on incrementalism – rights of foetuses, pregnant women and potential fathers

The incrementalism, that is the gradual finding of new elements in the rights guaranteed by the Convention, can be found in cases concerning the admissibility of abortion on as many as three planes. These are: the evolution of the scope of protection of the right to life under Article 2 of the Convention in the context of the regulation of the legal status of the fetus; the evolution of the extent of the prohibition of inhumane and degrading treatment under Article 3 of the Convention in the context of the level of distress suffered by a woman prevented from undergoing abortion legally; and, finally, the evolution of the scope of the right to the protection of private life under Article 8 of the Convention in relation to the legal situation of pregnant woman, as well as the right to the protection of private and family life in terms of the legal situation of the potential father. In all these ranges, incrementalism not only has an interpretative role but also an arguing role as reasoning to convince to the correctness of the judgment, even if the decision is not simply a consequence of the adopted scope of the right under consideration.

It is appropriate to begin with the evolution of the legal protection of the life of the foetus, however it is relatively subtly developed in the Court's case law under Article 2 of the Convention. In the *Brüggemann and Scheuten v. Germany* case, the Commission only decided about the necessity to restrict the right to privacy in relation to the decision to undergo abortion and the thread has not been developed further.[64] In the case of *X v. UK*, in view of the

64 Brüggemann and Scheuten v. Germany, p. 59. It is worth noting that it was a kind of response to the formulation contained in the judgment of the Federal Constitutional Court

allegation made by a potential father, the Commission focused largely on the interpretation of Article 2 of the Convention with regard to the guarantee of the foetus' right to life. It expressly excluded the possibility to interpret the Convention as providing the foetus with the absolute right to life,[65] but simultaneously has avoided specifying whether the foetus is entitled to any protection.[66] This statement was made more precise in the case *Boso v. Italy*, where the Court held that "in certain circumstances, the fetus might be considered to have rights protected by Article 2 of the Convention."[67] Bearing in mind that in previous cases the Court had merely acknowledged that the foetus is not entitled to absolute protection while avoiding to indicate whether it enjoys any rights under Article 2, this statement should be viewed as a decisive step in extending the guarantees of foetal rights.

In the subsequent rulings on abortion, this theme has not been further explored. The allegation of a breach of Article 2 of the Convention in abortion cases was no longer raised, which in turn relieved the Court of the need to decide on the issue. However, establishing the connection between the situation of the developing foetus and a woman's right to respect for her private life even in the earliest cases has left its mark on the scope of the guarantees granted to her and, in consequence, on the argumentation used to persuade the audience to the direction of the decisions taken. The potential rights of the foetus were in the background of all the Court's considerations on women's rights, although it was already proved in the section concerning margin of appreciation. The questions of beginning of life or of the rights of the foetus were not taken into consideration as those crucial for the determining the applicants' rights in later stages of the Court's case law.

The evolution of the prohibition of inhuman treatment and the right to privacy in the context of a woman's right to decide whether to continue or terminate a pregnancy presents a very different picture.

In the case of *R. R. v. Poland*,[68] the Court found that by virtue of the fact that the foetus had an incurable defect the applicant was in a situation of great vulnerability.[69] The Court has thus extended the catalogue of persons covered

of 1975 that "pregnancy belongs to the intimate sphere of the woman whose protection is guaranteed" (par. 58). The German Court ruled that the woman's right to free development of her personality, including right to decide against becoming a parent as expressly limited by the rights of others, the constitutional order and the moral code, must give away the pre-eminence of the protection of the life of the foetus.

65 X v. UK, par. 18. The Commission found that "general usage of the term 'everyone' . . . in the Convention . . . and the context in which this term is employed in Art. 2 . . . tend to support the view that it does not include the unborn," par. 9.

66 X v. UK, par. 23.

67 Boso v. Italy, par.1. p. 4.

68 The allegation of inhuman treatment contrary to Art. 3 of the Convention had already been raised in previous cases, but the Court did not find any violation of this provision in them. Cf. Tysiąc v. Poland, par. 108, A., B. and C. v. Ireland, par. 160–5.

69 R.R. v. Poland, par. 159.

by this concept.[70] The Court held that the manner in which the applicant had been treated by the medical personnel and the fact that she had been prevented from availing herself of the diagnostic facilities provided for by law and available nationally had caused the applicant's suffering to reach the minimum threshold of severity under Article 3 of the Convention.[71] This line of argument has reinforced the ECtHR's position considerably and, at the same time, has set a new framework for the protection of pregnant women whose foetus is burdened with foetal fatal anomalies.[72] Consequently, owing to the lack of effective implementation of domestic legal provisions, the infliction of suffering which may be suffered by a pregnant woman claiming the exercise of her legitimate rights, including, in the further alternative, a lawful abortion, was assessed for the first time as falling within the scope of the acts prohibited by Article 3 of the Convention.

The interpretation of the prohibition of inhuman and degrading treatment was developed in *P. and S. v. Poland.* Here, the Court indicated further elements allowing to consider that a pregnant woman is in a state of great vulnerability: low age (being a minor) and the pregnancy being the result of unlawful intercourse.[73] When assessing the threshold of severity inflicted upon the applicant by the authorities, in light of her vulnerability, the Court took into account cumulative circumstances such as: pressure put on her and her mother by medical personnel, priest and other third parties; institution of criminal proceedings; procrastination, confusion, and lack of proper and objective counselling and information; separation from her mother; and deprivation of liberty in breach of the requirements of Article 5 § 1.[74]

The collective analyses of the cases *Tysiąc v. Poland*; *A., B. and C. v. Ireland*; *R. R. v. Poland;* and *P. and S. v. Poland* in which Article 3 was raised (however not always successful) demonstrates an incremental broadening in the ECtHR approach to Article 3 in the context of abortion. The key factors determining the level of suffering by the applicants was their great vulnerability,

70 This issue is discussed in Chapter 1.

71 R.R. v. Poland, par. 160–1. More about the expansion of the concept of torture and inhuman and degrading treatment, see Alyson Zureick, "(En)Gendering Suffering: Denial of Abortion as a Form of Cruel, Inhuman or Degrading Treatment." *Fordham International Law Journal* vol. 38, issue 1: 101 and sub. The author points out that the ECtHR, by adjudicating violation of Article 3 only in certain cases applied implicit justifiability test proposed my Manfred Nowak to determine whether infliction of pain or suffering may be justifiable and thus not an act of inhuman and degrading treatment.

72 The potential for acknowledging a violation of Art. 3 in defining the scope of the right to abortion in the ECtHR case law is pointed by Bríd NÍ Ghrainne, Aisling McMahon, "Access to Abortion in Cases of Fatal Fetal Abnormality: A New Direction for the European Court of Human Rights?" *Human Rights Law Review* 19 (3) (2020): 561; as well as Molly Joyce, "The Human Rights Aspects of Abortion." *Hibernian Law Journal* 16 (2017): 27–41.

73 P. and S. v. Poland, par. 161–2.

74 P. and S. v. Poland, par. 161–9.

psychological distress and denial of medical treatment.[75] Declaring violation of Article 3 in some of the cases leaves the door open for the ECtHR to incrementally broaden its position on abortion rights in future case law.[76] It can be argued that in view of the observation that refusal of an abortion in the event of fatal foetal anomalies may be qualified as "inhuman and degrading treatment,"[77] the Court's willingness to use incrementalism is a step forward to stating a violation of the Convention in such a case.

The most significant evolution in the scope of protection has occurred within Article 8, which refers to the right to respect for private life.[78] The Commission's first findings in *Brüggemann and Scheuten v. Germany* focused on whether the issue of the availability of abortion fell within the scope of Article 8 of the Convention at all. The Commission stated only very generally that legislation regulating interruption of pregnancy touches upon the sphere of private life,[79] but that not every form of legislation regulating the termination of pregnancy constituted an interference with the right to respect for the private life.[80] It concluded that the German provisions allowing only for abortion in case of a threat to the life and health of the mother (both in the case of illness and on account of her mental state) and in the case of an embryopathological premise did not constitute such an interference with a woman's rights.[81] The Commission's position was significant in that it confirmed that future cases were not to be assessed solely within the framework of guarantees for the protection of a woman's private life, understood as the possibility of choosing to undergo an abortion. This perspective was therefore relatively conservative from the point of view of defining the limits of the right to autonomy.[82]

75 Ghrainne, McMahon, "Access to Abortion." 569–72. They indicate that the Court did not conclude that Art. 3 of the Convention in the first abortion case referred to it – *Tysiąc v. Poland* – because at that time it did not want to make such far-reaching assessments against the Polish authorities. Only in the absence of a fundamental objection in the European arena to the ruling given, although then only in terms of Art. 8 and its longstanding non-enforcement by the Polish authorities, have emboldened the Court to conclude on the violation of Art. 3.

76 Ghrainne, McMahon, "Access to Abortion." 573.

77 Ghrainne, McMahon, "Access to Abortion." 581 et seq.

78 The evolution of the right to respect for private life in abortion cases is also shown in a very concise way by Gerards, cf. Gerards, "Margin of Appreciation." 507–8.

79 Brüggemann and Scheuten v. Germany, Report of the Commission. 127.7.1977, par. 54.

80 Brüggemann and Scheuten v. Germany, par. 61.

81 Brüggemann and Scheuten v. Germany, par. 63.

82 The Commission's position, already very conservative regarding the protection of the decision-making autonomy of pregnant women, is strongly contested by Mr E.S. Fawcett in his dissenting opinion in favour of introducing more extensive foetal protection, stating: "'Private life' in Article 8 (1) must in my view cover pregnancy, its commencement and its termination: indeed, it would be hard to envisage more essentially private elements in life. But pregnancy has also responsibilities for the mother towards the unborn child, at least when it is capable of independent life, and towards the father of the child, and for the father too towards both. But pregnancy, its commencement and its termination, as so viewed is still part of private and family life, calling for respect under Article 8 (1)."

Although another important ruling on the definition of the constituent elements of Article 8 came with the *Boso v. Italy* case and concerned the rights of the potential father, the Court managed to "slip in" an important point concerning the de facto rights of women within Article 8 of the Convention. In assessing the applicant's challenge against the Italian regulations under which his wife had been able to terminate her pregnancy, to the detriment of the foetus, the Court found the regulations permitting abortion on the ground of risk to the woman's health to be compatible with the Convention because they correctly balanced the interests of the woman and of the foetus.[83] It seems that with this statement, the Court paved the way for the inclusion in Article 8 of the Convention of the right to demand that abortion regulations be shaped in such a way as to make abortion possible on account of a woman's health condition.

While deciding on *Tysiąc v. Poland*, the Court shaped the scope of Article 8 by expressly refusing to attribute a meaning to Article 8 that could constitute a basis for demanding an abortion. It stated that it is not its task to examine whether the Convention guarantees the right to undergo such a procedure.[84] At the same time, the Court stated that the issues raised in the abortion-related cases, especially in the case at hand, constituted a "combination of different aspects of private life," encompassing, *inter alia*, aspects of an individual's physical and social identity, as well as a person's physical and psychological integrity.[85] At this point, attention must be paid to the wording equating the importance of mental and physical integrity of the mother – even though the circumstances of the case clearly indicated the somatic illness of the pregnant woman, whose pregnancy could have resulted in severe disability. This aspect recognised in the *Tysiąc v. Poland* judgment has been extensively supplemented in subsequent judgments, especially Irish ones. It should be emphasised, however, that due to the choice of perspective in assessing the applicant's situation, that is assessing the State's fulfilment of positive rather than negative obligations, the Court did not expressly state in that case that the existence of legislation restricting the permissibility of abortion constituted an interference with the right to respect for private and family life. Undoubtedly, however, the indication of how broad the values or interests covered by that right are, constituted a further clarification of the scope of the guarantee under Article 8 of the Convention.

As we have mentioned, the Court applied in the *Tysiąc v. Poland* case the tool of proceduralisation examining the shape of the applicable law and assessing the decision-making process in relation to the applicant. Therefore, also the Court's position on incrementalism largely focuses on the required

83 Boso v. Italy, par. 1, p. 5.
84 Tysiąc v. Poland, par. 104.
85 Tysiąc v. Poland, par. 107.

content and manner of implementing the domestic provisions. However, this leads to conclusions concerning the already substantial right to autonomy.

Initially, the Court set out the general standard that the procedure provided for by the law and governing access to abortion must make it possible to clearly assess the legal position of a woman in terms of whether the conditions for carrying out the procedure are fulfilled. Most notably, a procedure must be in place for assessing the situation and reaching a decision in the event of a difference of opinion, either between the pregnant woman and her doctors or between the doctors themselves.[86] Resolving such disagreements should be entrusted to an independent body. In addition to this general obligation to create an adequate regulatory framework, the ECtHR has also formulated several procedurally specific requirements which significantly enrich the meaning of the right to privacy in the context of the admissibility of abortion. These include: the right of a pregnant woman to be heard in person and to have her views considered, the obligation incumbent upon the competent body to issue written grounds for its decision[87] and the procedures in place should ensure that decisions are made in a timely manner and not reviewed *post factum*.[88] The *Tysiąc v. Poland* case was the first case in which the Court highlighted that provisions regulating the availability of lawful abortion should be formulated in such a way as to alleviate the chilling effect, which may be caused by the fact that legal restrictions on abortion must be read in the light of criminal provisions penalising illegal abortions.[89]

Indicated constituent elements of Article 8 extracted by the Court specify the framework within which the legislature and subsequently the judiciary should operate to ensure that the regulations in force and their application comply with the requirements of the Convention.

Further specification of the content of the scope of guarantees under Article 8 stemmed from the *A., B. and C. v. UK* judgment. In stating so, it should be stressed that the Court drew a distinction between its assessment of the situation of applicants A. and B. who complained that they had been prevented from undergoing an abortion where this was not provided for by domestic law, and that of applicant C., who had been prevented from undergoing the procedure despite it being formally permissible. The Court expressly acknowledged, departing from the view expressed in *Brüggemann and Scheuten v. Germany*, that the prohibition of the termination of pregnancies sought for reasons of health or well-being amounted to an interference with their right to respect for their private lives.[90] That view was followed, however, by

86 Tysiąc v. Poland, par. 116.
87 Tysiąc v. Poland, par. 117.
88 Tysiąc v. Poland, par. 118, 127.
89 Tysiąc v. Poland, par. 116, 193.
90 A., B. and C. v. Ireland, par. 216.

the conclusion that, in the case of the applicants A. and B., the interference was justified in the exercise of the State's discretion. The Court held that it was permissible for the law on abortion to be framed in such a way so as to prohibit the procedure on the ground that it constituted a risk to health or well-being, but only if women were also entitled to travel abroad legally to have an abortion, with access to appropriate information and medical care in their country of origin.[91] The Court's conclusion regarding the shape of the abortion legislation as permissible under the Convention must be read within the context of *Boso v. Italy*, where the premise of the woman's health was recognised as legitimate under Article 8 of the Convention.

As far as applicant C. is concerned, abortion was theoretically permissible in that case, so the Court again – just as in the *Tysiąc* case – decided to conduct the analysis focused on fulfilling procedural obligations. As a result, the ECtHR's judgment did not include any assessment as to whether prohibiting abortion in the case of threat to a woman's life would constitute an interference with the right to respect for private life. Given the conclusions on the admissibility of abortion legislation under Article 8 of the Convention though, as formulated both in this and previous judgments, it is reasonable to conclude that legislation prohibiting abortion in cases where a woman's life is in danger would constitute infringement of the right to respect for her private life, although it would rather be assessed as an unjustifiable interference. However, this is a conclusion about the shape of guarantees under Article 8 and women's rights that cannot be directly derived from the judgment.

With regards to the grounds for permissibility of the termination of pregnancy under the Convention, it is worth noting one additional finding of the Court. Despite the government's use of the term "social reasons" in its reasoning to collectively designate all the grounds, the Court considered it important to distinguish between health (physical and mental) and other well-being reasons to describe why the applicants chose to seek abortion. Hence, it recognised the difference in those grounds and sought to distinguish their significance.

In *A., B. and C. v. Ireland*, the scope of Article 8 was further defined in terms of procedural obligations imposed on States, particularly in relation to the shape of legislation on abortion. The Court emphasised that it must be "shaped in a coherent manner which allows the different legitimate interests involved to be taken into account."[92] It thereby reaffirmed the scope of the right to respect for private and family life in the area of the obligation to respect the principles of fair legislation and proportionality. Additionally, the Court defined several criteria concerning the shape of the national regulation and its application. It pointed out the existence of the right to receive medical consultation, and that this right must be effective, including the possibility

91 A., B. and C. v. Ireland, par. 241.
92 A., B. and C. v. Ireland, par. 249.

of recourse to the courts in the event of disagreement between the woman and the medical personnel, among other things.[93] The necessity for generally binding and well-disseminated recommendations and standards setting out the specifics of the permissibility of abortion in situations where the existing legislation is very general, as in Ireland, was identified as another essential element. These State obligations simultaneously create new areas of entitlement under Article 8 – the right to initiate a procedure to clarify doubts about the admissibility of termination of pregnancy and binding indications specifying general constitutional standards for the protection of life. Having found a violation of Article 8 (in the case of applicant C.), the Court held that a pregnant woman's right to privacy therefore also contains those elements which substantiate the admissibility of the abortion and the procedure for clarifying doubts and disputes about it.[94]

In addressing the scope of the guarantees under Article 8 in *R. R. v. Poland*, the Court resorted to procedural tactics and case analysis concentrating on the fulfilment of positive obligations, just as it had done in *Tysiąc v. Poland*. In this context, it pointed to further requirements concerning the shape of the domestic law on abortion, including the need to provide the woman with full and reliable information on the foetus' health in particular.[95] When outlining the State's obligations towards situations in which doctors rely on the conscientious objection clause in order not to carry out the abortion procedure, the Court makes it clear that it is the State's duty to organise the medical care system in such a way that the medical personnel's exercise of their rights does not affect the effectiveness of the medical treatment received by patients.[96] This postulate does not only pertain to the abortion procedure, but to all other services available within the framework of health care. Indeed, in the context of abortion, the mechanism for ensuring access to diagnostic care and comprehensive information is intended to guarantee a fundamental right which the

93 A., B. and C. v. Ireland, par. 253.

94 It should be stressed that the ECtHR's incrementalism of the right to respect for family life in terms of the premise legalising abortion when a woman's life is in danger was heavily influenced by the incrementalism of the right to a woman's autonomy contained in a domestic judgment handed down in Ireland by the Supreme Court in the X case in 2002. This judgment was cited approvingly by the Court in *A., B. and C. v. Ireland*. The Irish court made the interpretation of Art. 40.3.3 of the Irish Constitution and presented a broad understanding of the premise of protection of the mother's life and health (including mental health), which extended to the content of the pregnant woman's right to access abortion. Thus, it can already be regarded as settled that a refusal to provide an abortion in a situation where a woman's life and health – including mental health – are at risk, whether for lack of an appropriate regulation (*A., B. and C. v. Ireland*) or because it is defective and poorly applied (*Tysiąc v. Poland*), will constitute a violation of the right to autonomy of the pregnant woman.

95 R. R. v. Poland, par. 200.

96 R. R. v. Poland, par. 206.

Court has derived in this very case from Article 8, namely the right to take an informed decision as to whether to seek an abortion or not.[97]

When reconstructing the substance of the "private life" to be protected, in addition to its previous findings including right to personal autonomy and personal development and right to a person's physical and psychological integrity, the Court referred in *R. R. v. Poland* to a new statement that the notion of private life applies to decisions both to have or not to have a child or to become parents.[98] This concept was first used by the Court in circumstances other than access to abortion, but citing it here seems to be a step towards a much broader understanding of the right to respect for private life in the context of deciding to terminate a pregnancy.[99]

In its decision for *P. and S. v. Poland*, the Court summarised its previous considerations on the availability of abortion in the context of the right to privacy, stating that the possibility of exercising personal autonomy depends on "effective access to reliable information on the conditions for the availability of lawful abortion, and the relevant procedures to be followed."[100]

The decision in *P. and S. v. Poland* was so far the last one brought against Poland (it appears that the change of law in Ireland is influencing the absence of new complaints), in which the Court addressed the scope of the right to privacy in the context of abortion. It is definitely not the last ruling, however, as there are as many as 13 pending complaints from potential victims who turned to the ECtHR after the Polish Constitutional Court de facto outlawed the embryopathological premise.[101] An individual case of a woman who was

97 R. R. v. Poland, par. 208.

98 This statement was first made in the judgment of *Evans v. the United Kingdom*, appl. no. 6339/05, par. 71.

99 R.R. v. Poland, par. 180. It is worth noting that in both cases, that is *R.R. v. Poland and P. and S. v. Poland*, Judge Gaetano – who submitted his dissenting opinions – expressed the view that the discussed issue should have been examined under Article 6. In his opinion, invoking Article 8 in such cases not only distorts the true meaning of "private life" but ignores the most fundamental of values underpinning the Convention, namely the value of life, of which the unborn child is the carrier.

100 P. and S. v. Poland, par. 111.

101 *K.B. v. Poland* and three other applications (appl. nos. 1819/21, 3682/21, 4957/21 and 6217/21), *K.C. v. Poland* and three other applications (nos. 3639/21, 4188/21, 5876/21 and 6030/21), *A. L. – B. v. Poland* and three other applications (nos. 3801/21, 4218/21, 5114/21 and 5390/21) and *M. L. v. Poland*, app. 40119/21. In addition to the comments on extending the meaning of privacy through incrementalism, it is worth referring to the judgment of the Polish Constitutional Tribunal in 2020. In that judgment, the CT declared the unconstitutionality of provision allowing abortion on the grounds that medical examination indicates a high probability of foetal damage or an incurable disease. The Constitutional Tribunal ruled that the challenged provision is inconsistent with the constitutional protection of life (Article 38) in the connection with the principle of proportionality (Article 31 [3] of the Polish Constitution). According to the Polish Tribunal's opinion, in the situation of an impairment or incurable disease of a child, there is no value that would allow for the child's life to be put as a value sacrificed for another good. In particular, it considered that such a value could not be regarded as the welfare of the mother – the protection of her health

prevented from having an abortion despite severe and irreversible foetal abnormalities is also pending.[102]

When summing up the evolution of the content of the right to private life facilitated by means of the incremental approach, it may be observed that the right to privacy does not yet imply, as a matter of fact, the right to request an abortion, to the effect that in none of the cases has it been established that there has been a substantive violation of Article 8 of the Convention. However, this right implies the right to the physical and psychological integrity of the woman, the right to decide whether or not to continue or terminate the pregnancy within the framework of domestic law, the procedural rights associated with that decision, and – by reference to a different decision in the new context – the right to decide whether or not to become a parent. The regulatory framework of adjudicatory and enforcement machinery protecting individuals' rights and the implementation, when appropriate, of specific measures is of paramount importance for the content and scope of so called reproductive self-determination. The evolution is thus not only noticeable, but extremely meaningful. Despite the Court's conservative stance on this issue, there is no denying that there has been a significant shift from declaring that abortion is not a private matter of the woman alone. The right to be or not to be a parent formulated in the case of *R. R. v. Poland* – although it is mentioned on the sidelines and in the context of other comments determining the content of the ruling – is, or at least may become, a milestone in the ECtHR case law. In the manner typical for the tool of incrementation, the Court may use the formulated scope of the Article 8 right, referring to the findings already made in its case law.

The concept of private life and family life with respect to the rights of a woman's partner – the potential father – has gone in a slightly different direction and has developed much less dynamically.

In the case *X. v. the United Kingdom*, the Commission examined the potential father's allegations of a violation of his rights guaranteed under Article 8 of the Convention from two angles. First, it acknowledged that the existence of legislation enabling a woman to take a lawful decision to terminate her pregnancy interfered with the applicant's right to respect for family life. It also confirmed that legal standing of a potential father falls within the right to respect for family life. In the circumstances of this case, however, proceeding

and life being a separate premise for a potential abortion. Therefore, the Polish Tribunal completely ignored the existence of the protected good in the form of the mother's condition and the fact that the child's life is connected with it. Thus, it reduced the scope of the mother's right to privacy to zero, ignoring the EctHR's findings on the right to private life, family life and the prohibition under Art. 3 of the Convention. It is therefore a unique voice in the usually observed dialogue between national courts and the EctHR, leaving the fate of the pregnant woman and her rights in a complete vacuum, while remaining completely outside the discourse – especially in Polish cases, including *R.R v. Poland* – on the need to embrace mother's protection in such cases. Por., CT judgment K 1/20 on October 22 2020.

102 B.B. v. Poland, appl. no. 67171/17.

with the abortion constituted interference justified by the rights of another person, namely the woman. The conclusion that the decision to perform an abortion constituted an interference with the rights of a potential father reflected the evolution that had taken place in relation to defining the scope of women's rights under Article 8. It should be remembered that back in *Brüggemann and Scheuten v. Germany*, regulations restricting the legality of abortion were not regarded by the Commission as constituting an interference with a woman's right. In the *X v. UK* case, the abortion was performed to avoid the risk of damaging the woman's physical and mental health. However, the Court did not clarify the issue of whether the need to respect the right to family life of a potential father would encompass the permissibility of abortion for other reasons.

A second angle for assessing the situation in light of the rights of a potential father was to recognise that the father's potential right to respect for his family life cannot be interpreted so widely as to embrace the right to be consulted or to apply to a court about the abortion which his wife intends to have performed on her.[103] The applicant's allegation concerning this issue was found in *X. v. the United Kingdom* to be incompatible *ratione materiae* with the Convention. By contrast, the Court had already taken a different approach in *Boso v. Italy*, de facto extending the scope of the partner's rights in the context of the possibility of co-participation in the abortion decision. Using the phrase "potential father's rights under Article 8," the Court did not regard the case as falling outside the material scope of Article 8 of the Convention, as it had done previously. The possibility of joint participation in decision-making was included within the material scope, since the ECtHR considered that it had assessed that any alleged interference with those rights was justified for the protection of the rights of another person – the woman.[104] Consequently, the right to be involved in the decision-making process was covered by the right to respect for private and family life, and the interference in the form of not granting a man the right to participate (veto) in the decision to perform an abortion was justified by the need to protect women's rights. This conclusion was reached under circumstances where the abortion procedure was performed on the basis of the need to protect the woman's health. On the other hand, it is difficult to determine the extent of the rights to which a potential father would be entitled in a situation in which a woman would express her will to undergo abortion for other reasons, such as connected to her well-being or without giving any reason.

Arguments based on proceduralisation – towards avoiding uncertainty

The Court's procedural turn is manifested in cases concerning access to abortion in two ways. First, it examines whether the State, in the course of

103 See X. v. UK, p. 254, and H. v. Norway, p. 170.
104 Boso v. Italy, par. 2, p. 5–5.

decision-making (judicial or administrative) in individual cases, has complied with procedural positive obligations and requirements guaranteeing procedural fairness and effective access to judicial remedies in terms of the implementation of abortion rights guaranteed by law (self-standing procedural rights).[105] Secondly, proceduralisation, as argued by the Court, seeks to assess whether the State has carried out an integrated procedural review of reasons and interests taken into account during the process of creating a legal framework for the permissibility (or rather impermissibility) of abortion (integrated procedural review).[106] It should be noted that in the case of abortion applications, the Court's procedural review of national decision-making procedures (medical, administrative and judicial) and integrated procedural review (procedural review of legislation) are closely linked. Not until the 2000s has the method of proceduralisation been applied in the Court's judgments.[107]

The Court used a two-way argumentation in *Tysiąc v. Poland*. It pointed to both deficiencies in the shape of the provisions regulating access to abortion (although not in terms of the prerequisites of admissibility) and to shortcomings in the decision-making process (in the broad sense) regarding the determination of the applicant's rights. The fulfilment of all those conditions must, however, be considered together, since their assessment depended on one another.

When reflecting on the requirements concerning the shape of the rules governing access to abortion, the Court made a general assumption as to the accepted diversity in the regulation of that issue at national level, referring that conclusion beyond the question of the conditions of admissibility.[108] In the *Tysiąc* case, precisely because it chose to decide the case in terms of the State's compliance with its positive obligations, the Court was the first to formulate a number of highly specific requirements as to what the desired shape of provisions allowing access to legal abortion ought to be, as discussed in the analysis of the incrementalism. As part of the argumentation under the method of proceduralisation, the Court examined the fulfilment of the requirements covered by Article 8 of the Convention, which it had previously pioneeringly formulated itself, often within the same case.

Having identified a number of deficiencies in virtually every patient's right during the domestic procedure, the Court concluded that it amounted to the failure of the State to comply with its positive obligations under Article 8 of

105 We use the procedural approach by distinguishing between self-standing procedural rights and integrated procedural review according to Kleinlein (Kleinlein, "The Procedural Approach." 92–3 and 96).

106 Fenwick, "The Modern Abortion Jurisprudence." 249–76.

107 In addition to the cases analysed in this chapter, it is worth mentioning for the sake of completeness that also in the already cited case *Vo v. France*, not involving abortion, but concerning the protection of foetal life, the Court decided to limit its examination to whether positive obligations in the sphere of public health and the protection of life were sufficiently fulfilled (par. 89–90).

108 Tysiąc v. Poland, par. 112 and 123.

the Convention and consequently found a violation of that right in respect of the applicant.[109] This conclusion referred specifically to the fact that the situation created for the applicant was of prolonged uncertainty[110]and it was not demonstrated that Polish law as applied to the applicant's case contained any effective mechanisms capable of determining whether the conditions for obtaining a lawful abortion had been met in her case.[111] In particular, the relevant regulations did not provide for any particular procedural framework to address and resolve cases where disagreement arises between the pregnant woman and her doctors, or between the doctors themselves.[112] Finally, according to the Court, the rules governing the exercise of the medical profession did not create any procedural guarantee for a patient to obtain such an opinion or to contest it in the event of disagreement.[113] Furthermore, retrospective measures whether criminal – aimed at identifying those guilty of negligence or law on tort – are not sufficient to provide appropriate protection for the physical integrity of individuals in such a vulnerable position.[114]

The procedural approach was also applied in the *A., B. and C. v. Ireland* case, although the Court drew attention to a wholly different context of domestic legal framework, namely the profound social acceptability of the regulations in force as a consequence of which restrictive regulations were adopted.[115] Not only did the Court go into great detail about the background to the prohibition of abortion in Ireland, but also thoroughly analysed the process that led to the adoption of the legislation as it stands. It emphasised that the protection afforded under Irish law to the right to life of the unborn was based on profound moral values concerning the nature of life which were reflected in the stance of the majority of the Irish people against abortion during the 1983 referendum. This is one of the few cases where the Court has explicitly invoked the premise of public morality as justifying the restrictions imposed on women's right to respect for their private lives resulting in severely restricted access to abortion.[116]

The Court took notice of the fact that the process of adopting the existing legislation involved significant consultation and considered numerous

109 The Court's conclusion about the violation of Art. 8 was done from a purely procedural point of view. This was met with considerable opposition in a separate opinion of Judge Borrego, who disagreed with the finding of a breach of positive duties as being based on the applicant's subjective fear.

110 Tysiąc v. Poland, par. 124.

111 Tysiąc v. Poland, par. 124.

112 Tysiąc v. Poland, par. 121.

113 Tysiąc v. Poland, par. 122.

114 Tysiąc v. Poland, par. 125–8.

115 A., B. and C. v. Ireland, par. 245.

116 A., B. and C. v. Ireland, par. 222. Cosentino draws attention to the line of argument as to whether the legislation of the State concerned is democratically legitimate in these cases but places this type of argumentation as an element of the margin of appreciation. See Cosentino, "Safe and Legal Abortion." 573, 575–7.

constitutional and legislative options and reflected profoundly differing opinions and demonstrated the sensitivity and complexity of the question of extending the grounds for lawful abortion in Ireland. The conclusion that the Irish provisions on the permissibility of abortion were the product of diligent parliamentary debates was common to the situation of all three applicants. By contrast, the other conclusions need to be viewed individually.

The Court analysed the situation of the first and the second applicant as regards the fulfilment of the State's negative obligations, that is whether the shape of the legislation in force constituted an excessive, unjustified interference with their right to respect for private life. Examination of the quality of the legislation in force became one of the most fundamental elements of the review. The Court focused on due care taken in the national procedures leading up to the limitation of the right to avoid the necessity of balancing conflicting rights. In this regard it accepted choices made by the national legislator and confirmed the absence of a breach of the guarantees conferred on them by the Convention.[117] This case was therefore a fine example of the fact that appropriate quality of domestic legislative process results in a positive assessment of the fulfilment of States' obligations.[118] Judgment issued in *A., B. and C. v. Ireland* confirmed that the Court is much more inclined to attach value to the quality of legislative process (either as a part of analyses of the fulfilment of negative or positive obligations) in cases concerning sensitive issues, here concerning difficult moral dilemmas.[119]

Conversely, the situation of the third applicant, who complained about not being able to undergo abortion legally because of life-risk reasons, was evaluated from the point of view of the State's compliance with its positive obligations. This decision immediately turned the Court's arguments towards investigating the quality of the procedures by which the applicant's situation was to be decided, and as a result the argument of the social legitimacy of the shape of the law ceased to play an important role. The Court's conclusion in terms of practical exercise of rights in this respect was negative and led to finding a violation. The reason for the Court's negative assessment was the absence of implementing any legislative or regulatory regime providing an accessible and effective procedure by which the third applicant could have

117 Still, in this case the Court also curiously dives into the division of powers as to the regulation and policy of abortion. It states that the constitutional courts are not the appropriate forum for the primary determination as to whether a woman qualifies for an abortion which is lawfully available in a State; they are not appropriate to set down on a case-by-case basis the legal criteria by which the relevant risk to a woman's life would be measured and, further, to resolve through evidence, largely of a medical nature, whether a woman had established that qualifying risk. The constitutional courts themselves have underlined that this should not be their role (par. 258).

118 Similar examples are provided by Kleinlein, "The Procedural Approach." 100.

119 Such a thesis was put forward by Gerards in relation to cases concerning complex choices in socio-economic policy and moral dilemmas. Cf. Gerards, "Procedural Review." 146–8.

established whether she qualified for a lawful abortion in Ireland.[120] This conclusion should be supplemented by the Court's assessment of the government's argument according to which the procedure by which the applicant could have established the existence of the right to abortion was an action before the constitutional court. The Court assessed such a plea of the Government as "equally inappropriate."[121]

The Court concluded that the uncertainty generated by the lack of legislative implementation of Article 40.3.3, and more particularly by the lack of effective and accessible procedures to establish a right to an abortion under that provision, has resulted in a striking discordance between the theoretical right to a lawful abortion in Ireland on the ground of a relevant risk to a woman's life and the reality of its practical implementation.[122] It therefore points to the unfulfilled positive obligations of the legislature towards interpretation of the Constitution that permits abortion under certain circumstances.

Our study of the Court's reasoning shows that it carried out both positive and negative procedural legislative review at the same time but focused on other elements conditioning the shape of the legislation. It is significant that, in the case of the applicants A. and B., the element of social legitimacy of the applicable legislation prohibiting abortion played a key role in their cases. With regards to applicant C., the Court shifted the focus of its considerations to the vagueness of the provisions already at the statutory level which were intended to make it possible to determine whether the conditions for carrying out the procedure were met.[123]

The *R. R. v. Poland* case, like *Tysiąc v. Poland*, was examined in the context of the fulfilment of positive obligations by the State.[124] In its judgment, the ECtHR concentrated on the assessment of the applicant's situation in the light of the requirements, clarified under Article 8 of the Convention, the observance of which must be ensured by the State in order to guarantee procedural fairness, both in the theoretical dimension of the shape of the legislation and in the practical one – that is, the decision-making process in a particular case. Keep in mind that the Court, in applying the tool of incrementalism, specifically indicated the need to provide the woman with full and reliable

120 A., B. and C. v. Ireland, par. 267–8. It is worth pointing out that the analysis of the applicant's situation with regards to the insufficient implementation of the constitutional provisions allowing abortion in the event of a life-threatening situation was based on the findings of the domestic courts. See, B. Daly, p. 278.

121 A., B. and C. v. Ireland, par. 259.

122 A., B. and C. v. Ireland, par. 264.

123 The difference in approach between applicants A. and B., who complained about the lack of regulation permitting abortion, and, on the other hand, applicant C., who complained about the lack of adequate regulation against constitutionally permissible abortion in her case, is pointed out by Federico Fabbrini, "The European Court of Human Rights, the EU Charter of Fundamental Rights, and the Right to Abortion: Roe v. Wade on the Other Side of the Atlantic." *Columbia Journal of European Law* 18(1) (2011): 1–54, 37.

124 R. R. v. Poland, par. 188.

information on the foetus' health and pointed to the requirement that the use of the conscientious objection clause by medical personnel should not lead to the suppression of women's rights to undergo a legitimate procedure. The purpose of fulfilling these as well as other requirements arising from earlier case law was to ensure the right to take an informed decision as to whether to seek an abortion or not.[125]

According to the Court, the infringement of the applicant's rights consisted in denying her timely access to medical procedures (genetic tests), enabling the applicant to acquire full information about the foetus' health.[126] This state of affairs was the result of abstruseness and reluctance on the part of some medical staff (including the use of the conscience clause) and a certain organisational and administrative confusion in the health system at the material time as to the procedure.[127] Furthermore, the privacy protection instruments provided by civil law were deemed to be insufficient.[128] The Court's negative procedural review thus concerned both the shape of the national legislation, the medical decision-making process affecting the applicant and the potential for privacy protection to be implemented at the civil level.[129]

By contrast, in *P. and S. v. Poland*, the Court did not challenge the shape of the legal framework.[130] As a matter of fact, the applicant had undergone a legal abortion in compliance with Polish law, so the Court focused on the quality of the decision-making process instead. It found that the process was characterised by numerous irregularities. First of all, the events surrounding the determination of the first applicant's access to legal abortion were marred by procrastination and confusion.[131] The applicants were given misleading and contradictory information; they did not receive appropriate and objective medical counselling which would have due regard to their own views and wishes; no set procedure was available to them under which they could have had their views heard and properly taken into consideration with a modicum of procedural fairness; and decisions were not taken in the right timeframe, which proved to be a critical factor.[132]

The aforesaid analysis clearly reveals that, at least with regard to cases involving abortion issues, the method of proceduralisation is strongly linked to incrementalism. As regards the Court's indication of the positive obligations incumbent upon the States, such as in terms of identifying standards for the shape of legislation and decision-making processes, these methods will mirror each other, meaning that the fulfilment of the requirements formulated

125 R. R. v. Poland, par. 208.
126 R. R. v. Poland, par. 188.
127 R. R. v. Poland, par. 198, 206.
128 R. R. v. Poland, par. 209.
129 R. R. v. Poland, par. 210–4.
130 P. and S. v. Poland, par. 83.
131 P. and S. v. Poland, par. 108.
132 P. and S. v. Poland, par. 111.

by the ECtHR within the framework of the incrementalism tool will be reviewed and assessed by means of the proceduralisation. At this point, it needs to be emphasised that, on more than one occasion, in judgments in which the Court formulated certain requirements under Article 8 of the Convention explicitly for the first time, it also carried out the first test of the State's fulfilment of these obligations.[133] This prompts the question whether this practice is correct, since the State which is the subject of the judgment has no practical means of implementing the Court's guidelines before a complaint is filed against it. On the other hand, the adoption of this method makes it possible to present specific (sometimes even casuistic) elements of the protected right, which results in clarification of their content and predictability of subsequent decisions.

Having analysed the Court's use of the tool of proceduralisation in abortion-related cases, one must note that the judgments support its use as an effective means of argumentation. Since the Court did not undertake substantive review (which would imply the necessity of balancing competing values on its own) and instead focused on procedural review, it did abstain from expressly addressing the issue of admissibility of abortion. The Court seems to say that the law may regulate the admissibility of abortion, according to moral and social values presented in society, but it must shape the situation of a woman in an unambiguous way and give her the guarantees of fairness and certainty. This kind of judicial reasoning largely replaces the substantive review and, from this perspective, it is very convenient and safe approach. This course of action can be criticised, as it shows that the Court avoids complicated matters and focuses on procedural safeguards instead of substantive issues.[134] On the other hand, in relation to applicant C. in the case against Ireland and in the cases against Poland, the Court draws a negative inference from the non-observance of procedural obligations.[135] Detailed analysis of provisions in force in these States allowed for the recognition of non-compliance with the Convention at the level of drafting (only the C. case with regard to the substantiation of constitutional norms) and application of law. Accordingly, these judgments undoubtedly took the situation of individuals into account by considering their allegations as well-founded. The decisions in the abortion cases focused on the fulfilment of procedural requirements are unquestionably an illustration of the thesis that the tool of proceduralisation is more neutral (but of course not entirely) towards the political choices of States in sensitive

133 In this context, it is worth paying attention to the position of Fenwick, who expressed the view that the procedural obligations formulated in the *Tysiąc* and *R. R.* cases are so far-reaching in the context of the regulations in force in Poland that de facto their implementation would mean the necessity to extend the current access to abortion. Cf. Fenwick, "The Modern Abortion Jurisprudence." 262.

134 Brems, "Procedural protection." 159.

135 Brems, "Procedural protection." 159.

matters than substantive review requiring from the Court independent proportionality assessment or balancing test.[136]

Employment of the proceduralisation in abortion-related cases also serves as a response to the views expressed in the doctrine that, in cases in which the Court grants States a wide margin of appreciation, it should attach particular importance to incorporating an assessment of domestic procedures in its judgments.[137] However, it should be stressed that the identification of procedural deficits has not led to an explicit conclusion on the narrowing of the margin of appreciation granted to States in any of the cases listed.[138] This is yet another argument that the concept of margin of appreciation should be treated as an argumentative and not merely an interpretative tool.[139]

Arguments based on plasticity and assimilation of concepts – "foetus" v. "unborn child"

In abortion-related cases, the arguments based on plasticity and assimilation of concepts are primarily linked to the question of recognising the foetus as a human being and thus as a subject of the rights guaranteed under the Convention.[140] Defining what a foetus is and, in particular, whether it is a subject of the right to life, has been a key problem in deciding abortion cases so far. From the beginning, the Court – and earlier the Commission – have both consistently failed to answer this question.[141] Therefore, we analysed in which form and in which contexts the subjects – that is, the foetus and the woman – are referred to in the Court's rulings. In our opinion, these terms are indicative and contribute to certain conclusions in the Court's reasoning.

Already in the initial phase of determining the limits of the right to privacy in the light of the protection of (foetal) life, the Commission made the telling choice in *Brüggemann and Scheuten v. Germany* to refer to the foetus

136 Leonie M. Huijbers, "Procedural-Type Review: A More Neutral Approach to Human Rights Protection by the European Court of Human Rights?" 2017 European Society of International Law Conference Paper No. 6/2017, 17.

137 Brems, Lavrysen, "Procedural Justice." 177–200. Kleinlein even points out that there exist "a direct link that between the degree of proceduralisation and the breadth of the margin of appreciation." Kleinlein, "The Procedural Approach." 96.

138 Cf. Part II, item 2, previously listed.

139 The need for a correlation between the width of the margin of appreciation and the fulfilment of obligations of a procedural nature is indicated by Brems, Brems, "Procedural protection." 160.

140 Gestational time – an extremely important factor in assessing the admissibility of abortion in national systems, but one that has so far received little attention in ECtHR case law – is left out of the discussion. Erdman, JN., "Theorizing time in abortion law and human rights." *Health and Human Rights Journal* 19(1) (2017): 29–40.

141 For more about the discussions about the status of the foetus as a subject of the right to life cf. Fenwick, "The Modern Abortion Jurisprudence." 255.

as an "unborn child."[142] Also, in the cases involving "partners" of pregnant women, in particular in *X v. the United Kingdom*, the Commission used the term "unborn" when commencing its consideration of whether Article 2 of the Convention could be applied prenatally.[143] However, starting from the part of the justification in which, as a result of linguistic and systemic analysis, the Commission answered this question negatively, it began to use the term "foetus" in a more frequent manner,[144] citing the term "unborn" only once.[145] The two terms were at that time used interchangeably, although the term 'foetus' was used more often than "unborn" and the term "unborn child" was not used at all. Also, the collocations "right to life of the foetus"[146] and, in relation to the complainant, "father of the foetus" remain in regular use.[147]

Accordingly, only the term "foetus" is used *in Boso v. Italy*. When the Court considered that it was not required to determine whether the foetus may have been qualified for protection under the first sentence of Article 2, as well as when it stated that even supposing that, in certain circumstances, the foetus might have been considered to have rights protected by Article 2 of the Convention, pregnancy was terminated in compliance with domestic law.

What is interesting, however, is that in *Tysiąc v. Poland*, the first case in which the Court came to the conclusion that Article 8 had been violated in that the applicant was deprived, as a result of the actual actions of medical personnel, of the opportunity to make a choice about the continuation of her pregnancy, the Court used the term "unborn child" at a crucial stage in its deliberations on balancing the interests of the mother and the child. The interests, or rights and freedoms of the "unborn child," are used to balance the woman's right to respect for her private life.[148]

In this judgment, the Court also outlined the position of the woman rather specifically. When describing the need to balance privacy and the public interest in the context of the positive obligations of the State to secure the physical integrity of the woman, the Court used the term "mother-to-be" and not, for instance, "pregnant woman".[149] It is hard to dismiss the impression that the use of the phrases "unborn child", "unborn life" and "mother-to-be" indicates

142 The approach to this problem in a non-abortion case, although concerning the life of the foetus, is very similar in *Vo v. France*. The Court – using both terms (unborn child and foetus) – concludes that it is convinced that it is neither desirable, nor even possible as matters stand, to answer in the abstract the question whether the unborn child is a person for the purposes of Article 2 of the Convention (par. 85).

143 X v. UK, par. 5.

144 X v. UK, para. 9, 10, 12, 17, 18, 19, 21, 22.

145 "The general usage of the term 'everyone' ('toute personne') used in Article 2 of the Convention did not include the unborn." X v. UK, par. 7.

146 X v. UK, para. 23, 25.

147 X v. UK, par. 25.

148 Tysiąc v. Poland, par. 106.

149 Tysiąc v. Poland, par. 107. The formulation as well as this part of the argument is also quoted in the justification of *R. R. v. Poland* (par. 189).

and emotionally orientates the reader towards motherhood in its traditional worldview context that is dominant in Poland, at least on the official level of disputes about abortion.

The Court echoed this practice in the *A., B. and C. v. Ireland* case, in which the use of both terms is symptomatic, but with a distinct preference for the terms "unborn" or "unborn child", which presupposes, already at the linguistic level, the existence not only of a life but also of a human being.[150] When mentioning the protection afforded by Irish law, the Court pointed out "that the protection afforded under Irish law to the right to life of the unborn was based on profound moral values concerning the nature of life."[151] When it concluded that the legitimate aim of the protection of morals impugned the protection of the right to life of the unborn in Ireland, it was also writing about the "unborn" and about "unborn life", not about the "foetus".[152] This term also appears when discussing a fair balance between the protection of that public interest, notably the protection accorded under Irish law to the right to life of the unborn, and the conflicting rights of the applicants to respect for their private lives.[153]

Meanwhile, in *D. v. Ireland*, the term "unborn" in the assessment of the Court is used only sparingly. In fact, it does not appear until the case law of the Irish courts is discussed.[154] The term "unborn" was put in inverted commas, as used in Article 40.3.3 of the Irish Constitution, and is applied in that context. The inverted commas are, of course, formally justified because the concept is used in the Court's decision as a normative concept taken from the Irish Constitution. The Court also considers its meaning in terms of Irish practice. It is not difficult to see, however, that in its considerations the Court uses the term "foetus" in most of its formulations – it appears as many as 20 times – even in a rather specific context, that is, when indicating how its rights may be expressed.[155]

150 A., B. and C. v. Ireland, par. 213.
151 A., B. and C. v. Ireland, par. 222.
152 A., B. and C. v. Ireland, para. 227, 230.
153 A., B. and C. v. Ireland, para. 231 and 233.
154 D. v. Ireland, par. 90.
155 D. v. Ireland, par. 101. In the context of that decision attention should be drawn to the position of the Committee on the Elimination of Discrimination against Women under article 7, paragraph 3, of the Optional Protocol to the Convention on the Elimination of All Forms of Discrimination against Women (Communication No. 22/2009, Views adopted by the Committee at its fiftieth session, 3 to 21 October 2011); here only the term foetus appears in the context of termination of pregnancy. Additionally, attention may be drawn to the statements of the Human Rights Committee in its decisions on Irish FFA cases. In views adopted by the Committee under article 5 (4) of the Optional Protocol concerning a communication on termination of pregnancy in a foreign country, the Committee justified its decision by balancing the competing interests of the foetus and the woman (7.3, 7.8). While doing the balancing exercise it underlined the difficult and vulnerable position of a pregnant woman carrying a foetus with fatal foetal anomalies: (7.4) a pregnant woman is in a highly vulnerable position after learning that her much-wanted pregnancy was not viable; she has to choose between continuing her non-viable pregnancy or travelling to another country

In both recent Polish cases, *R. R. v. Poland* and *P. and S. v. Poland*, the term "foetus" has become completely dominant. The term "foetus" is used 34 times in the Court's assessment in *R. R. v. Poland*. The word "unborn" in this part of the justification appears only once – and eight times in the dissenting opinion of Judge Gaetano. It may be assumed that the use of this very term is somehow intuitively connected with the tragic circumstances of this case, as the Court indicated "the foetus was affected with an unidentified malformation."[156] This does not mean, however, that in previous proceedings, especially the Irish cases, the use of this concept was not equally justified. It is also notable that wherever the trauma of the pregnant applicant is mentioned, the terms "foetus" health and "foetus condition" are used.[157] Citing previous findings, the Court notes that the decision of a pregnant woman to continue her pregnancy or not belongs to the sphere of private life and autonomy. Consequently, legislation regulating the interruption of pregnancy also touches upon the sphere of private life, since whenever a woman is pregnant her private life becomes closely connected with the developing foetus. Let us repeat that the term "unborn" was used in such a context in previous cases (such as *Tysiąc v. Poland*). The term "foetus" is also used when quoting former rulings, although there the terms unborn and foetus were used interchangeably as equivalents.[158] And when the Court made the significant decision that was crucial for the conclusion of the judgment to redefine the scope of the margin of appreciation, it recognised the consensus of the European States for a resolution of the conflicting rights of the foetus and the woman in favour of greater access to abortion, using the phrase "foetus" and not the "unborn".[159]

The reasoning of the Court in the case of *P. and S. v. Poland* uses only the term "foetus". With regards to the applicant and her situation, only the term pregnancy is used ("unwanted pregnancy" or "termination of pregnancy"). When, on the other hand, the Court speaks of a consensus between States on wide access to abortion, it merely states that a fair balance between individual rights and the public interest has been maintained without going into detail

while carrying a dying foetus at her personal expense and separated from the support of her family, and returning while not fully recovered; the shame and stigma associated with the criminalisation of abortion of a fatally ill foetus; a woman is forced to leave the baby's remains behind and later having them delivered to her by courier. Communication no. 2324/2013, Amanda Jane Mellet v. Ireland, 31, views adopted on March 2016. Similarly, the Committee considered this issue in Whelan case – Views adopted by the Committee under article 5 (4) of the Optional Protocol, concerning communication No. 2425/2014, Siobhán Whelan, Ireland, 17 March 2017.

156 R.R. v. Poland, par. 153.

157 R.R. v. Poland, par. 159.

158 R.R. v. Poland, par. 181.

159 R.R. v. Poland, par. 186. In this case, Judge de Gaetano's dissenting opinion (the term unborn child is consistently used therein) is significant. The judge writes about balancing the interests of the unborn child and the mother, noting that the unborn child's right to life remains in limbo.

as to what this public interest consists in.[160] The partly dissenting opinion of Judge de Gaetano, whose conclusions are worth quoting at the end of this section, is especially significant in this regard. The judge emphatically states that "calling the unborn child a fetus does not change the essential nature of what is at stake and of what an abortion entails."

These remarks are not intended to demonstrate that the terminology is flawed or biased. On the contrary, the phrases are perfectly justified by individual circumstance of the cases, by their use in medical and colloquial communication, and partially also by the national conditions. Their use in specific context strongly reinforces the argumentation in favour of the stated position. The terminology has a strong persuasive effect by acting on the emotions and empathy of the reader, paints a certain image of the case, the fate of the applicant and her ability to make decisions, and the extent to which she decides – or is deprived of the possibility to do so – and is condemned to a fate that is sometimes tragic. From the logical and legal point of view, interchanging "foetus" with "unborn child" is irrelevant. These terms have the same meaning. The *logos*, which can be equated with the search for a rational solution, is the same, whereas from the perspective of the *pathos* – to make an impression on the recipient – the difference is significant and deliberate.[161] This persuasive aim is ultimately placed above the *ratio* of using the terms not in isolation from the terminology used in legal cultures in the signatory States.

In the first case against Poland, *Tysiąc*, the Court shyly referred to notions such as "mother-to-be" or "unborn child", thus meeting both the language used in public discussions as well as State's conservative attitude towards abortion. In the following judgments issued in face of growing unavailability of abortion in Poland, the Court used language that was more representative of a woman's attitude and feelings, thus it referred mainly to "foetus". In the first case against Ireland, *A., B. and C.*, the Court's distinct preference for the terms "unborn" or "unborn child" strongly reflected the unborn's standing in the domestic legislation. However, in order to mitigate the effect of such a strong confirmation of its legal position, in the latter case *D.*, the Court used that word only in inverted commas, using the neutral word "foetus" more frequently.

160 P. and S. v. Poland, par. 97.

161 It is worth comparing these observations with the wording of the Polish judgment of the Constitutional Tribunal of 22 October 2020. Due to significant differences in the structure of the justification of the judgments of the ECtHR and the Constitutional Tribunal, a quantitative comparison is pointless, but it should be noted that the Polish judgment includes, inter alia, categorical statements: Termination of pregnancy is also associated with the deprivation of human life – a child in the prenatal period (16, 161). This wording clearly shows that the Polish Tribunal neither recognises nor intends to notice competitive interests on the mother's side and does not consider either goods falling within the scope of private or family life, or the risk of violating the prohibition of cruel treatment by excluding the exception of criminalising abortion on the grounds of fatal foetal anomalies.

Summary

The Court has attempted to avoid a categorical resolution of the most difficult problems relating to access to abortion at the European level at all costs. As the judges in the dissenting opinion accurately observed in *A., B. and C. v. Ireland*: "the Court refrains from playing its harmonising role, preferring not to become the first European body to legislate on a matter still undecided at European level."[162]

The ECtHR case law in the area under examination serves as an excellent example of the use of several ways of argumentation and their combination into motifs that are characteristic almost exclusively of this sphere of jurisprudence. The pursuit of proper argumentation takes place on two planes.

First, by applying tools from the deontological group related to the identification of positive obligations of the State in the sphere of protection of life and privacy and shaping the content of the Convention rights by way of incrementalism. The ECtHR applied the "sensible incremental approach" in the judgments in question, expanding the scope of guarantees for pregnant women under Articles 3 and 8 of the Convention slowly but consistently, supplementing these guarantees by applying the proceduralisation.[163] It seems that the Court's hitherto conservative approach to the issue of abortion was undermined by the *R. R. and P.* and *S.* cases, which can be interpreted as heading in the same direction as the decidedly more progressive jurisprudence of the Human Rights Committee.[164] There is no doubt, however, that in deciding to make extensive use of incrementalism, the Court followed the basic guideline underlying it, namely that in each of its judgments it presented the most far-reaching argumentation that it believed would be acceptable to certain audiences.[165]

The second plane of argumentation is the turning to authority. The Court's application of the margin of appreciation to the sphere of assessing the beginning of human life is of particular interest. The Court thereby shifts its scope of application. Usually, the application of the margin of appreciation leaves the interpretation of the limits of the Convention rights and freedoms to the States, which allows them to retain the discretion as to how to implement

162 A., B. and C. v. Ireland, Joint partly dissenting opinion of Judges Rozakis, Tulkens, Fura, Hirvelä, Malinverni and Poalelungi, p. 5.

163 Some authors even point out that the lengthy development of the right to respect for private life in the area of abortion stands in contrast to how it has been implemented in other areas, such as the rights of homosexual persons, cf. Cosentino, "Safe and Legal Abortion." 586.

164 Ghrainne, McMahon, "Access to Abortion." 581; Zureick, (En)Gendering Suffering." 112 et seq. Indeed, several authors point to the Court's recent judgments as laying the foundations for the future formation of a right to safe and legal abortion. Cf. Cosentino, "Safe and Legal Abortion." 588.

165 More on the Court's arguments to build its legitimacy and ensure the enforceability of its judgments: S. Dothan, Judicial tactics in the European Court of Human Rights, p. 117 et seq.

the obligations of the Convention in accordance with the specificity of local conditions.[166] The use of the margin of appreciation instrument to allow States the discretion to determine the moment in time when life begins – and thus to grant to the foetus in their domestic legislations the status of an Article 2 rights holder – allows both a liberal and a very restrictive approach to the legality of abortion to be accepted under the Convention.

Finally, teleological arguments are completely absent. It turns out that it is possible to adjudicate at the deontological level, primarily through the skilful application of the margin of appreciation and proceduralisation in combination with the pragmatic argument concerning the migration for the purpose of exercising the right in a broader scope than the one permitted in the country of residence. The latter argument largely replaces the teleological argumentation by reference to the consequences of a possible ruling on the future direction of the implementation of rights.

Bibliography

ASTRA. *Network on Reproductive Health and Rights in Central and Eastern Europe for the European Population Forum.* ASTRA, 2004.

Brems, Eva. "Procedural protection – An examination of procedural safeguards read into substantive Convention rights." In *Shaping Rights in the ECHR – The Role of the European Court of Human Rights in Determining the Scope of Human Rights*, edited by Janneke Gerards and Eva Brems, 137–161. Cambridge University Press, 2013.

Brems, Eva and Laurens Lavrysen. "Procedural justice in human rights adjudication: The European Court of Human Rights." *Human Rights Quarterly* 35 (2013): 177–200.

Cosentino, Chiara. "Safe and legal abortion: An emerging human right: The long-lasting dispute with sovereignty in ECHR jurisprudence." *Human Rights Law Review* 15(3) (2015): 569–590.

Daly, Brenda. "Access to abortion services: The impact of the European convention on human rights in Ireland." *Medicine and Law* 30(2) (2011): 267–278.

Dothan, Shai. "Judicial tactics in the European Court of Human Rights." *Chicago Journal of International Law* 12(1) (2011).

Dzehtsiarou, Kanstantsin. "European consensus and the evolutive interpretation of the ECHR." *German Law Journal* 12(10) (2011): 1730–1745.

Erdman, Joanna N. "Theorizing time in abortion law and human rights." *Health and Human Rights Journal* 19(1) (2017), 29–40.

Fabbrini, Federico. "The European Court of Human Rights, the EU charter of fundamental rights, and the right to Abortion: Roe v. Wade on the other side of the Atlantic." *Columbia Journal of European Law* 18(1) (2011): 1–54.

166 Garlicki, "Wprowadzenie." 5. On the margin of appreciation, see generally Legg, *The Margin of Appreciation*; Letsas, "Two concepts."; Yourow, *The Margin of Appreciation*, 192; Gerards, "Margin of Appreciation." 498.

Fenwick, Daniel, "The modern abortion jurisprudence under article 8 of the European Convention on Human Rights." *Medical Law International* 12(3–4) (2012): 249–276.

Garlicki, Lech. "Wprowadzenie" [Introduction] In *Konwencja o ochronie praw człowieka i podstawowych wolności. Komentarz do artykułów 1–18* [Convention on the Protection of Human Rights and Fundamental Freedoms. Commentary on Articles 1–18], edited by Lech Garlicki, 3–12. Wydawnictwo C.H. Beck, 2011.

Gerards, Janneke. "Margin of appreciation and incrementalism in the case law of the European Court of Human Rights." *Human Rights Law Review* 18(3) (2018): 495–515.

Ghrainne, Bríd NÍ and Aisling McMahon. "Access to abortion in cases of fatal fetal abnormality: A new direction for the European Court of Human Rights?" *Human Rights Law Review* 19 (3) (2020): 561–584.

Huijbers, Leonie M. "Procedural -type review: A more neutral approach to human rights protection by the European Court of Human Rights?" *European Society of International Law Conference Paper No.* 6/2017, Research Forum (Granada), SSRN: https://ssrn.com/abstract=3045270 or http://dx.doi.org/10.2139/ssrn.3045270

Irvine, Nigel. "A time to regulate: Possible implications of European Human Rights Law on abortion in Northern Ireland." *Medical Law International* 5(2) (2001): 127–140.

Janneke, Gerards and Eva Brems. *Procedural Review in European Fundamental Rights Cases*, 230–262. Cambridge University Press, 2017.

Joyce, Molly. "The human rights aspects of abortion." *Hibernian Law Journal* 16 (2017): 27–41.

Kleinlein, Thomas. "The procedural approach of the European Court of Human Rights: Between subsidiarity and dynamic evolution." *International & Comparative Law Quarterly* 68 (2019): 91–110.

Lawson, Rick. "The Irish abortion cases: European limits to National sovereignty." *European Journal of Health Law* 1(2) (1994): 167–186.

Legg, Andrew. *The Margin of Appreciation in International Human Rights Law: Deference and Proportionality.* Oxford University Press, 2012.

Letsas, George. "Two concepts of the margin of appreciation." *Oxford Journal of Legal Studies* 26 (4) (2006): 705–732.

McGoldrick, Dominic. "A defence of the margin of appreciation and an argument for its application by the human rights committee." *International and Comparative Law Quarterly* 65(1) (2016): 21–60.

Rhinehart, Morgan A. "Abortions in Ireland: Reconciling a history of restrictive abortion practices with the European Court of Human Rights' ruling in A., B. & C. v. Ireland." *Penn State Law Review* 117(3) (2013): 959–978.

Sealy, Thomas Richard. "Abortion law reform in Europe: The European Commission on Human Rights upholds german restrictions on abortion – Bruggemann and Scheuten v. Federal republic of Germany." *Texas International Law Journal* 15(1) (1980): 162–186.

Sunstein, Cass. *Designing Democracy: What Constitutions Do.* Oxford University Press, 2001.

Synthesis Report of the European Union Network of Independent Experts on Fundamental Rights. *Conclusions and recommendations on the situation of fundamental rights in the European union and its member states in 2004.* MEMO/05/260, Brussels, 15 July 2005.

Yourow, Howard Ch. *The Margin of Appreciation Doctrine in the Dynamics of European Human Rights Jurisprudence.* Martinus Nijhoff Publishers, 1996.

Zureick, Alyson. "(En)Gendering suffering: Denial of abortion as a form of cruel, inhuman or degrading treatment." *Fordham International Law Journal* 38(1): 100–140.

5 Ways of reasoning in end-of-life situations

Introduction

The question of how legitimate it is to decide to terminate the life of a person who wishes to die or is in a terminal state is more and more often leaving the sphere of personal, moral decisions.[1] The present-day advancement of medicine and the regulation of specific medical practices and patient behaviour, as well as the rise of claims to protect one's autonomy, have brought about a significant increase in such issues. Dying has been institutionalised and professionalised more than ever before; as such, it turns out that it requires decisions on the part of legislators and courts.

Matters that have so far been settled quietly and discreetly at the bedside of a terminally ill or hopelessly distressed patient have become the subject of legal regulations. Such regulations occurred in Netherlands,[2] Belgium[3] and in Luxembourg.[4] Euthanasia has been legal since 2021 in Spain[5] and Portugal.[6] In Switzerland – the well-recognised European centre of assisted dying – euthanasia has still not been directly regulated, but assisted suicide

1 Walter M. Bortz, "The Trajectory of Dying. Functional Status in the Last Year of Life." *Journal of American Geriatric Society* 38 (1990): 146. After: Dougherty, "The Common Good." 155.

2 The Dutch "Euthanasia and Assisted Suicide Act" came into force on April 1, 2002. The Act amended the Criminal Code with Article 293 and Article 294 para. 2 (termination of life upon request and assistance in suicide respectively) which since this time have not been considered punishable offences if they are performed by a physician with particularly mentioned requirements. The law also enabled children (12–18, since 2013 even newborns) to request euthanasia. For patients aged under 12, the parents or guardians must give their consent.

3 Act on Euthanasia permits a physician to carry out euthanasia on request under certain conditions. Since the 2014 amendment came into force, minors of any age have been able to request assisted suicide from their attending physician under certain circumstances.

4 Loi du 16 mars 2009 sur l'euthanasie et l'assistance au suicide.

5 The Organic Law for the Regulation of Euthanasia came into force as approved by the Cortes Generales on 18 March 2021.

6 The law legalising medically assisted suicide was passed in November 2021. The previous regulation was passed in 2020 but declared unconstitutional by the Portuguese Constitutional Court at the request of the president. In November 2021, the Parliament again passed a law allowing assisted suicide.

DOI: 10.4324/9781003375999-6

is considered an offence when done with selfish reasons.[7] In other countries there has been a long discussion concerning regulating euthanasia and assisted suicide. There were cases in Germany,[8] Austria[9] and France.[10] In most of countries, active euthanasia is banned, like in the UK where assisted suicide remains illegal under Section 2 of the Suicide Act 1961, despite intense and lengthy debate on the subject in both the English and Scottish Parliaments.[11]

As this brief overview demonstrates, resolving these issues became the subject of decisions by national legislatures and judicial decisions as late as the last century due to their extremely controversial moral implications. In both case law and statutory law, end-of-life situations are usually approached by weighing the autonomy of the will and the dignity of the person wishing to die against the duty to protect life, which is considered to be the ultimate good to protect.[12] Consequently, the strict legal obligation to protect life is starkly confronted with the decisions of those who wish to die – or with the situation of those who are in the persistent vegetative state, with no hope of regaining consciousness or the ability to lead an independent existence. Addressing this collision is not just difficult, it is among the most challenging of issues, requiring a particular kind of competence in decision-making as well as the ability to properly reason about its validity. As Lord Sumption concluded in one such case, "judges tend to avoid addressing the moral foundations of law and to lay down principles of morality, in some cases, however, it is unavoidable – and this is one of them."[13] Sumption referred there to British judges, yet there is no doubt that this reluctance is all the more apparent in the decisions of the Court, which is faced with the arduous task of determining whether there has been a breach of rights protected under the ECHR in a situation of consent or non-consent to assisted dying.

7 Verleitung und Beihilfe zum Selbstmord, Art. 115 of Swiss Criminal Code 1989.

8 In 2015, the Bundestag passed the law amending Article 217 of German Criminal Code (Strafgesetzbuch), which criminalised assistance in another person's suicide (relatives of the dying person and physicians are excluded from the penalty in specific cases). In its ruling of 26 February 2020, the Federal Constitutional Court declared the relevant sections of Act 217 unconstitutional.

9 VfGH-Erkenntnis G 139/2019 vom 11 Dezember 2020.

10 In 2002, France saw the adoption of the "Loi n° 2005–370 relative aux droits des malades et à la fin de vie," amending the Code de la santé publique (Public Health Code) to the effect that passive euthanasia (interruption of medical treatment at the patient's request) is not penalised under certain circumstances. Work has been going on for years to pass a law on assisted suicide. In April 2021, a proposal to legalise assisted death for people suffering from terminal illnesses was blocked in the French Parliament.

11 The bill entitled "End-of-life Assistance (Scotland) Bill (SP Bill 38)" was debated by The Scottish Parliament on 21 January 2010 and rejected.

12 About "de-absolutisation" of the value of life, see Diego Zannoni, "Right or duty to live? Euthanasia and Assisted Suicide from the Perspective of the European Convention on Human Rights." *European journal of legal studies* (12)(2) (2020): 181.

13 Nicklinson and Lamb, appl. no. 2478/15 and 1787/15, judgment of 23.06.2015, par. 207.

Judgments of the ECtHR issued in the context of end-of-life situations have been the subject of numerous analyses for a long time. This chapter will therefore discuss the elements of reasoning contained in the judgments pertaining to two situations: claims related to assisted suicide and interruption of life support for patients incapable of expressing their own will.

One of the first such decisions of the ECtHR was that in *Sanles Sanles v. Spain.*[14] The case concerned the right to painless and voluntary death of a man who had been paralysed and unable to live independently for 30 years and wished to end his life with the assistance of third parties, and who succeeded. He died during an assisted suicide in January 1998. However, before that happened in the absence of a clear decision of his case in the proceedings before the domestic courts, the patient filed an application with the ECtHR, which was upheld after his death by his sister. In its judgment, the Court held that the complaint's allegations of violation of Articles 2, 3, 5, 6, 8, 9 and 14 of the Convention and of the right to life and death with dignity could not be examined because the complaint was inadmissible due to non-transferable character of the rights that were subject of the application.

In the case of *Pretty v. UK*, one of the fundamental cases in this category,[15] the applicant, who was terminally ill and incapacitated, complained, invoking Articles 2, 3, 8, 9 and 14 of the Convention, that her husband had been prevented from assisting her to commit suicide without risking prosecution by the United Kingdom authorities under the Suicide Act (which made assisting suicide punishable). The Court found no violation of the provisions of the ECHR.

In *Haas v. Switzerland*,[16] the applicant, suffering from severe bipolar affective disorder, wished to end his life and complained about his inability to obtain the lethal substance without a medical prescription that had been required, which constituted a violation of his right to personal autonomy. The Court found that there had been no violation of Article 8.

In *Koch v. Germany*[17] the claim alleging violation of private and family life regarded the authority's refusal to allow the applicant's paralysed and artificially ventilated wife to take a lethal dose of medication. Initially, the requests were rejected by German medical services and authorities. Eventually, the woman committed suicide in Switzerland using the services of the Dignitas clinic. The Court found a breach of Article 8 in the refusal of the domestic courts to rule on the merits of the applicant's motions.

The *Gross v. Switzerland*[18] case was partially similar in terms of circumstances and allegation, in which the applicant, seeking to commit suicide by

14 Sanles Sanles v. Spain, appl. no. 48335/99, decision of 25.10.2000.

15 Pretty v. the United Kingdom, appl. no. 2346/02, judgment of 29.04.2002.

16 Haas v. Switzerland, appl. no. 31322/07, judgment of 20.01.2011.

17 Koch v. Germany, appl. no. 497/09, judgment of 19.07.2012.

18 Gross v. Switzerland, appl. no. 67810/10), judgment of 14.05.2013, the majority ruled 4 to 3 (with joint dissenting opinion of Judges Raimondi, Jociene and Karakas).

taking poison (without being in a terminal or incapacitated state) unsuccessfully sought a prescription for the drug. She alleged a violation of Article 8 by the fact that the State had failed to provide sufficient guidelines defining whether and under what circumstances medical practitioners were authorised to issue a medical prescription to a person in the applicant's condition. The Court decided that the absence of clear and comprehensive legal guidelines had violated the applicant's right to respect for her private life under Article 8 of the Convention.

The *Nicklinson and Lamb v. the UK* case[19] concerned the ban on assisted suicide and voluntary euthanasia in the UK. Both patients (the first applicant was the wife of a patient) wished to end their lives and were unable to commit suicide without assistance. The ECtHR declared the application inadmissible in regards to the first applicant due to the fact that the domestic courts did deal with the substance of the claim and in regards to the second applicant for failure to exhaust domestic remedies.

The second group of cases is concerned with the administration or withdrawal of treatment. In *Glass v. the UK*,[20] the applicants complained that diamorphine administered by hospital physicians to their sick child without their consent and the "do not resuscitate" order contained in its medical records constituted a violation of Articles 2 and 8 of the Convention. The Court found that their complaint was manifestly ill-founded under Article 2 of the Convention. However, it considered that there had been a violation of Article 8 of the Convention because of the lack of opportunity to challenge the doctors' decisions before the Court.

In the *Burke v. the United Kingdom* case,[21] the applicant suffered from an incurable degenerative brain condition and feared that the guidance applicable in the United Kingdom could lead in due course to the withdrawal of artificial nutrition and hydration. The applicant then requested protection in the form of guarantees that there would be no ending of life support. The Court declared his application, lodged under Articles 2, 3 and 8 of the Convention, inadmissible as being manifestly ill-founded. Also, in *Ada Rossi and Others v. Italy*,[22] the complainants (relatives, friends of severely disabled persons joined by doctors, psychologists and lawyers who assist the persons concerned, together with a human rights association), filed complaints claiming that a decision allowing for the requested authorisation to stop feeding young women who were in a coma or in a vegetative state violated Articles 2 and 3 of the Convention. The Court held that the applicants' complaints were inadmissible under Articles 2 and 3.

19 Nicklinson and Lamb v. the UK, appl. no. 2478/15 and 1787/15, judgment of 23.06.2015.
20 Glass v. the UK, appl. no. 61827/00, judgment of 9.03.2004.
21 Burke v. the United Kingdom, appl. no. 19807/06, judgment of 11.07.2006.
22 Ada Rossi and Others v. Italy, appl. nos. 55185/08, 55483/08, 55516/08, 55519/08, 56010/08, 56278/08, 58420/08 and 58424/08, decision of 22.12.2008.

Subsequent ECtHR judgment, by far the most significant, on the withdrawal of artificial nutrition and hydration was delivered in the *Lambert and Others v. France* case.[23] The applicants included the relatives of Vincent Lambert, a tetraplegic with the state of total dependence. A controversy arose between his relatives and their dispute proceeded before the French courts, where the conclusions were not unanimous. The Administrative Court reiterated the decision to withdraw artificial nutrition and hydration as a "serious and manifestly unlawful violation of [his] right to life," whereas the Conseil d'État held that the provision of the French Public Health Code authorising physicians to withdraw and withhold "unreasonably futile" treatment should be applied instead. The ECtHR found no violation of Articles 2 and 8 of the ECHR.

The next case that involved withholding life sustaining treatment is *Gard v. the UK* (2017),[24] which is the case of a baby boy suffering from a terminal illness whose life-sustaining treatment was stopped in accordance with the best interests of the child – and against the wishes of his parents. The European Court of Human Rights declared the application by the child's parents on the ground of alleged violations of Articles 2, 5, 6 and 8 of the ECHR, also on behalf of their son, inadmissible.[25]

This list of judgments is not exhaustive, nevertheless, these cases are exceptionally significant as well as interesting in terms of argumentation. At the very outset, it is worth mentioning that the vast majority of end-of-life situations cases at the ECtHR fail to provide evidence of a violation of the complainants' rights. With the exception of the violations of Article 8 in the *Glass*, *Koch* and *Gross* cases, no violation of the Convention was found in any of these cases. In contrast, the only violations of Convention rights observed in these cases concerned violations of the right to judicial protection – non-existence of a procedure to review decisions of medical authorities or administration/authority. The Court therefore found a violation of the procedural, not substantive, content of Article 8 of the Convention.

In addition to ECtHR judgments, the decisions of domestic courts will also be indicated in this category. Among these are judgments delivered in British cases[26] shaping the right to assisted suicide[27] and the judgment of

23 Lambert and Others v. France, appl. no. 46043/14, judgment of 5.06.2015.

24 Charles Gard and Others v. the United Kingdom, appl. no. 39793/17, judgment of 27.06.2017.

25 The decisions of the ECtHR in the cases of *Afiri and Biddarri v. France* (dec.), appl. no. 1828/18, 23.01.2018 and *Haastrup v. the UK* (dec.), appl. no. 9865/18, 6.03.2018 resembled the decision of the ECtHR in the case of *Charlie Gard*. Both cases concerned the decision to withdraw the life-sustaining treatment to minor patients in a vegetative state.

26 We refer particularly to Airedale National Health Service Trust v. Bland [1993] AC 789, 1 All ER 821 at 836 and R (Purdy) v. DPP [2009] UKHL 45. Other British cases and the shaping of the right to euthanasia will not be discussed in detail, since it was done in other works cited herein, such as Michael Freeman, "Denying Death Its Dominion: Thoughts on the Dianne Pretty Case." *Medical Law Review* 10, No. 3 (Autumn 2002): 245–70.

27 The applicant sought a verdict that the prohibition of assisted suicide (sec.2.1 Suicide Act 1961) interfered with her right to respect for personal autonomy and right to self-determination in

the German Federal Constitutional Court (Bundesverfassungsgericht) of 26 February 2020.[28]

Arguments referring to authority

A considerable part of the ECtHR's reasoning in end-of-life situations is taken up by references to external authorities. Several types of argumentation can be distinguished here. Some of them simply invoke international law sources as well as domestic law regulating the issue of dying. The Court makes extensive reference to these regulations, treating them not only as a determinant of the legal order, but also as an argument (sometimes sufficient) to recognise the chosen line of interpretation of the rights guaranteed under the Convention. Others rely on epistemic authority – the knowledge of physicians about the condition of the person concerned.

Arguments referring to external (beyond the ECHR) law sources – where is the standard?

In its reasoning, the Court has often referred to the content of international documents addressing the legal and ethical issues appearing in connection with the end-of-life situations.[29] Special rank is given to the Convention for the Protection of Human Rights and Dignity of the Human Being with regard to the Application of Biology and Medicine from 1997 (the so-called the Oviedo Convention on Human Rights and Biomedicine)[30] and two soft

---

cases of the suicide of a terminally ill or severely and incurably disabled person, who wishes – capable to take freely and with full understanding such a decision – to receive help to travel to a country where assisted suicide is lawful – is not "in accordance with the law" as required by Article 8(2), in the absence of an offence-specific policy (the Code for Crown Prosecutors). The House of Lords found the Director of Public Prosecutions was required to issue specific guidelines as to when prosecution would be recommended for a person who had assisted another to commit suicide.

28 The FCC declared the prohibition of assisted suicide services violates the general right of personality in conjunction with human dignity (Article 2[1] and 1[1] of Grundgesetz) in its manifestation as the right to a self-determined death of persons who choose to end their own life, 2 BvR 2347/15, 2 BvR 651/16, 2 BvR 1261/16, 2 BvR 1593/16, 2 BvR 2354/16,2 BvR 2527/16.

29 International documents on the subject have been issued since the 1970s, including Resolution 613 of the Parliamentary Assembly CoE (1976), which declares that dying patients, for the most part, wish to die in peace and with dignity and, as far as possible, in the comfort and support of their loved ones. Another document is PA Recommendation 779 (1976) in which Parliament states that "prolongation of life should not be the sole aim of medical practice, which must include the relief of suffering with equal concern." These documents therefore emphasise the right to die in dignity and the danger of "artificial prolongation of life." None of these documents is of binding nature.

30 The convention was ratified by 29 Member States of the Council of Europe, while it has not been ratified by, among others, Germany, Austria, Belgium, Sweden, the Netherlands, Italy and the United Kingdom, as well as Poland. Source: https://rm.coe.int/inf-2019-2-etat-sign-ratif-reserves-bil-002-/16809979a8 (10.11.2020). It guarantees patients the right

law documents: the Parliamentary Assembly Recommendation 1418 (1999) "Protection of the human rights and dignity of the terminally ill and the dying" and the Parliamentary Assembly Resolution 1859 (2012) "Protecting human rights and dignity by taking into account previously expressed wishes of patients," which echo the principles of the Oviedo Convention. These documents have created the entitlement known as the right to die with dignity, also in relation to persons who are unable to express their will. In doing so, they create a new paradigm of the right to die which stems from human dignity. At the same time, they stress the guaranteed protection of the right to life, that is, the prohibition on deliberately taking it away.

References to indicated sources of law are quite frequent in the Court's judgments and they serve rather differentiated purposes.

The argument of reference to external law sources works well when it is aimed to approve the alleged practice by recognising that it does not violate the limits set by international law drawn up by the Council of Europe, albeit outside the Convention. The Court followed such an approach in the case *Glass v. the UK*.[31] Here, the Court made extensive reference to sources of international law relating to the protection of children, including Article 3(1) of the United Nations Convention on the Rights of the Child,[32] as well as Article 24 of the European Union's Charter of Fundamental Rights.[33] Among relevant benchmarks the Court also indicated Article 6 of the Oviedo Convention, describing the issue of protection of persons not able to consent[34]

---

to give their consent to all therapeutic interventions and actions (Article 5) and, in the case of persons incapable of making their own decisions, a procedure of surrogate consent (Article 6). In order to implement the principles of the Oviedo Convention, a "Guide on the decision-making process regarding medical treatment in end-of-life situations" has been prepared by the Committee on Bioethics of the Council of Europe, containing an extensive section on "The question of limiting, withdrawing or withholding artificial hydration and nutrition."

31 Glass v. the UK, par.75.

32 "In all actions concerning children, whether undertaken by public or private social welfare institutions, courts of law, administrative authorities or legislative bodies, the best interest of the child shall be the primary consideration."

33 Article 24 – The rights of the child

1 "Children shall have the right to such protection and care as is necessary for their well-being. They may express their views freely. Such views shall be taken into consideration on matters which concern them in accordance with their age and maturity.
2 In all actions relating to children, whether taken by public authorities or private institutions, the child's best interests must be the primary consideration.
3 Every child shall have the right to maintain on a regular basis a personal relationship and direct contact with both his, or her parents, unless that is contrary to his or her interests."

34 Article 6 – Protection of persons not able to consent

1 "Subject to Articles 17 and 20 below, an intervention may only be carried out on a person who does not have the capacity to consent, for his or her direct benefit.
2 Where, according to law, a minor does not have the capacity to consent to an intervention, the intervention may only be carried out with the authorisation of his or her representative or an authority or a person or body provided for by law.

and the Guide on the decision-making process regarding medical treatment in end-of-life situations.[35] All these documents contain the same phrase which was used in this judgment to construct a certain standard – it is a reference to the "best interest" of child or of patient. Through this reference, the Court anchors its argument about entrusting decisions concerning the life of the patient in unclear and contentious situations to those authorised to assess the best interest of patient, such as physicians (as discussed later in the chapter). Such references in *Glass v. the UK* were made by the Court to show that the national legislation corresponding with the challenged action is not incompatible with the standards set by the Convention on Human Rights and Biomedicine. Similar reference was made in the *Gard v. the UK*, where, citing the findings in *Glass v. the UK*, the Court held that there was no reason to conclude that the regulatory framework in place in the United Kingdom is in any way inconsistent with the standards laid down in the Convention on Human Rights and Biomedicine in the area of consent.[36]

All three acts – The Biomedical Convention, the Resolution and the Recommendation – co-form the essential background of the ECtHR's decision in *Lambert and Others v. France*. The Court cites their content with painstaking precision and emphasises the principles and guidelines for national regulation arising from the Guide (2014) and Resolution (2012). Based on this, the Court has largely built its argumentation on the State's obligations regarding the conditions for the admissibility of the discontinuation of life-sustaining measures.[37] The Guide was used by the Court to argue that artificial nutrition and hydration (ANH) ought to be equated with medical treatment, thereby placing the decision as to its continuation in the hands of physicians.[38]

The opinion of the minor shall be taken into consideration as an increasingly determining factor in proportion to his or her age and degree of maturity.

3 Where, according to law, an adult does not have the capacity to consent to an intervention because of a mental disability, a disease or for similar reasons, the intervention may only be carried out with the authorisation of his or her representative or an authority or a person or body provided for by law.

The individual concerned shall take part in the authorisation procedure as far as possible.

4 The representative, the authority, the person or the body mentioned in paragraphs 2 and 3 above shall be given, under the same conditions, the information referred to in Article 5.

5 The authorisation referred to in paragraphs 2 and 3 above may be withdrawn at any time in the best interests of the person concerned."

35 The Guide on the decision-making process regarding medical treatment in end-of-life situations was drawn up in 2014 by the Committee on Bioethics (DHBIO) of the Council of Europe in the course of its work on patients' rights and with the intention of facilitating the implementation of the principles enshrined in the Convention on Human Rights and Biomedicine (Oviedo Convention, ETS No. 164, 1997), https://rm.coe.int/CoERMPublicCommonSearchServices/DisplayDCTMContent?documentId=090000168039e8c5.

36 Gard v. the UK, par. 89.

37 Lambert and Others v. France, par. 59–71.

38 Lambert and Others v. France, par.155.

Nonetheless, both in the *Lambert* case and in the remaining proceedings, the argument based on the wording of the cited documents does not carry any normative value – it cannot, since the documents are predominantly of a non-binding nature (even the Oviedo Convention has not been ratified by many states that are parties to the ECtHR proceedings). In fact, it is worth pointing out that these documents contain wording that allows for a wide range of interpretations and actions. Citing them creates a well-established and resounding interpretative context in which the procedures applied by the state in relation to end-of-life situations are examined. Thus, referring to external sources of law, mainly by indicating that the action of the State remained within the framework set by these acts, strongly supports and serves the arguments developed by the Court, which is hesitant and very reticent in assessing the behaviour of States, their administration and medical services.

One very interesting reference to a legal order external to the Convention, but of an entirely different nature, is the citation of the Canadian Supreme Court's judgment in the *Rodriguez* case (1993) provided in the justification of decisions concerning the admissibility of euthanasia.[39] The facts and claims in this case are almost identical to the European cases on the permissibility of assisted suicide. In Justice Sopinka's opinion, there is an assumption that the decision to die voluntarily falls within the sphere of human autonomy, but there are also three basic arguments put forward against the permissibility of assisted suicide. Firstly, the prohibition of assisted suicide meets the very important objective of protecting the vulnerable and is reflective of fundamental values at play in the society. Secondly, it is grounded in the State interest in protecting life and reflects the policy of the State that human life should not be depreciated by allowing life to be taken as a part of our fundamental conception of the sanctity of life, which "has never been adjudged to be unconstitutional or contrary to fundamental human rights, is not arbitrary or unfair." Thirdly, creating legislative attempts to create any *exceptions are unsatisfactory and tend to support the theory of the "slippery slope" as relaxing the clear standard of the protection of life.*[40]

The reasoning employed in Justice Sopinka's opinion has been used substantively to a large extent by the ECtHR and the British courts. However, from this perspective, it is also notable that the Court referred to this decision as an important voice in the resolution of euthanasia cases, a position taken by the court external to the European human rights order. By invoking this standpoint, it has thus shown that it is not charting a new path, but following one already mapped out after an insightful and multifaceted argument, the

39 Rodriguez v. British Columbia (Attorney General), Judgment of 30 September 1993, Report [1993] 3 SCR 519. The case involved a woman in a deteriorating state of inertia who requested assisted suicide when there has been a long-standing blanket prohibition of assisted suicide in Canadian Criminal Code, p. 241(b). Her request was not successful.

40 Ibidem, p. 192–3.

very opinion it cites extensively. These threads appear clearly in the argumentation of the European courts; this ruling and argumentation was referred to first by the British courts,[41] and this line of argument was later repeated and endorsed by the ECtHR in *Pretty v. the UK*.[42]

The argumentation described here based on the reference to external sources is an argument building a connection with others argumentative tools, particularly with a margin of appreciation.

Arguments from the margin of appreciation – five issues of deference

The restraint observed in interfering with the decisions of domestic medical authorities in end-of-life cases is possible primarily through resorting to one of the Court's most important ways of reasoning: the granting of a margin of appreciation.[43] This well-known interpretative doctrine used in the ECtHR case law has been analysed dozens of times. Here, however, we will focus on it as a certain strategy of persuasion towards the position adopted in the ruling, usually accepting the approach taken by domestic authorities. What is particularly noteworthy here is the great persuasive potential to remain reticent in adjudication, and clear appeal to the audience by emphasising the diversity of attitudes of the international community and the legitimacy of national authorities to regulate matters of such sensitivity in accordance with moral and social attitudes existing locally.

Undoubtedly, it is clear that the issue of the termination of life has always been a highly sensitive and emotionally charged matter, both in terms of ethics and of acceptable social and, consequently, legal practices. However, at no point and in no judgment does the Court refer to this sensitivity, going beyond merely stating scientific, legal and ethical doubts[44] or the importance

41 Lord Cornhill in the opinion on *Pretty (The Queen on the Application of Mrs Dianne Pretty (Appellant) v. Director of Public Prosecutions (Respondent) and Secretary of State for the Home Department (Interested Party)* called Rodriguez's judgment 'The most detailed and erudite discussion known to me of the issues in the present appeal" (p. 19). For a full exposition of this argument, see Lord Hope's opinion in the same case (para 96). The judgment of the Federal Court of Switzerland on 3 November 2006 in the *Haas* case cites not only the ECtHR judgment in *Pretty v. the UK*, but also the Rodriguez judgment (paras. 6.2.2–6.2.3) – although the circumstances of that case are vastly different from those of the cited decision (the ECtHR did not refer to the *Rodriguez* case in its assessment).

42 Pretty v. UK, par. 66.

43 It should be noted, however, that the application of the margin of appreciation mechanism in cases involving violations of Article 2 (and 3) of the Convention, that is involving rights that cannot be limited and are absolute in nature, is in principle excluded. These rights do not allow for any deference to be paid to the national authorities. See J. Gerard, Margin of appreciation, p. 501. The author also explains there are certain exceptions to this rule in case law.

44 For instance: Lambert v. France, par.144: "in the context of the State's positive obligations, when addressing complex scientific, legal and ethical issues concerning in particular the beginning or the end-of-life, and in the absence of consensus among the member States, the Court has recognised that the latter have a certain margin of appreciation."

of "interest at stake."[45] It is therefore impossible to decipher why this issue is considered particularly sensitive. One gets the impression that the Court either takes it completely for granted and, as it were, primary to further considerations, or avoids naming and analysing the taboo issues, refraining from penetrating the structure of the moral and legal conflict that may come into play here.

Hence, highlighting the subtlety and sensitivity of the subject matter and the importance of conflicting interests gets mentioned in the reasons for ECtHR judgments, but the predominant argument is that there is no consensus at the level of the Member States as to the assumptions behind the solutions and their axiological underpinnings.[46] The consensus on regulations existing between the States and parties to the Convention is among the factors conditioning the granting of the margin of appreciation and is one of the basic determinants of its scope. The documents of international law on end-of-life situations previously mentioned, as well as comparisons of regulations of European states, allow the Court to make certain assumptions regarding the European consensus in this area. However, in each case, the Court finds that the wide margin of appreciation granted to the states is partly attributable to the lack of such a consensus on the end-of-life – or rather, human participation in it. Therefore, the Court does not find a *commonly accepted standard*[47] which would allow for this kind of designation of the degree of protection at European level – be it the right to life, the right to privacy or the right to die in dignity.

There are at least five issues in the case law on end-of-life situations where the Court leaves it up to the States to shape regulation and practice.

The first of these relates directly to the fact that there is no consensus regarding the acceptability of assisted dying. In the context of the ECHR, the Court emphasises the impossibility of reaching a pan-European compromise on the admissibility of such interference in end-of-life situations, which calls for the exercise of utmost caution in setting limits or legal frameworks for behaviour which could be considered a violation of the rights guaranteed under the Convention. Such a lack of consensus in cases of assisted suicide was indicated by the Court in the cases of *Haas v. Switzerland*[48] and *Koch v. Germany*.[49] As

45 Pretty v. the United Kingdom, par.70: in determining whether an interference is "necessary in a democratic society" the Court will take into account that a margin of appreciation is left to the national authorities, whose decision remains subject to review by the Court for conformity with the requirements of the Convention. The margin of appreciation to be accorded to the competent national authorities will vary in accordance with the nature of the issues and the importance of the interests at stake.

46 Emily Wada, "A Pretty Picture: The Margin of Appreciation and the Right to Assisted Suicide." *Loyola of Los Angeles International and Comparative Law Review* 27(2) (2005): 281–7.

47 As it was set out in Tyrer v. UK, appl. no. 5856/72, judgment of 28.04.1978.

48 Haas v. Switzerland, par. 55.

49 Koch v. Germany, par. 70.

the Court has scrupulously pointed out in these judgments,[50] the issue of the admissibility of assisted suicide in European countries is far from being settled unanimously; in the vast majority of countries (36 out of 42, to be precise)[51] any form of assistance to suicide is strictly prohibited and criminalised by law. Only four Member States[52] allow doctors to prescribe lethal drugs in specific circumstances, as long as certain safeguards are observed.

The second issue which the Court leaves explicitly to the discretion of the States is the regulation governing the type and use of medical treatment and life-sustaining treatment. The most controversial issue is permitting the withdrawal of artificial life-sustaining treatment. This problem was identified by the Court in *Lambert v. France*, noting that the majority of States appear to allow it. Although the precise arrangements for withdrawal of treatment vary from country to country, there is a consensus that the will of the patient is paramount in the decision-making process, regardless of the way in which it is expressed.[53]

By contrast, in *Gard v. the United Kingdom*, involving the withholding of life-sustaining treatment as well as the lack of consent to proceed with experimental therapy, the Court noted that the lack of consensus on access to experimental medical treatment for the terminally ill meant that the margin of appreciation in this area was wide.[54] This was subsequently used to support the argument that the decision to refuse consent for this type of therapy to a sick boy was correct. Another issue in this respect was addressed by the Court in *Burke v. the United Kingdom*, where the application alleged, *inter alia*, a violation of the prohibition of discrimination through the possibility of treating an incompetent patient against his will – as opposed to a competent patient. In its decision, the Court stressed that "the Contracting States enjoy a margin of appreciation in assessing whether and to what extent differences in otherwise similar situations justify a different treatment." This principle means that in this case neither a competent nor an incompetent patient can require a doctor to administer treatment which in that doctor's opinion is not clinically justified and thus no difference of treatment arises in that regard. Insofar as

50 Koch v. Germany par. 26 and Haas v. Switzerland. par. 29–31, 55.

51 These are: Albania, Andorra, Austria, Azerbaijan, Bosnia and Herzegovina, Bulgaria, Croatia, Cyprus, Czech Republic, Denmark, Estonia, France, Georgia, Greece, Hungary, Ireland, Latvia, Lithuania, the Former Yugoslav Republic of Macedonia, Malta, Moldova, Monaco, Montenegro, Norway, Poland, Portugal, Romania, Russia, San Marino, Spain, Serbia, Slovakia, Slovenia, Turkey, Ukraine and the United Kingdom. In Sweden and Estonia, assistance to suicide is not a crime, but Estonian medical practitioners are not allowed to prescribe a drug to facilitate suicide. Since the Lambert judgment, however, the situation has changed in Spain and Portugal, and also as a result of decisions by the constitutional courts of Germany and Austria, as mentioned at the beginning of the chapter.

52 At the time of adjudication these were: Switzerland, Belgium, the Netherlands and Luxembourg.

53 Lambert and Others v. France, par. 147.

54 Gard and Others v. UK, par. 122.

a competent patient is able to participate in the consultation process and an incompetent patient is not, such patients, for self-evident reasons, cannot be regarded as being in a relevantly similar situation. The extremely wide-ranging subject-matter of the margin of appreciation in that case therefore allowed the Court to conclude that the patients who would be affected by that difference in treatment are not in a similar situation, even though the doctor is required, in respect of both categories, to respect the duty of giving duly justified treatment.

The third issue to which the Court applies the margin of appreciation is the question of determining the beginning or the end-of-life. This type of argumentation can be found in *Lambert v. France*, where the Court, in formulating its observations on positive obligations, states that their scope is determined by the States within their margin of appreciation "when addressing complex scientific, legal and ethical issues concerning in particular the beginning or the end-of-life, and in the absence of consensus among the member States".[55] The Court made an even clearer reference to the lack of consensus among European States in *Gard v. the United Kingdom*. It referred more broadly to the lack of agreement with regard not only to whether the withdrawal of artificial life-sustaining treatment should be authorised or not, but also with regard to how a balance can be struck between protecting patients' right to life and safeguarding their right to respect for their private life and personal autonomy.[56] Consequently, in this case, the Court granted the margin of appreciation for balancing the patient's right to protection of life and privacy, with reference to this understanding of the purpose of the margin as in *A, B and C v. Ireland*.[57] Due to that very indication of differences and disagreements about the limits of life, the Court, with respect to Article 2, allowed the sphere of permissible differences in domestic legal orders as to the balancing between protected rights and the assessment of legitimate aims.

This is evident in the reasoning developed in *Lambert v. France*. While considering the alleged violation of the right to the protection of life, the Court admittedly stipulated that this margin of appreciation is not unlimited and the Court had the power to review whether or not the State has complied with its obligations under Article 2,[58] but at the same time it reiterated the statements concerning the lack of consensus concerning the beginning and the end-of-life and the balance between the protection of patients' right to life and the protection of their right to respect for their private life and their personal autonomy.[59] It is worth noting that this is a significantly used balancing test since

55 Lambert and Others v. France, par. 144.
56 Gard and Others v. UK, par. 84
57 *Mutatis mutandis* A., B. And C. v. Ireland, appl. no. 25579/05, judgment of 16.12.2010, par. 237, 238.
58 Lambert and Others v. France, par. 148.
59 Ibidem.

in the circumstances of this case, both rights were held by the same person – though represented in the case by relatives with radically opposing stances regarding the protection of the patient's interests and related claims based on allegations of either a violation of Article 2 or of Article 8.

A different area was addressed in the Court's assessment in *Pretty v. the United Kingdom*. In the course of evaluating the criminalisation of assisted suicide, the Court found that the law in issue (section 2 of the 1961 Suicide Act) was designed to safeguard life by protecting the weak and vulnerable and especially those who are not in a condition to take informed decisions against acts intended to end life or to assist in ending life. Thus, the Court placed it in the discretion of the State and the domestic legal order to assess the risk and the probability of incidence of abuse if the general prohibition on assisted suicides was relaxed or if exceptions were to be created, notwithstanding arguments as to the possibility of safeguards and protective procedures.[60] This led the Court to conclude that the prohibition imposed by British law did not constitute a violation of Article 8 of the Convention, as it was a regulation left to the discretion of the domestic authorities, which had a wide margin of appreciation to assess the danger and risks of abuse.

The argumentative use of the margin of appreciation is almost always engaged in end-of-life cases for the purpose of arguing the rightness of asserting the absence of a violation of law. Thus, it comes as no surprise that in cases in which the Court decided that there had been a procedural violation of Article 8, the topic of the margin of appreciation does not appear because it is unusable there as an argumentative instrument. For example, in *Gross v. Switzerland* it does not appear at all, but it is repeatedly mentioned as an instrument that should be used in dissenting opinions of judges who decided that the violation should not be declared.[61]

It is legitimate to note in this context that the use of the instrument of the margin of appreciation as an argumentative tool triggers the same controversies as it does in the traditional field, that is as an interpretative tool. Doubts are raised especially by treating it instrumentally, with the effect of avoiding statements on the merits, and consequently relativising and renationalising the scope of guaranteed rights.

In the context of the lack of consensus between the European States concerning the authorisation of assisted suicide it is necessary to notice one more phenomenon, which lies at the root of many cases in this category decided both by the ECtHR and domestic courts, called in one of the judgments (following the Swiss government) "suicide tourism."[62] This is the practice of

60 Ibidem, par. 74.

61 In their view, the margin should be applied because there is no consensus between the States to the Convention, either as to the relative importance of the interest at stake or as to the best means of protecting it, particularly where the case raises sensitive moral or ethical issues. p. 6–8 of dissenting opinion, see footnote 18.

62 Gross v. Switzerland, par. 53.

migrating to countries with liberal rules permitting such suicide (mainly to the Dignitas clinic in Switzerland). This concept, in other cases described in the book categorised as a "right to travel," is almost omitted in ECtHR judgments concerning end-of-life questions, thus it is of great practical importance. This issue arose in the *Pretty* case and is also significant in the *Koch* case, yet it remained discreetly ignored by the ECtHR in its findings on the scope of the implementation of the applicants' rights. On the other hand, it resounded very strongly in the aforementioned judgment of the German Federal Constitutional Court.[63] The German Court noted that the State cannot simply conclude that the realisation of the right (to suicide) is possible in other countries. The State's task is to guarantee the protection of fundamental rights within the framework of its legal order (par. 300).[64] The Court was thus sceptical of the strategy of washing one's hands of the matter by quietly allowing people to travel to clinics and centres offering professional services for assisted suicide.

It is worth noting that expectations to allow States to be at liberty in these matters met expectations of domestic courts, which is also clearly articulated in their decisions, and in a way pre-empted the findings made by the Court in this regard. This was expressed with remarkable accuracy by Lord Steyn in the *Pretty* case,[65] who formulated the concern that these issues should not be decided in a manner which compelled States to take certain steps, saying that it is "necessary to take into account that in the field of fundamental beliefs the European Court of Human Rights does not readily adopt a creative role contrary to a European consensus, or virtual consensus."[66]

Argument from epistemic authority – the best interest of the patient

Another type of argument referring to external authority in end-of-life cases is the strategy of appealing the expertise of physicians and medical personnel. This tool allows the decision to be entrusted to an entity other than the court, essentially aiming to demonstrate the competence of that very decision-making entity. This time, however, the authority is not based on a sovereign decision by an entity empowered to do so in light of accepted principles of interpretation and the limits of Convention protection, but rather on the science and scientific research. Much like in the cases in which the ECtHR referred to the margin of appreciation and extra-conventional standards in euthanasia cases, here the argument is aimed at demonstrating the court's lack of competence to

63 Judgment of 26 February 2020, see footnote 513.

64 Ibidem, par. 300. The State may also not simply refer the individual to the option of using suicide assistance offered in other countries. Under Art. 1(3) GG, the State must guarantee protection afforded by fundamental rights within its own legal order.

65 The Queen on the Application of Mrs Dianne Pretty (Appellant) v. Director of Public Prosecutions (Respondent) and Secretary of State for the Home Department (Interested Party), House of Lords judgment on 29.11.2001, [2001] UKHL 61.

66 Ibidem, par. 56.

decide a particular aspect of the case that is outside its cognizance (argument *ad verecundiam*). The appeal, which concerns the attribute of knowledge and experience, as well as assumptions about the high ethical qualifications of physicians finds its fullest expression in the reliance on the concept of one of the distinguished commonplaces: "the best interest of patient."

According to well-established British case law, in order to assess whether treatment is lawful in a situation where the patients are unable to express their will regarding it, it is necessary to establish that such action is in the best interest of patient.[67] This principle has also been extended to decisions to discontinue treatment if it is not in the patient's best interests.[68] Currently, English law explicitly acknowledges that in particular circumstances it may be in the best interests of a patient (child or adult) to withhold and withdraw medical treatment.[69]

The best interest criterion is also included in the Oviedo Convention on Human Rights and Biomedicine,[70] as well as in the "Guide on the decision-making process regarding medical treatment in end-of-life situations." It states that in the context of collective decision-making, when patients are unable or no longer able to express their will, physicians are the persons who, following the involvement of all concerned health professionals, are responsible for making a clinical decision based on the best interests of the patient, with certain requirements to consider any other relevant factors.

The term the best interest of patient is used with great versatility in case law and in a variety of categories of cases in which it is impossible for the patient to express their wishes for whatever reason (such as lack of mental capacity).

67 The standard set out in Bolam v. Friern Hospital Management Committee [1957] 2 All ER 118, Re F (Mental Patient: Sterilisation) 2 WLR 1025 (HL). Broad and in-depth discussion of the criteria and applications: Helen J. Taylor, "What are the "Best interests? A Critical Evaluation of 'Best Interest' Decision-Making in Clinical Practice." *Medical Law Review* 24(2) (2016): 176–205.

68 Aintree University Hospital NHS Trust v. James [2013] UKSC 67.

69 Part 3B of the British Medical Association guidance "Withholding and withdrawing medical treatment: guidance for decision making.": ".where there is reasonable uncertainty about the benefit of life-prolonging treatment, there should be a presumption in favour of initiating it, although there are circumstances in which active intervention (other than basic care) would not be appropriate since best interests is not synonymous with prolongation of life. . . . If the child's condition is incompatible with survival or where there is broad consensus that the condition is so severe that treatment would not provide a benefit in terms of being able to restore or maintain the patient's health, intervention may be unjustified. Similarly, where treatments would involve suffering or distress to the child, these and other burdens must be weighed against the anticipated benefit, even if life cannot be prolonged without treatment." Paragraph 15.2 of the 2001 British Medical Association guidance "Withholding and withdrawing life-prolonging medical treatment" states: "The law has confirmed that best interests and the balance of benefits and burdens are essential components of decision making and that the views of parents are a part of this. However, parents cannot necessarily insist on enforcing decisions based solely on their own preferences where these conflict with good medical evidence."

70 Art. 6 par. 2 and 5.

However, case law has repeatedly expressed doubts as to whether the category of "best interest" of patients, allowing decisions to be made without explicitly expressing a wish to end life, is a purely medical concern, to be decided solely on the basis of such an assessment.[71] Certain ineptitude can be observed in unambiguous classification of the decision to end life by withholding therapy or ANH as a decision based solely on medical grounds.[72] However, the best interest assessment – viewed as a tool to essentially equip physicians with adjudicative competence – continues to be the primary source and basis for the adjudication in numerous cases involving the discontinuation of therapy or life support.[73]

Essentially, the reasoning is reduced to the assumption that thanks to their qualifications and impartiality, only physicians are able to assess what is in *the best interest of the patient* and how their condition predisposes them to consider a therapy unnecessary or even harmful from the point of view of their condition, rights and self-determination. Hence, there is a certain shift in this doctrine, from releasing from responsibility for making certain medical decisions (and assessing whether they were made with the best interest in mind) to transferring the competence to adjudicate, to determine what the best interest is and, consequently, what decision has to be made by the court.

It is an instrument for entrusting another entity with the decision by appealing to its authority. However, at least two other features must be taken into consideration. First, its primary feature is its great persuasive potential

71 Specifically, this problem was widely considered in the case of *Airedale NHS Trust v. Bland*. Lord Goff in his opinion (United Kingdom House of Lords (4 Feb, 1993) concludes: "The best interests principle, as applied by the English courts, requires treatment decisions to be made in accordance with a responsible and competent body of professional opinion, since in an appeal of James Munby Q.C. for the Official Solicitor counter-arguments were put: The best interests and substituted judgment arguments are moral or ethical; they are not medical. That gives rise to two difficulties. If the doctor can withdraw feeding without first applying to the court for permission, it is placing upon a doctor a moral or ethical duty of judgment. If the matter is dealt with out of court then the decision is taken by doctors out of court who are not experts in moral and ethical issues. If it is taken by the court it is taken by judges who are similarly not experts on moral and ethical issues)."

72 Robert G. Lee & Derek Morgan, Regulating Risk Society: Stigmata Cases, Scientific Citizenship & (and) Biomedical Diplomacy, 23 *Sydney Law. Review* 297 (2001), p. 297.

73 It is hard to resist the impression that the use of the best interest argument in judgments handed down by British courts also seems to constitute a paraphrase of the state and inevitability of the death of the people concerned, of which the judges are convinced. This is confirmed by the rhetoric of the judgments, which are full of great empathy and the utmost sympathy for the dying and their relatives, both in the *Bland* and *Gard* case and in the case of *Alfie Evans* (the case has not yet been mentioned, but is similar in its circumstances and outcome), in which the judge not only expresses his thanks and utmost respect for the parents and relatives of the child, but also writes movingly about the care and feelings that accompany these people. These judgments seem to explain to loved ones that their child is dying and nothing can help them, and that any hope is illusory – they have great persuasive power and emotional charge. In this respect, Justice Hayden's vote in the ruling in the *Alfie Evans* case stands out (decision of 20.02.2018, [2018] EWHC 309 (Fam).

through the use of the phrase "best." It is immediately obvious that the decision made in the best interest of the patient is going to be the right one. This purely rhetorical device becomes possible because of the use of the concept employed in physicians' rules of conduct and medical criteria. It ensures that decisions made in agreement and to achieve the best interest of patient are not only professional, they are also the best.

Secondly, the analysis present in the courts' justification of the decision as to whether the best interest criterion was met is somewhat illusory. It is intended as a criterion for physicians – a recommendation of what should guide their actions in relation to the patient. However, the generic character of this phrase let the courts delegate the power to decide to the medical personnel without further inquiry into their expertise and the criteria for reaching it. The content of the decision to discontinue life-sustaining treatment itself remains a matter of medical judgment. Thus, it is apparent that there has been a certain shift in meaning and thus a reversal of function. Instead of examining what falls within "the best interest," the courts cede this sphere to the medical profession, thereby avoiding taking its own position. As a result, the best interest formula makes it possible to hand over the competence from judge to doctors by acknowledging their epistemic authority.

This standpoint has been criticised as not only carrying the risk of relegating decision-making entirely into the hands of medical personnel, but also as inevitably leading to assessment and balancing of quality of life – to the extent that this life does not deserve to be sustained.[74] In ECtHR jurisprudence, however, this doubt has not been expressed clearly.

In cases involving substantive adjudication of the merits of an alleged violation of Article 2 by the discontinuation of life-sustaining treatment, reflection on the nature and extent of the best interest did not receive due consideration. In *Glass v. the UK*, the Court merely concluded that the action taken by the hospital staff was intended, as a matter of clinical judgment, "to serve the interests of the first applicant."[75]

The use of this argument[76] can be easily traced in the case of Charlie Gard, but towards a slightly different direction. Having analysed the category of best interest in the context of this case and referring to previous decisions,[77] the British courts decided that this term must be used in the widest sense (not just medical but social and psychological) and include non-exhaustively every kind of medical, emotional, sensory (pleasure, pain and suffering) and instinctive (the human instinct to survive) considerations capable of impacting on

74 In particular, the appellant's position in *Bland J. Munby* and the opinions of the judges in that case, including Lady Hale (§ 39).

75 Glass v. UK, par. 77–78.

76 On quality of life as *leitmotiv*, see Zannoni, "Right or duty." 186–7.

77 NHS Trust v. MB (A Child represented by CAFCASS as Guardian ad litem) [2006] 2 FLR 319, 44.

the decision. Yet they entrusted taking the decision to medics and experts, on whose opinion the court had to rely in this respect.

In turn, although the ECtHR recalled three norms of international law that refer explicitly to the category of best interest: Article 3(1) of the United Nations Convention on the Rights of the Child,[78] Article 6(5) Convention on Human Rights and Biomedicine on the consent of the patient or the patient's representatives[79] and Article 24 of the European Union's Charter of Fundamental Rights,[80] it only concluded that the domestic courts decisions were, "in line with general consensus" – the only criterion for assessing whether the national authorities have acted correctly.[81] Thereby it entirely omitted the reference to the best interest of the patient, replacing it with a vague notion of "general consensus."

It has to be stressed, however, that the Court does not mention "the best interest" concept very often in its assessment of the cases, citing only phrases which in their established wording refer to unquestionable legal and moral value. For the purposes of assessing the allegation of a violation of Article 2 of the Convention, it carries out a test which in essence amounts to entrusting judgment to medical practitioners: the Court recalls that Article 2 cannot be interpreted as imposing any requirements for obtaining an agreement of the relatives of the child and the medical personnel as to the decision.[82] Rather, the Court accepts that the national courts had ensured that the patient's wishes

78 Art. 3(1) In all actions concerning children, whether undertaken by public or private social welfare institutions, courts of law, administrative authorities or legislative bodies, the best interests of the child shall be the primary consideration.

79 Art. 6 – Protection of persons not able to consent:

3 Where, according to law, an adult does not have the capacity to consent to an intervention because of a mental disability, a disease or for similar reasons, the intervention may only be carried out with the authorisation of his or her representative or an authority or a person or body provided for by law.

The individual concerned shall as far as possible take part in the authorisation procedure.

4 The representative, the authority, the person or the body mentioned in paragraphs 2 and 3 above shall be given, under the same conditions, the information referred to in Article 5.

5 The authorisation referred to in paragraphs 2 and 3 above may be withdrawn at any time in the best interests of the person concerned.

80 Art. 24

1 Children shall have the right to such protection and care as is necessary for their well-being. They may express their views freely. Such views shall be taken into consideration on matters which concern them in accordance with their age and maturity.

2 In all actions relating to children, whether taken by public authorities or private institutions, the child's best interests must be a primary consideration.

3 Every child shall have the right to maintain on a regular basis a personal relationship and direct contact with both his, or her parents, unless that is contrary to his or her interests.

81 Gard v. UK, par. 108.

82 Lambert and Others v. France, paras. 91, 162.

were expressed by the patient's guardian, appointed by the domestic courts, and that the opinions of all the medical personnel involved had been carefully considered.[83] In the Court's judgment in the *Gard* case, this means that the condition of due consideration for the life of the child was met. The Court goes on to say that the hospital's decision was presented to the court, which then rendered its decision accordingly, and thus the procedural requirement (underlying the finding of infringement in the *Glass* case) was fulfilled. The Court concluded that the medical due diligence is in fact the only relevant authority to make the substantive decision; thus, the authority was in face delegated to the medical personnel.[84]

By contrast, in the *Lambert* case, the concept of "the best interest" is mentioned only marginally. Admittedly, the Court recalls that the withdrawal of treatment requires some conditions to be met, among others that the treatment must no longer be in the patient's best interests, but this aspect was not further developed. On the other hand, not only did the Court extensively describe the entire legal procedure concerning the patient's case, but it also quoted the opinions of experts and ethical bodies used by the French Conseil d'État[85] which have proven to be an important factor in national decision-making processes and an appreciated contribution by national authorities.[86] What is important from the perspective of the Court's argument is that these entities commented on the interpretation of the law. The National Medical Academy and the National Ethics Advisory Committee shared their analyses and positions on the understanding and scope of the law and the notions of unreasonable obstinacy, treatment and sustaining life artificially, and addressed the ethical issues arising out of such situations. This line of reasoning is similar to the appeals to authority presented earlier, for it consists in invocation of the positions of bodies professionally engaged in ethical issues. Thus, the Court seems to exclude ethical issues of resolving end-of-life doubts from its cognition.

While considering the applicants allegations under Article 2 of the Convention that their arguments had not been considered in the course of domestic proceedings, the Court observed that although the procedure under French law is described as "collective," including several consultation phases and the patient's wishes to be taken into account, it was the doctor in charge of the patient alone who had been responsible for the decision to withdraw treatment.[87] Then, it declared that the consultation procedure as required by the French law satisfied the requirements under Article 2 of the Convention.[88] This part of the justification is clearly based on delegating the burden of decision-making

83 Ibidem, par. 92–4.

84 Gard v. UK, par. 67.

85 These were: National Medical Council, Mr Jean Leonetti, rapporteur for the Law of 22 April 2005, the National Medical Academy and the National Ethics Advisory Committee.

86 Lambert and Others v. France, par. 44.

87 Ibidem, paras 163–4.

88 Ibidem, par. 168.

to physicians since they are the only ones capable of an autonomous, impartial and professional assessment not only of the patient's condition and the medical procedure, but also of the decision to keep the patient alive.

In justifications of the Court's rulings on end-of-life situations, arguments from authority play a more significant role than just ornamentation. Skilful application of the margin of appreciation coupled with external sources of law make it possible to build the conviction that, first of all, the matters of end-of-life decisions are not only subject to the interpretation of the Convention, thus allowing to distribute the burden of the decision to other actors and sources of law. Secondly, the skilful employment of provisions and phrases contained in acts of international law allow for the strengthening of the argumentation, particularly one based on the doctrine of the margin of appreciation. In turn, recourse to the knowledge and experience of physicians assessing the condition of the patient, in combination with the use of the commonplace category of "the best interest," constitutes an argument that reinforces the conviction that the decisions made are correct and at the same time is completely transcendent to the order of the Convention.

Deontological argumentation

Deontological modes of judicial reasoning aim at demonstrating what is right and proper in the light of rules, reproduced in the course of interpreting the norms of the Convention. This type of argumentation is the most traditional of all the types presented here, and the closest to the well-known methods of interpretation, especially the recreation of the scope of rights and the corresponding duties of States. These rules may seek to indicate and develop various solutions, but the point is that by using this type of argumentation the Court remains within their scope, indicating not so much the appropriateness of the solution to the problem itself as the suitability and rightfulness of the path that leads to it.

This group of arguments used in end-of-life cases includes the proceduralisation, which consists in the attempt to reduce the necessity of adjudication to creating a catalogue of obligations on the part of the State, which sometimes requires deep insight into the structure of the rights which are the subject of the application. Another type of argument described here is incrementalism, which involves expanding the scope of the right, or creating a new principle within it – often without identifying a violation of the right in specific circumstances. The third argumentative tool distinguished here is argumentation, which consists of a skilful use of the known concepts for the purposes of particular argumentation by means of assimilation, change of meaning or a new field of application.

Arguments based on proceduralisation – duties of States to ensure the right to die

The first way of reasoning identified in end-of-life cases consists in determining the obligations incumbent upon States to respect and protect the right to the protection of life and the right to privacy. What is most distinctive in this category is the focus on interpretation, as well as in reasoning, on positive duties that relate to taking measures to effectively prevent violations of the rights set forth in the Convention. Procedural duties occupy the central position among them, and these involve creation of appropriate legal instruments and their actual implementation, so that the party seeking protection can actually and effectively pursue it. The Court creates a certain catalogue of State obligations in the context of end-of-life situations mainly by examining the observance of procedural fairness. This is essentially what the conclusions of the judgments in which the ECtHR found a violation of Article 8 of the Convention in the context of end-of-life situations boil down to. In none of the cases in this category did the Court find a violation of negative obligations with regards to the protection of the right to life, nor the right to private and family life.

In cases concerning the withdrawal of life-sustaining treatment with respect to patients incapable of making an independent decision, the obligations primarily concern the creation of a legal framework guaranteeing the predictability of medical behaviour in the decision-making process and the resolution of possible disputes between the standpoints taken by the medical staff and the patient's relatives. In terms of the Court's reasoning, the catalogue of these obligations serves primarily to determine whether States have complied with them, and it is interesting to see that they usually concern either Article 2 of the Convention, or Articles 2 and 8 of the Convention, in line with the Court's position on the need to read the system of the Convention "as a whole."

The Court's initial attempt to reconstruct positive duties was addressed in *Glass v. UK*, where the allegation concerned a breach of Article 8 (rather than Article 2), but the Court's considerations also apply in large part to the right to life. The Court found that it was the State's duty to develop the regulatory framework which would be firmly predicated on the duty to preserve the life of a patient, save in exceptional circumstances.[89] The Court stated that in order to provide such protection, the legal framework must prioritise the requirement of parental consent (since the patient was a minor) and, save in emergency situations, require doctors to seek the intervention of the courts in the event of parental objection. In doing so, the Court has formulated a canon of three positive obligations: the existence of a regulatory framework in domestic law and practice, judicial review in situations of doubt about the decision to be made and considering the opinion of the patient's relatives alongside that of medical personnel.

Consequently, the Court established only a violation of the procedural aspect of the Article 8 right in that the decision of the authorities to override the mother's objections to the proposed treatment had been made in the absence

89 Glass v. UK, par. 74.

of authorisation by a court.[90] The violation came therefore from the doctors' decision-making process, not from the intervention itself nor from the legal framework.

The content of the State's obligations under Articles 2 and 3 of the Convention in withdrawal of life-sustaining treatment was again addressed by the Court in ***Burke v. the UK***. However, these obligations were formulated very cautiously and with a considerable level of generality.[91] The Court emphasised the right of appeal to the court should there be a need to solve any conflict or doubt as to the applicant's best interests. But the role of the court (here the Court referred to the explanation given by the Court of Appeal) is not so much to authorise medical action as to determine whether the proposed action is lawful. The physician is held accountable for a decision, being fully subject to the sanctions of criminal and civil law, and is therefore encouraged to seek legal advice in addition to an informed medical opinion where a particular course of action is in some way controversial. Any stricter legal obligation would, in the Court's view, be normatively burdensome for doctors and would not necessarily entail any greater protection. The obligation of judicial review involves scrutiny of the legality of doctors' conduct, not a transfer of powers and decisions to the court.

Similarly, in ***Lambert v. France***, the Court referred to the issue of creating a proper legislative framework and a framework for proper decision-making. In this case, the Court examined the allegations in terms of the violation of Article 2 of the Convention, finding that the allegation of the violation of Article 8 was "engulfed by the allegations raised by the applicants under Article 2 of the Convention."[92] The Court made it clear at the beginning that the case did not concern a breach of negative obligations under Article 2, and examined only fulfilment of positive obligations.[93] It defined them in the public-health sphere as requiring States to make regulations compelling hospitals, whether private or public, to adopt appropriate measures for the protection of patients' lives.[94] However, in this case, it concentrated its analysis not so much on the shape of the legal framework as on the process of interpretation of the law by the Conseil d'État,[95] as one which established important safeguards of patients' interests.[96] The Court stressed that the case was the subject of an in-depth examination in the course of which all points of view could be expressed and all aspects were carefully considered. Also, the procedure consisting in

90 Ibidem, par. 83.

91 The ECtHR made references to *Pretty v. UK*, paras. 61–67.

92 Lambert and Others v. France, par. 184

93 Ibidem, paras 117, 118, 119, 124.

94 It is worth noting that these obligations and, at the same time, the ECtHR's assessment criteria also stem from the Council of Europe's "Guide on the decision-making process regarding medical treatment in end-of-life situations."

95 Lambert and Others v. France, par. 158.

96 Ibidem, par. 159.

determining the patient's wishes and consulting those close to him or her as well as other medical personnel was considered compatible with Article 2.[97] The Court also pointed out all the procedural circumstances: that the Conseil d'État had examined the case sitting as a full court and considered it necessary to have the fullest information possible regarding patient's state of health[98] specifically to clarify the concepts of "unreasonable obstinacy" and "artificial life support."[99] In such circumstances, the Court observed that the case had been examined and the judgment prepared "in great depth,"[100] and that the State thereby fulfilled its obligations to protect life.[101]

This kind of reasoning allows the Court to use the detailed description of the process of interpretation of the law by the Conseil d'État to cover the ambiguity of the law, which was the focus of the complaint. By describing the process of decision-making and judicial review, also with reference to the opinions of medical and ethical bodies, the Court is in a way relieved of its responsibility for the substantive content of the decision, which it ultimately found to be lawful.

The case law on the withdrawal of life-sustaining treatment seems to be permanently shaped by this range of obligations. The same catalogue was reproduced in *Gard v. the UK*,[102] where the Court also held that all required obligations were fulfilled and therefore there had been no violation of Article 2,[103] which is particularly interesting as there had been no allegation of a violation of Article 2 in the complaint.[104] The situation was different from that of the *Lambert* case in that the child had never had the opportunity to express their own wishes (even implicitly or by implication from the testimony of those close to it), but the Court found that the appointed guardian had fulfilled his duty and did not identify any shortcomings which could have breached the obligation to protect life.[105] So it is not the content of the law but the design of the relevant procedure that is at the heart of the considerations on the scope of the States' obligations in the end-of-life context. In this case, the Court also addressed the positive obligations of the State in the sphere of access to experimental therapy and concluded that Article 2 of the Convention

97 Lambert and Others v. France, par. 162.
98 The author and initiator of amendments to the law governing conditions of withdrawal.
99 Lambert and Others v. France, par. 173.
100 Lambert and Others v. France, par. 174.
101 Ibidem, par.181. It is worth noting that this conclusion was, however, very strongly discredited in the joint partly dissenting opinion of Judges Hajiyev, Šikuta, Tsotsoria, De Gaetano and Griтco, in which (§ 7) the judges observed that French law was not sufficiently clear in this respect and that the assumption of positive obligations for the protection of life was insufficient.
102 Lambert and Others v. France, par. 80.
103 Lambert and Others v. France, paras. 85–98.
104 Ibidem, par. 88.
105 Ibidem, paras. 91–2, 96.

cannot be interpreted as requiring that access to unauthorised medicinal products for the terminally ill be regulated in a particular way.[106]

The Court's arguments in euthanasia cases must foremost deal with the question of whether, on the basis of the Convention, it is possible to construct an obligation on the part of the State to guarantee the right to death to a person who expresses such a wish. The path of argumentation demarcating the sphere of positive obligations in these cases relates exclusively to Article 8 of the Convention. Already in the first case in this category, *Pretty v. the UK*, the Court took the view that it was not legitimate to develop the right to die in dignity on the basis of Article 2, as it was not a reversible right. And, in the Court's view, no positive obligation arises under Article 3 of the Convention to require the respondent State to not prosecute the applicant's husband if he assisted her to commit suicide or to provide a lawful opportunity for any other form of assisted suicide.[107] Eventually, the Court did not formulate a catalogue of obligations under Article 8 in this case, presumably because the applicant built her case by inferring not so much a right, but a freedom to die under Article 2.[108]

In contrast, the argument concerning the positive obligations of the State emerged in its entirety in *Haas v. Switzerland* (2011). According to the Court, that case no longer concerned the "freedom to die," but rather whether the State must ensure, under Article 8 of the Convention, that the applicant can obtain a lethal substance without medical prescription, by way of derogation, in order to commit suicide painlessly and without risk of failure.[109] It can be understood as the right to die and the responding State's duty to facilitate exercising this entitlement. The Court then examined the applicant's claim from the perspective of the positive obligation imposed on the State to take the necessary measures to permit a dignified suicide. However, the issue was not resolved categorically. The Court eventually considered that, *even assuming that the States have a positive obligation to adopt measures to facilitate the act of suicide with dignity*,[110] the Swiss authorities had not failed to comply with this obligation in this case. By using the phrase *even assuming such a positive obligation exists*, the Court has avoided giving a definitive answer to the question formulated in the plea in law of the application – that is, whether it is the obligation of the State to provide free (over-the-counter) access to a lethal substance to a person wishing to commit suicide, something which could be regarded as interference with the right to die with dignity from the point of view of negative obligations.[111] Instead, the Court went on to con-

106 Gard v. UK, par. 78.
107 Pretty v. UK, par. 56
108 More in: Antje Pedain, "The Human Rights Dimension of the Diane Pretty Case." *Cambridge Law Journal* 62(1) (2003), p. 187.
109 Haas v. Switzerland, par. 52.
110 Ibidem, par. 61.
111 Haas v. Switzerland, par. 53, 61.

sider whether the State had failed to provide sufficient guidance as to whether and, should the answer be affirmative, under what circumstances doctors had the authority to issue a prescription to a person in the applicant's condition. Consequently, only the requirements of creating and maintaining an adequate procedure in which the applicant could act were explored.[112]

In subsequent cases on the admissibility of euthanasia, a violation of the procedural aspect of Article 8 was also examined. In *Gross v. Switzerland*, the Court decided to limit itself to the conclusion that the absence of clear and comprehensive legal guidelines violated the applicant's right to respect for her private life under Article 8 of the Convention, without in any way taking up a stance on the substantive content of such guidelines.[113] This lack of clear legal guidance, according to the Court, can have a discouraging effect on doctors and introduces uncertainty about a particularly important aspect of life which leads to considerable anguish suffered by the applicant.[114] This conclusion led the Court to a statement about a violation of Article 8, but only in its procedural aspect.

A similar conclusion about the violation of a procedural aspect of Article 8 was reached in *Koch v. Germany*, where the Court held that it constituted a violation of Article 8 when the administrative courts refused to review the merits of the claim originally brought by patient.[115] On the other hand, as far as the scope of the right to privacy in relation to the right to die in a dignified manner was concerned in this case, the Court adopted a very cautious approach. Referring to the decision in the *Haas* case and the opinion "Even assuming that the State was under an obligation to adopt measures facilitating a dignified suicide" the Court considered that "Article 8 of the Convention may encompass a right to judicial review even in a case in which the substantive right in question had yet to be established."[116] Then, the Court did not exclude the existence of such an obligation *a priori*, but neither did it rule against it. As a result, it asked the domestic courts to assume jurisdiction to rule on the substance of the right to assisted suicide – even though that obligation was not expressly formulated as a positive obligation derived from the wording of Article 8 of the Convention. Quite the contrary, the context recalled from the *Hass* case concerning the assumed existence of such a right on the part of the applicants explicitly calls for a position to be taken by the domestic courts.

112 It is important to add that in this case the Court engaged in a weighing of the different interests at stake, in the context also of rights other than Article 8, that is, Article 2 of the Convention, "which creates a duty for the authorities to protect vulnerable persons, even against actions by which they endanger their own lives" (par. 54), and thus went beyond the limits of proceduralisation without relying exclusively on the balancing made by the national authorities.

113 Gross v. Switzerland, par. 69.

114 Gross v. Switzerland, paras. 65–6.

115 Koch v. Germany, paras. 53–4.

116 Koch v. Germany, par. 53.

A response from the German Federal Constitutional Court came several years later. In its judgment, the FCC laid down precise requirements for the legislature in terms of shaping the limits of the right to assisted suicide in order to protect against the risk of excessive expansion of such practices,[117] requesting, among other things, the creation of an appropriate legal framework for full, comprehensive palliative care with reference to the legal acts regulating the exercise of the medical profession.[118] In doing so, it shaped the sphere of positive obligations, in particular those regulating the guarantee of the undisturbed scope of the essence of the right to self-determination.[119]

Due to the use of proceduralisation, the European Court of Human Rights gets the opportunity to justify its decisions not by verifying the decisions themselves, but the legal framework that underpins them together with the decision-making process, leaving the substantive assessment of the admissibility of end-of-life measures to the States within the framework of the created legal order. Perhaps the strongest message the Court gives in the *Koch* case is that it entrusts these matters to domestic authorities and courts, giving itself very strict limits to decide on the substantive elements of right to privacy and the scope of State obligations in this matter. Substituting such an assessment with the catalogue of positive obligations to create a sufficiently clear legal framework and transparency of the decision-making procedure with primacy of the doctors' opinion in life-withdrawal cases and the patient's will allows for the creation of the impression of objectivity of this assessment, although in fact it is only a partial response to the claims raised in the applications. Still, the nature of positive obligations also allows ECtHR rulings to remain subsidiary to national legislative and judicial action without substantive resolution of end-of-life issues.[120]

The second line of argument within proceduralisation makes it possible to use the strategy of entrusting decisions to those actors who have the appropriate tools and democratic procedures suitable for resolving such difficult and complex issues, not only of legal, but of a social and ethical nature as well. This was already done by the Court in *Pretty v. UK*, where in the reasoning of the judgment it expressly acknowledged – following the position of the British House of Lords and also citing its own judgment in *Laskey, Jaggard*

117 Federal Constitutional Court judgment on 26.02.2020, paras 229, 233, 235, 249, 250 i 278.

118 Ibidem, paras 284–95.

119 It is worth noting, however, that the Federal Constitutional Court sees a very clear negative obligation on the part of the State to refrain from interfering in the sphere of the right to privacy, including the right to suicide, and deems the criminalisation of such an act as violating the constitutional right to self-determination (par. 219–27).

120 British case law corresponds with such an established view as to the scope of positive obligations, particularly in the sphere of Article 2. In the *Pretty* case, Lord Cornhill drew attention to the social and cultural conditioning, and thus social relativism, of positive duties, stating that actions in the sphere of positive obligation are more judgmental, different in States, as more dependent on the opinions and beliefs of the people and less susceptible to any universal injunction.

and Brown v. UK – the right of States to decide where the limits of crimes against the life and safety of others lie, also in regard to assisted suicide.[121] Thus, the ECtHR indicated that it is up to national authorities to establish the boundaries of decision-making in end-of-life situations and also accepted the right of the domestic court to leave this issue to the legislature. This was well-illustrated in the ECtHR's judgment in *Nicklinson and Lamb v. UK*, where the Court affirmed the right of national courts to leave this issue to Parliament.[122]

The argument about surrendering decisions on such difficult and sensitive matters to the legislature is also reflected in the case law of the British courts.[123]

121 Pretty v. UK, par. 74.

122 Nicklinsosn and Lamb v. UK, par. 84.

123 In the decisions of the British Supreme Court (until 2009 this function was held by the Appellate Committee of the House of Lords as the highest court in the United Kingdom) on end-of-life situations, one can easily recognise the scepticism towards the resolution of such cases by the courts as matters of considerable moral – rather than legal – weight. These rulings emphasise very clearly the need for the legislature to decide on the punishability of specific acts and the limits of assisted suicide. Most notably, in the *Pretty* case, Lord Steyn expressed a clear position on this point, referring to parliaments' democracy and the need for democratic debate on assisted suicide and decision-making by legislatures (§ 57), as well as Lord Hope of Craighead (§ 85) and Lord Cornhill who indicated the need "to limit the power of judges in relation to requests that are the subject of profound and fully justified concern to very many people. . . . The task of the committee in this appeal is not to weigh or evaluate or reflect those beliefs and views or give effect to its own but to ascertain and apply the law of the land as it is now understood to be."

In other judgments, UK judges have been equally clear in leaving the room for such a determination to the legislative body; this happened, for example, in the *Purdy* case, concerning a claim that assisted euthanasia was not unlawful (par. 26). The most comprehensive elaboration on this point was made by Lord Sumption in his judgment in the *Nicklinson* case, who stated that it was "a classic example of the kind of issue which should be decided by Parliament," as it involved a choice between two fundamental but mutually inconsistent moral values, upon which there is at present no consensus in the society; and such choice is inherently legislative in nature . . . and should be solved by those who represent the community, since it is not appropriate for professional judges because their personal opinions on matters of this kind lack constitutional legitimacy (paras 230–32). Again, Lord Hughes used an argument about the exclusive legitimacy of parliament in this matter, with reference to the separation of powers and the jurisdiction of that forum (par. 325), explicitly denying the judicial power to make the moral judgment necessary in this situation. Nevertheless, it is necessary to stress the completely different position and argumentation presented in the judgment of the German FCC of 26 February 2020. It is a verdict of the body responsible for examining and contesting the acts of the legislator as inconsistent with the Fundamental Law, thus the position taken by the FCC cannot be based exclusively on argumentation ad auctoritatem, which is inadequate in this situation. The German FCC, however, expresses a very strong opinion not only on the examined right, but also on other obligations of the legislature in relation to the issues of drawing the boundaries of assisted suicide and other obligations related to guaranteeing the right to bodily autonomy, self-determination and practical issues of medical care, palliative care, etc. (par. 277). Consequently, the German Court formulates here precise regulatory obligations of the legislature, determines not only the scope but also the direction of the decisions that should be made by the parliament, unobtrusively assuming the role of a positive – and not only negative – legislator. Although in terms of direction this approach is

Arguments based on incrementalism – even assuming such right exists

As far as the argumentation of the scope and content of protected rights is concerned, incrementalism allows for the gradual identification of new elements within the framework of the rights protected by the Convention. As part of this tool, the Court and the domestic courts engage in a complex and dynamic dialogue in an attempt to define mutually acceptable positions.

But incrementalism in end-of-life cases has a much broader dimension and one must start with the arguments refusing to recognise the broader scope of the right guaranteed by the Convention, in this case the right to the protection of life – that is, to establish what this right is not. Already at the level of domestic judgments, attempts to argue that the right to life can also mean the right to take life have been rejected. In other words, that it is a kind of reversible right, in the same way that the right to expression can also mean the right to remain silent – or not to be heard. A broad consideration of the scope and nature of the right to life appeared in the domestic proceedings in the *Pretty* case as part of the Lord Cornhill's opinion.[124] Again, in the same case, Lord Hope states that the scope of the right to life does not include the right to choose death.[125]

This was fully and unequivocally confirmed by the ECtHR in this case, stating that it was *not persuaded that "the right to life" guaranteed in Article 2 can be interpreted as involving a negative aspect and did find no right to die, whether at the hands of a third person or with the assistance of a public authority, can be derived from Article 2 of the Convention.*[126] The right to the protection of life was also not made transferable, as confirmed by the ECtHR in the *Sanles Sanles v. Spain* case.[127]

The scope of the right to respect for one's private (and family) life as an element of right to privacy guaranteed in Article 8 has evolved considerably in

diametrically opposed to the argumentation used by the British courts in favour of limitation of power of the judiciary, in terms of method of argumentation it still amounts to the use of persuasion concerning the characteristics and role of parliament as the only body and forum competent to decide on the limits of assisted suicide.

124 Whatever the benefits which, in the view of many, attach to voluntary euthanasia, suicide, physician-assisted suicide and suicide assisted without the intervention of a physician, these are not benefits which derive protection from an article framed to protect the sanctity of life. The Queen on the Application of Mrs Dianne Pretty (Appellant) v. Director of Public Prosecutions (Respondent) and Secretary of State for the Home Department (Interested Party), House of Lords judgment on 29 November 2001, [2001] UKHL 61, par. 6.

125 Ibidem, par 87: It does not say that every person has the right to choose how or when to die. Nor does it say that the individual has a right to choose death rather than life. What the first sentence does – and all it does – is to state that the right to life must be protected by law. Also, the contributions of Lord Bingham and Lord Steyn on this issue. More in: Bernard McCloskey, "The Right to Life – Human Rights at British and Death." *Commonwealth Law Bulletin* 37, no. 2 (June 2011): 231.

126 Pretty v. UK, paras. 39, 40–1.

127 Sanles Sanles v. Spain, decision, p. 7.

euthanasia cases. At the beginning, in *Sanles Sanles*, the Court declared it was not obliged to lay down the rule as to whether there exists a right to die in dignity under the Convention.[128]

This ruling was referred to by the Court in *Koch v. Germany*, but the Court went on to rule that the right to die with dignity, *even assuming that such right existed*, was of a non-transferable character.[129]

With respect to end-of-life situations, the content and scope of the right was primarily influenced by the decision in *Pretty v. UK*. It is worth to study this argumentation because it is a perfect example of reasoning which consists in creating a new scope of a right without establishing a violation of this right in a specific case. The ECtHR's reasoning runs as follows: The ECtHR held that although no previous case had established as such any right to self-determination as contained in Article 8 of the Convention, the notion of personal autonomy was an important principle underlying the interpretation of its guarantees. The right to self-determination was therefore considered to be an element of the right to privacy.[130] It pointed to previous decisions (*Laskey, Jaggard and Brown v. the United Kingdom*) in which the ability to engage in activities perceived to be physically or morally harmful or dangerous was considered to be part of the right,[131] and considered that even if death in this case was to be the consequence of a choice arising from personal autonomy it did not change this rule.[132] In consequence, the Court commented in a very cautious manner on the content of the law so reconstructed. It stated that it was "not prepared to exclude that this constitutes an interference with her right to respect for private life as guaranteed under Article 8 § 1 of the Convention."[133] The Court thus stopped short of concluding that it could not have excluded that opting for suicide as a means of ending one's life in states of advanced physical or mental decrepitude which conflict with strongly held ideas of self and personal identity is subject to the guarantee of the right to private life. At the same time, however, it must be recalled that despite this observation, the Court failed to find a violation of Article 8 in this case. Thus, the Court used the technique of argumentation, carefully extending the scope of the right to privacy without concluding that there had been an violation of that right. On the one hand, the use of this type of argumentative tool made it possible to emphasise the sanctity of life (par. 65), "respect for human dignity and human

128 The Court considered it important to point out from the outset that "it is not required to rule on whether or not there is a right under the Convention to a dignified death or a dignified life." Ibidem.

129 Par. 78. Daria Sartori, "End-of-life issues and the European Court of Human Rights. The value of personal autonomy within a 'proceduralized' review," *Questions of International Law* 52 (2018): 23–43.

130 Pretty v. UK, par. 61.

131 Ibidem, par. 62.

132 Ibidem, paras. 63–4.

133 Ibidem, par. 67.

freedom," and at the same time to pave the way for shaping a new scope, a standard of right henceforth covered by the guarantees of Article 8 of the Convention, soon to be called the right to die in dignity.

The Court's cautious but essentially progressive approach to the issue soon led to the development of a new meaning and scope of the right in Article 8 in subsequent judgments. The Court was more daring in subsequent judgments on euthanasia, clearly confirming that Article 8 of the Convention includes the right to decide how and when a life will end (then: right to die), and in particular the right to avoid a distressing and undignified end to life, provided that the decision is made freely. It followed that in *Haas v. Switzerland*, where it held that in the light of its case law, Article 8 encompasses an individual's right to decide in which way and at which time his or her life should end, provided that he or she was in a position to freely formulate own will and to act accordingly.[134] In this case, the Court indicated that the issue at stake was whether, under Article 8 of the Convention, the State had to ensure that anyone could obtain a lethal substance without a medical prescription in order to commit suicide painlessly and without risk of failure.[135] Despite this wording of the extent of the right – here again it stated that "even assuming that the State was under an obligation to adopt measures facilitating a dignified suicide"[136] – the Court found no violation of Article 8 of the Convention in this case.

In another euthanasia death case, *Koch v. Germany*, the Court invoked the scope formulated in *Pretty v. UK* and *Haas v. Switzerland*[137] and further held that *Article 8 may encompass a right to judicial review even in a case in which the substantive right in question had yet to be established.*[138] By using the phrase "may encompass" and referring to the right that is to be established, the Court created the framework for the scope of the right to self-determination based on two (seemingly) unresolved presumptions – one as to (substantive) content and one as to judicial protection. Meanwhile, it was the absence of substantive review of the right in this case that led to the finding of a violation of Article 8 of the Convention. The right was thus already not fully established, yet sufficiently outlined to allow for the recognition of a violation. Moreover, the *Koch* case laid down the principle that a person close to a person wishing to take his or her own life and involved in his or her suffering and desire to die has an

134 Haas v. Switzerland, par. 51: In the light of this case law, the Court considers that an individual's right to decide by what means and at what point his or her life will end, provided he or she is capable of freely reaching a decision on this question and acting in consequence, is one of the aspects of the right to respect for private life within the meaning of Article 8 of the Convention.

135 Ibidem, par. 52.

136 Ibidem, par. 61.

137 Koch v. Germany, paras. 46, 51 and 52.

138 The Court referred to Schneider v. Germany, appl. no. 17080/07, judgment of 15.09.2011, par. 100.

individual right to privacy encompassing such a claim.[139] This was confirmed by the Court in the case *Gross v. Switzerland*, citing previous findings that the applicant's wish to be provided with a dose of sodium pentobarbital allowing her to end her life fell within the scope of her right to respect for her private life under Article 8 of the Convention.[140]

Ten years after the ruling in the *Pretty* case, the issue was no longer contentious. The standard and scope of the right to request the end-of-life under particular circumstances was established through the consolidation of the content and scope of the right to self-determination. However, there is still no positive obligation for the State to assist people in anticipating their own death, nor is there a clearly established right for individuals to die.[141]

Argumentation based on plasticity and assimilation of concepts – what is the medical treatment?

Another argumentative tool used in the Court's judicial reasoning aims at convincing recipients of the rulings to the decision by appropriately naming and defining the acts and behaviours which are the subject of it. There are quite a few of them in respect to the end-of-life, as the problems that arise in this

139 Koch v. Germany, par. 43–6.

140 Gross v. Switzerland, par. 60.

141 Zannoni, "Right or duty." 197. The scope of the right to privacy as agreed at the level of domestic courts corresponds with these findings. The right to choose when and how to die as part of the right to privacy was expressed in the rulings in the *Pretty* case as a right of self-determination. Similar findings were also made in the *Purdy* case (2009). The phrasing of the scope of the right to privacy in the *Bland* case (House of Lords) is also noteworthy, with the sentence "The right to privacy of a patient includes the right to be let alone by doctors, nurses, or strangers with no public interest to pursue," referring to one of the most famous sentences defining the right to privacy as the right to be let alone in an article by Warren and Brandeis. Consequently, there is little controversy about the scope of the right to privacy and its constituent element in the form of the choice to end it, especially when there is real fear of discomfort and suffering. The right to suicide as an element of the right to self-determination was most emphatically and extensively confirmed in the mentioned above judgment of the German Federal Constitutional Court of 26 February 2020, in which the Court held, referring in its findings also to the ECtHR case law, such as the *Pretty, Haas and Koch* cases (§ 304, 305), that the right to privacy in connection with the obligation to protect human dignity guarantees the right to choose, self-determination to take one's own life based on an informed and deliberate decision and to make use of the assistance of third parties when doing so. This right was explicitly defined as a right to suicide (§ 203,204). Furthermore, the German CC held that the right to a self-determined death, as an expression of personal freedom, is not limited to situations defined by external causes. The right to determine one's own life is not limited to serious or incurable illness, nor does it apply only in certain stages of life or illness. Restricting the scope of protection to specific causes or motives would essentially amount to an appraisal of the motives of the person seeking to end their own life, and thereby a substantive predetermination, which is alien to the Basic Law's notion of freedom (§ 210). Thus, the German CC has gone to great lengths to establish the right to suicide, unconditioned by any circumstances, as well as the right of the person committing suicide to request assistance in committing it (par.212 bb and 213).

context concern determining the scope and legal qualification of termination of life, as well as the treatment of life-sustaining treatment and euthanasia, passive or active.[142] At the same time, the way certain behaviours are defined facilitates their legal and socially accepted assessment. This line of argumentation is subtle and difficult to follow, as it often concerns the indication and naming of the elements of the factual state in a manner oriented towards an almost subliminal persuasion about the rightness of the decisions made. It is all the more interesting to trace how the Court presents the circumstances surrounding end-of-life situations in order to convince of the rightness of the adopted solutions.

One of the most controversial issues regarding eligibility and its implications is the way in which life-support activities are treated, especially artificial nutrition and hydration (ANH). Nonetheless, it is a relatively rare subject of consideration in ECtHR decisions. Usually, the definition of such activities is omitted as an element of factual description which is obvious and essentially easy to qualify as a form of treatment,[143] which makes it possible in most disputed cases to assume that it can be considered a form of futile therapy. The inclusion of ANH among matters committed to medical decision-making prompted another question and plea in the *Burke* case, for example. Yet the Court avoided explicitly categorising ANH as treatment, although it relied on the UK's "Withholding and Withdrawing Life-prolonging Treatments: Good Practice in Decision-making," published by the General Medical Council in August 2002, and held that carrying on with it or withholding it was a decision falling within the scope of medical decision-making in consultation with the patient and their relatives.

In *Lambert and Others v. France*, the question of the qualification of life-sustaining treatment also escaped clear classification. In its assessment, the Court notes that according to the CoE Guide, treatment comprises not only interventions whose aim is to improve a patient's state of health by acting on the causes of the illness, but also interventions which concern only the symptoms and not on the aetiology of the illness, or which are a response to a body organ dysfunction. Then, artificial nutrition and hydration are provided to a patient following a medical indication and imply choices concerning medical procedures and devices (perfusion, feeding tubes).[144] Although the Court has stressed that decisions on the admissibility of its withdrawal are subject to a margin of appreciation, it is always the patient's wish that counts when making

142 On the meaning of the terms passive and active euthanasia: John Coggon, "Ignoring the moral and intellectual shape of the law after Bland: the unintended side-effect of a sorry compromise." *Legal Studies* vol. 27, no. 1 (March 2007); John Keown, *Euthanasia, Ethics and Public Policy – An Argument Against Legalisation* (Cambridge University Press, 2002), 110.

143 Regarding doubts about the use of the word treatment – cf. John Keown, *The Law and Ethics of Medicine: Essays on the Inviolability of Human Life*, (Oxford University Press, 2012), 330–2.

144 Lambert and Others v. France, par. 155.

such a decision[145] as well as the State's fulfilment of the positive obligations formulated in this respect. This was reiterated in *Glass v. the UK*[146] and *Gard v. the UK*.[147] Both judgments relate to the existence of a regulatory framework in national law and practice that complies with the requirements of Article 2. However, as the argument goes, the rules of conduct in all cases regarding ANH concerned the duties incumbent on medical personnel and such is the nature of the withdrawal decision.

It is worth noting that the question of whether ANH should be considered a medical practice falling under the responsibility of doctors remains a source of much controversy – both in the literature[148] as well as occasionally in the voices coming from the court, especially in British rulings. As early as the 1990s, in the UK ruling in *Airedale NHS Trust v. Bland*, [149] the court gave extensive consideration to the problem of withholding ANH from patients in a permanent vegetative state. The court went on to conclude that although this is a medical procedure, as it is not possible without the intervention of medics and their expertise and equipment, it has no medical purpose – that is, its purpose is merely to maintain vital functions in the absence of any hope of improvement in the patient's condition.[150] Therefore, the court ruled in this case that the decision to withhold or continue nutrition was based on the doctors' opinion based on the best interest assessment – not compassion, assessment of values or lack thereof – just a decision to provide treatment or similar. At this second instance, the Court also responded positively to the question: *Do nutrition and hydration constitute medical care or treatment?* This prejudiced the decision to entrust the decision to doctors capable of assessing the best interest of the patient. It should be noted, however, that in this case, Lord Goff denied that nutrition could be regarded as treatment and called such an approach an oversimplification, which would condemn patients to be treated in a paternalistic manner by doctors. By contrast, in the *Nicklinson* case, where the national court considered the question of the admissibility of suicide, Lord Neuberger drew a comparison between the two situations – that is, requesting assisted suicide and withdrawing life-sustaining treatment, finding that the latter is a "more drastic interference in that person's life and

145 Ibidem, paras. 124, 147 and 148.
146 Glass v. UK, paras. 75,76, 79, 83.
147 Gard v. UK, paras 80, 84, 89, 90.
148 Such as: Glanville Williams, *The Sanctity of Life and the Criminal Law*, (Keown, 1957), Keown, *The Law and Ethics of Medicine*. In the latter book, Keown calls such action: *intentionally killing by dehydration* (Chapter XXI passim).
149 Airedale National Health Service Trust v. Bland [1993] AC 789. Decision of the Court – 1 All ER 821 at 836.
150 Ibidem, p. 836–7. The court referred to previous decisions including Re Conroy (1985) 98 NJ 321 and Re J (a minor) [1992] 4 All ER 614, [1993].

more extreme moral step than assisting in a suicide where the person wanting to die is clearly in command."[151]

This problem was expressly stated in the dissenting opinion to the *Lambert* judgment, in which the judges referred to the assumptions on the meaning of the concept of ANH that were at the root of the ECtHR's arguments, exposing the ease and far-reaching consequences of manipulating their use in order to achieve a particular outcome. Firstly, they highlighted the ambiguity of the qualification between ordinary and extraordinary treatment, and the difficulty in properly distinguishing between what amounts to unreasonable obstinacy, and, more critically, what amounts to prolonging (or sustaining) life artificially. They point out that the nutrition of a helpless person incapable of expressing own will is an act of ordinary care and withholding or withdrawing food and water is followed by inevitable death. Therefore, withholding nutrition and hydration is an act leading to death and, although it consists only of withholding action and not actively performing it, it should be assessed as such. They also question the appropriateness of using the term "artificial" for nutrition and hydration – as they point out "every form of feeding . . . is, to some extent, artificial, as the ingestion of the food is being mediated."[152]

A second concept with great persuasive potential – a keyword for reasoning about end-of-life issues – is the term "medical futility" (futile medical care). The term has gained popularity in the final years of the last century. Futile treatments are therapies that are deemed by the physician to be ineffective given the patient's condition and as such may be withdrawn or withheld, even against the desires of the patient and his family. There is a well-established view that there are reasons why it is necessary and reasonable to discontinue a treatment deemed to be persistent when a persistent vegetative state or a near minimally conscious state does not promise improvement.[153] However, it is argued in the literature that this term is far from precise [154] and, even though it wields great persuasive power, it is not very effective when applied in a meaningful way. First of all, it is not clear how to measure the effectiveness of therapy – what is its purpose or the chances of achieving the expected effect – whether it is to cure the patient and, for example, to reduce suffering or to prolong life.

151 Nicklinson and Lamb v. UK, par. 94. see further: Rob Heywood, Alexandra Mullock, "The value of life in English law: revered but not sacred?" *Legal Studies* 36(4) (2016): 671.

152 John Coggon, "Ignoring the moral." 9. On dichotomy between passive or active euthanasia (depending on whether it is killing by an omission or an act) see further: Keown, *Euthanasia,* 110.

153 Teneille Ruth Brown, "Medical Futility and Religious Free Exercise." *First Amendment Law Review* 15 (2016) 86.

154 Francisco Javier Insa Gómez, Pablo Requena Meana, "Is Medical Futility an Ethical or Clinical Concept?" *National Catholic Bioethics Quarterly* 2 (2017): 262; Raj K. Mohindra, "'Medical futility: a conceptual model." *Journal of Medical Ethics* 33 (2007): 71; Nancy S. Jecker, Robert A. Pearlman, "Medical futility: who decides?" *Archives of Internal Medicine* 152 (1992): 1140; Heywood, Mullock, "The value." 661.

Secondly, the term therapy itself is vague, like with medical treatment, and the doubts as to how to qualify ANH point well to this dilemma.

Meanwhile, it was precisely the consideration of this *futility* that became one of the axes of argumentation in the *Lambert* case. The argumentation of the Conseil d'État showed that no therapeutic measures (artificial nutrition and hydration were included in this category) could lead to "unreasonable obstinacy" and they could be discontinued when they became futile or disproportionate in the artificial support of life.[155] This is also what the Conseil d'État believes must be the interpretation of the Public Health Code standards.[156] This reasoning and way of thinking is shared by the Court. It pointed out that, under French law, there were factors which make it possible to classify therapy as futile. They included: the medical factors (which had to cover a sufficiently long period, be assessed collectively and relate in particular to the patient's current condition, the change in that condition, his or her degree of suffering, and the clinical prognosis) and the non-medical factors, namely the patient's wishes, regardless of the way they are expressed, to which the doctor had to "attach particular importance," and the views of the person of trust, the family or those close to the patient. The Court found that these provisions constitute a legal framework which is sufficiently clear and concluded that the State put in place a regulatory framework apt to ensure the protection of patients' lives.[157]

Finally, it is worth noting the very lexical connotation of this phrase. The term "obstinacy" or "futile" is used in many cases involving withdrawing life-sustaining treatment,[158] though it should be noted that the ECtHR usually leaves the assessment of this futility (obstinacy) to national authorities and medical knowledge. However, the very use of a term evocative of something

155 Lambert v. France, par. 33.

156 Article L. 1110–5 of Public Health Code amended by the "Leonetti Act." (The Law of 22 April 2005 on patients' rights and end-of-life issues):

> "Every individual . . . shall be entitled to receive the most appropriate care and to be given the safest treatment known to medical science at the time to be effective. Preventive or exploratory acts or care must not, as far as medical science can guarantee, subject the patient to disproportionate risks in relation to the anticipated benefits.
>
> Such acts must not be continued with unreasonable obstinacy. Where they appear to be futile or disproportionate or to have no other effect than to sustain life artificially, they may be discontinued or withheld. In such cases, the doctor shall preserve the dignity of the dying patient and ensure his or her quality of life by dispensing the care referred to in Article L. 1110–10.
>
> Everyone shall be entitled to receive care intended to relieve pain. That pain must in all cases be prevented, assessed, taken into account and treated.
>
> Health-care professionals shall take all the measures available to them to allow each individual to live a life of dignity until his or her death."

157 Lambert and Others v. France, par. 158.

158 Such as in Gard and Others v. the UK, paras. 6, 21 and 28.

burdensome and futile leads *prima facie* the recipient of such persuasion to make a tacit assumption of a legitimate need to discontinue it.

The aims of deontological tools of argumentation

The employment of the discussed tools of reasoning, especially by combining them, makes it possible to achieve the persuasive effect – albeit only to a limited extent. The Court benefits from its privileged position, however, as it enjoys the status and advantage of having already taken such decisions. It only examines the scale and manner of the authorities' actions from the point of view of their compliance with the established standard, and so pursues its argumentation in the light of criteria it deems convenient. The ECtHR uses these arguments to point out that the issues to be decided are largely determined by national discretion and domestic law, and that verification of whether States are meeting their obligations to protect and respect Convention rights is in fact limited to checking whether positive obligations are met, with particular attention paid to the appropriate level of a clear legal framework and decision-making process and access to court. It also develops the elements of the right to self-determination very carefully and without significant interference in national systems as of yet. This comfort, however, is not available to domestic courts and to the authorities of States when the ECtHR takes a position on a case. The courts do so as reluctantly as the ECtHR, trying to avoid ideological entanglements with questions about the sources of the moral order, an individual's obligations to his or her community, and a person's place in the world. In this respect, argumentative tools from the deontological group are extremely difficult to employ. This immanent difficulty of striking the right balance between understanding and empathy for a suffering person, sometimes under extreme circumstances, and the minimum social morality – reduced in law to the balance between individual and public interest – is constantly present as the background to the relevant considerations. This basic dilemma, however, is much more apparent in the use of tactics from the teleological group used to justify the adjudication of end-of-life cases.

Teleological arguments – rights of the weak and vulnerable viewed as the limits of autonomy

The ECtHR's decisions in several of its end-of-life rulings are particularly worthy of attention because of the deliberations they contain regarding the public interest, which in turn may lead to the crystallisation of a certain moral minimum established in these cases in regards to the principle of the protection of life. Identifying the public interest as a reason for restricting the exercise of the right to privacy proves to be extremely difficult. In matters that divide society and concern taboos or issues strictly connected with personal, private life, it is overly complicated to define such an interest – and thus the good or the purpose – since it requires an answer to the question of what kind of society we want to live in and what is the projection of the Court that decides the case in this respect. All of this requires *the assumption of some pre-existing moral theory or overarching moral principle to guide and justify*, and this is particularly challenging in cases of this nature, which is why courts are wary of defining this public interest in opposition to the interest of the individual patient claiming the right to die. This recurring theme appears most clearly in the rulings on the possible decriminalisation of assisted suicide, regarded as an offence under criminal law.[159] This public interest, referred to as the State's interest in preserving human life,[160] as well as described by reference to the principle of sanctity of life[161] or reverence for life,[162] or simply – as in the judgment of the German FCC – as the protection of life as such,[163] sets the boundary in liberty to make decisions about life by a person suffering and wishing to die. However, it has not been defined, particularly in relation to the moral minimum or the requirement to live in the community. Recognition of the need to balance public and private interests leads to arguments that rationalise this kind of fear of infringement of human life or individual privacy in a broader way than before.[164] These ways of reasoning, however, have completely different connotations from ethical ones; they take on a rather utilitarian and pragmatic character.

To this end, the ECtHR resorts to particular argumentative tools, referring to the outcomes of its decisions. Firstly, it has to be mentioned in the context of end-of-life cases the argumentative mechanism known as "the slippery slope." In a nutshell, this argument presents the risk of future consequences of the decision taken, and it comes down to considering what effect it will have on subsequent cases. In fact, the slippery slope concept abstracts completely from the circumstances and claims of the parties presented in the decided case; it is an extrapolation of the *ratio decidendi* to subsequent cases and other circumstances, which, in the Court's opinion, would be unduly far-reaching. It therefore goes beyond an appraisal of those circumstances and those standards that are relevant to the case. It refers rather to the pragmatic significance of the

159 This was the case in British law (Suicide Act 1961) and for some time in German law. Broadly on the evolution of the attitude of common law to the issue of suicide and mercy-killing: Neil M. Gorsuch, "Right to Assisted Suicide and Euthanasia." *Harvard Journal of Law & Public Policy* 23(3) (2000): 599–710.

160 Lord Hope in the *Pretty* case (par. 97) wrote about the State's interest in protecting the lives of its citizens. The juxtaposition of private and public interests expressed by the values considered in these cases (autonomy and protection of the weak and vulnerable) was also noted by Lady Hale in the *Purdy* case (par. 75).

161 About this rule in common law: Gorsuch, "Right to assisted." 702–6.

162 About this argumentation as seen, *inter alia*, in the opinions of Lord Sumption and Lady Hale, see Heywood, Mullock, "The value." 673

163 German FCC judgment of 26.02.2020, par. 227.

164 On philosophical connotations and the discussion see further: Gorsuch, "Right to Assisted." 669–77.

precedent of the judgment, instructing the Court to restrict itself in formulating its thesis.

US courts have employed this argument in euthanasia cases for years,[165] while in European jurisprudence, the argument appears in a rather camouflaged way in the context of end-of-life situations.[166] In fact, it would be difficult to extract it in a pure form. For one thing, these cases are already so difficult and final that they are, figuratively speaking, at the bottom of this slippery slope and the danger inherent in them is already great enough, especially when it comes to deciding the case at the level of the ECtHR. The risk of "dangerous precedent" already exists to an extreme degree in the case at hand – not in a future case.

Arguments of this kind are therefore formulated explicitly rather rarely and sparsely – in principle primarily in the positions of the parties[167] or in national rulings.[168] This type of reasoning underpinned the Swiss court's ruling and the Swiss government's position in *Haas v. Switzerland.* The Swiss government argued before the ECtHR that it was therefore necessary to ***draw a distinction*** between the desire to commit suicide as an expression of illness and the desire to commit suicide as an autonomous, deliberate and permanent decision.[169] Given the complexity of mental illness and its uneven development, such a distinction cannot be made without a thorough analysis over a period of time that would allow the consistency of the desire to commit suicide to be reviewed.

In its decision, the Court referred to the interpretation of the right to privacy as expressed in its previous judgments on assisted suicide (notably *Pretty v. UK*) and, in view of this, held that it was an individual's right to decide by what means and at what point his or her life would end, provided

165 Yale Kamisar, "Some Non-Religious Views Against Proposed Mercy-Killing Legislation." *Minnesota Law Review* 42 (1958): 969, 1015, 1023, 1027, 1030–37; Frederick Schauer, "Slippery slopes." *Harvard Law Review* 99(2) (1985): 361–83. On the US court arguments in these cases, as well as utilitarian and ethical considerations, see Gorsuch, "Right to Assisted." 599–710.

166 This term is used more frequently in commentaries and literature, cf. Keown, *Euthanasia*, 76, Zannoni, "Right or duty." 212.

167 The position of James Munby Q.C. (for the Official Solicitor) in *Airedale NHS Trust v. Bland* serves as an excellent example. He drew attention to the subsequent decisions which represent the legal but also social consequences of previously adopted solutions and their alarming course of evolution. As he pointed out, the first step was to hold that a mentally incompetent adult could be sterilised: In re F. [1990] 2 AC 1. The next development was the holding that life-sustaining treatment could be withheld from the dying: In re C. (A Minor) (Wardship: Medical Treatment) [1990] Fam. 26. The third step was the holding that life-sustaining treatment could be withheld from the patient who was not dying, on the ground that he should be spared pain and suffering (In re J. [1991] Fam. 33). However, Lord Goff of Chieveley, who delivered the opinion in the case, did not share this argument and, in addressing Munbye's concerns, pointed to the explicit provisions prohibiting euthanasia.

168 On the Supreme Court's use of this tactic in the *Pretty* case, see: Pedain, "The Human Rights." 200–1.

169 Haas v. Switzerland, par. 47.

that he or she was capable of deciding freely on the matter. It considered that the *Haas* case contained an important difference consisting of the applicant's condition – his ability to act independently and his lack of a terminal condition. The Court also considered that since the State adopts a liberal approach in this regard, adequate measures to implement such an approach and preventive measures are necessary to prohibit assisted suicide organisations from acting illegally and in secret, with significant risk of abuse. The Court recognised that the risk of abuse associated with a system that facilitates access to assisted suicide should not be underestimated.[170] Thus, one can see a slippery slope resulting from limits to "the right to suicide", should an applicant try to formulate such a right on the basis of the Convention. The Court has therefore clearly separated this case from its previous decision in the Pretty case, in which it recognized that the right to privacy is only restricted by legitimate aims *of protecting everybody from hasty decisions and preventing abuse.*[171] In doing so, the Court identified the need to protect everyone from rash decisions – as it were, from themselves – as the reason for limiting the right of access to lethal injection, and thus formulated an extremely important and fresh interpretation of legitimate aim, which has not been explicitly qualified among the rights and freedoms of others, but which must be included in this category. The Court, however, did not elaborate on the arguments concerning this protection, its real reasons and the basis for limiting certain behaviours, which belong to the sphere of the realisation of human rights, so that this dangerous effect could have been avoided.

In order to explain the argumentative significance of such an appeal, it is worth referring to the second distinguished argumentative instrument, called "secondary effects." As has already been pointed out in Chapter 2, the application of such an appeal to the undesirable effects of certain decisions will allow the Court in the future to convince and persuade the audience to decisions made in a way that appeals to the common sense through the prism of threats faced by the community and attempts to overcome them, rather than by indicating an arbitrary (by its very nature) moral choice. It has an often implicit element of ethical evaluation and addresses the question of measuring evil, expressed through the risk of undesirable social consequences. At the same time, however, it does not evoke fears connected with moral majoritarianism, ideological threats or others, which are imminently connected to moral reasoning. Because it is undertaken from a purely utilitarian position, it allows rationalising moral choices and judgments by indicating their rational and pragmatic grounds.

This tool resonates in the most widely represented type of argumentation in end-of-life situations, leading to reduced interference in the sphere of life

170 Haas v. Switzerland, par. 58.

171 Ibidem, par. 56. Here, the ECtHR referred to *mutatis mutandis* Tysiąc v. Poland, par. 116.

termination. The reason behind the limitation of the right to assisted suicide is often given in the jurisprudence as consideration for other members of society – those who are sensitive for certain reasons to the possible abuse of the law that could occur if the claims of those seeking consent or assistance in ending life were granted.[172] This kind of reasoning was first invoked by the British courts. The argument of the need to protect the weak and vulnerable from the risk of abuse of assisted suicide was particularly voiced in the *Pretty* case, where the weak and vulnerable group was defined as the terminally ill and those suffering great pain from incurable illnesses, and the risk itself meant that assisted suicide may be abused in the sense that such people may be persuaded that they want to die or that they ought to want to die.[173]

This line of argumentation was noticed and acknowledged by the ECtHR in the judgment in this case (*Pretty v. UK)*, with emphasis on its precedent-setting nature and prudence needed in making decisions which will inevitably result in certain legal and further social consequences. The Court fully shared the conclusion about the purpose of the regulation criminalising assistance in suicide, which was designed to safeguard life by protecting the weak and vulnerable[174] and especially those who are not in a condition to take informed decisions against acts intended to end life or to assist in ending life.[175] It was pointed out that many terminally ill patients might be vulnerable, and this vulnerability of that group grants the State the right to assess the risk and probability of abuse if the general prohibition of assisted suicide was relaxed or if exceptions were created. The Court held that national law is entitled to intervene in the protection of the life and safety of others, including in so far as it restricts personal autonomy with a view to protecting the weak and vulnerable.[176] It is supported by the public interest, concretised in this defence of the weak and vulnerable against the risk of abuse and social pressure which might arise if such an act were not penalised.[177]

In the *Pretty* case, the Court also implicitly referred to the mechanism and the concern typical of this argumentative tool. It notes that although the applicant's individual case remains to be decided, judgments issued in individual cases establish precedents, albeit to a greater or lesser extent, and the decision

172 A forerunner in this respect was the judgment and accompanying justification in the *Rodriguez* case (Canada, 1993), often cited in UK and ECtHR judgments, in which Justice Sopinka formulated the effective protection of life and those who are vulnerable in society as the reason for the generally accepted prohibition on assisted suicide.

173 Lord Steyn's opinion draws attention to the utilitarian nature of this argument and refers to the mechanism of the slope (such views are countered by those who say it is a slippery slope or the thin end of the wedge). Another secondary effect noted in his opinion is the risk of loss of trust in medical personnel.

174 Once again, with a reference to the ruling handed down in the *Rodriguez* case.

175 Pretty v. UK, par. 74.

176 Pretty v. UK, par. 74.

177 Pretty v. UK, par. 76.

in this case could not have been, either in theory or practice, framed in such a way as to prevent application in later cases.[178] The Court further argues that the ruling in favour of the applicant's interests, that is to say, one which denies the right to interfere with the individual's autonomy as to the choice of the moment of death and which removes criminal liability from an accessory, would have set a precedent of broader scope.[179]

This argument has been revisited and thoroughly analysed and presented in the decision of the UK Supreme Court in the *Nicklinson and Lamb* case, and then fully endorsed (in respect of the first applicant) in the ECtHR decision in that case.[180] The British court's judgment, diligently cited in the ECtHR judgment, illustratively formulates the reason for the continued penalisation of suicide on the grounds of protecting the weak and vulnerable. It is therefore a *direct concern* about weak and vulnerable people who might feel:

> that they have some sort of duty to die, or are made to feel (whether intentionally or not) that they have such a duty by family members or others, because their lives are valueless and represent an unjustifiable burden on others.

One concern that was also formulated there was that such an evolution of the right to suicide would send a *more general message* to other people in a similar situation who are not motivated to commit suicide,[181] dubbed by Lord Sumption in the same case for the Commission on Assisted Dying as an "*indirect social pressure*."[182] It would be difficult to encapsulate this line of argument better than he did by writing:

> People in this position are vulnerable. They are often afraid that their lives have become a burden to those around them. The fear may be the result of overt pressure, but may equally arise from a spontaneous tendency to place a low value on their own lives and assume that others do so too. . . . In a world where suicide was regarded as just another optional end-of-life choice, the pressures which I have described are likely to become more powerful.

178 Pretty v. UK, par. 75.

179 As indicated by ECtHR (par. 75): judgments issued in individual cases establish precedents albeit to a greater or lesser extent and a decision in this case could not, either in theory or practice, be framed in such a way as to prevent application in later cases.

180 The decision of the Supreme Court of 25.06.2014, [2014] UKSC 38, UKSC 2013/0235, cited in: Nicklinson and Lamb v. UK, par. 85.

181 Lord Neuberger opinion in the British Supreme Court decision (see footnote 665), par. 86.

182 Lord Sumption opinion, ibidem, par. 228.

Lord Sumption clearly places this argument as coming from the realm of moral and social values fundamental to the State.[183] This argument is also referred to by Lord Hughes, who drew attention to the fact that the protection of vulnerable persons, those who feel that their lives are worthless or that they are a burden on others, should be classified under Article 8 of the Convention as "protection of health" or as "protection of the rights of others," especially the right to life protected under Article 2.[184]

In the *Nicklinson and Lamb* case, the Court (in respect of the first applicant) stopped short of concluding that the British court had given proper and careful consideration to the competing values. However, the argumentation about the need to protect the weak and vulnerable was fully accepted by the ECtHR. Also, in the judgment in *Haas v. Switzerland* there was some room for this line of argumentation. This time, however, the Court strengthened the argument. It referred to the content of Article 2 of the Convention, which obliges to protect the vulnerable against actions that may endanger their lives.[185] It stated that the content of Article 2 obliges the national authorities to prevent an individual from taking his or her own life if the decision has not been taken freely and with full understanding of what is involved.[186]

183 Ibidem, par. 229. The relative importance of the right to commit suicide and the right of the vulnerable to be protected from overt or covert pressure to kill themselves is inevitably sensitive to a state's most fundamental collective moral and social values.

184 Ibidem, par. 311.

185 On this point, the Court referred to *Keenan v. the United Kingdom*, appl. No. 27229/95, judgment of 3.04.2001, par. 91.

186 It is interesting to compare this argumentation of the EctHR with the one presented in the German CC ruling of 26.02.2020 (which finds the penalisation of assisting in suicide incompatible with the right to autonomy and human dignity). In the CC's argumentation, the threat to the common good (public interest) by making assisted suicide a "regular service in the healthcare system" that could prompt people to end their lives is recognised (par. 229, 233), but, in the Court's opinion, the fear of making death by suicide a common thing (par. 229) does not lead to the necessity of criminalising assisted suicide. The German Court has analysed this premise quite meticulously, citing research on the frequency of suicides, the attitudes of people who commit suicide and would-be suicides, comparing it all also with data from countries where such suicide is permitted within certain limits (par. 263). It is therefore a recognition of a socially undesirable issue, but this concern is marginalised by dismissing the empirical data as not providing evidence of this type of correlation (par. 256 (ββ). After a careful analysis of both the individual motives for committing suicide, the medical control over the prescription of lethal drugs, the professional standards of doctors and medical personnel, the CC comes to the conclusion that this legitimate aim does not justify such a profound interference in the right to commit suicide as envisaged by the unconstitutional Article 217 of the German Criminal Code. This time, therefore, the balancing of the two interests: the individual, or the execution of the will to take one's own life, and the common good, or the social attitude of respect for life, and finally the fear of social pressure on persons who might find themselves in a situation particularly susceptible to it, led the German court to the conviction that the act of assisting in suicide was excessive and did not need to be criminalised.

The discussed application of the categories of *the weak and vulnerable* in the jurisprudence on the limitation of the right to privacy in the execution of a request for assisted suicide or euthanasia death raises several observations.[187] The first remark concerns the circle of people who fall into this category. These are people who are terminally ill, in a vegetative state or awaiting such an inevitable state, dependent on external aid, living with the feeling of being a burden on others, fearing senility, suffering or having already experienced it. Attention is drawn to the hypothetical – and not real – nature of this distinction. In relation to the vulnerable groups classified so far in ECtHR jurisprudence, this is certainly a potentially disadvantaged and particularly sensitive group of people, but it is difficult to label them as discriminated against or stigmatised. They do not share the characteristic of social odium, isolation and cultural attitudes that would have condemned them to stigmatisation in the past – quite the contrary. The only thing they have in common is their openness to being hurt, and this is probably the reason for using the term in the sense used so far in ECtHR case law. This is, however, an imaginary and *ad hoc* group and therefore marks a significant semantic shift in using the term "vulnerable," used hitherto to describe groups who are susceptible because of the stigmatisation or discrimination they have suffered.

Secondly, this time – unlike the previously used category of the vulnerable – it is a group opposed to the interests and welfare of the complainants. It is the interests of the weak and vulnerable that justify the restriction of the applicant's right, who paradoxically also belongs thereto. The application of this category is different from that used up until now. What we have here is a situation in which we limit the rights of the applicants – rights that exist and are infringed in their opinion – by placing an abstract and hypothetical value of a certain group of people who are not identified individually and are difficult to classify unequivocally and who are at risk of harm by virtue of a possible decision against them.

It should also be noted that this kind of argumentative tool in the case of end-of-life situations (differently than before) is taken from the justifications of domestic courts, which is especially visible in the British cases presented (*Pretty, Nicklinson and Lamb*). Here, the ECtHR shares the argumentation of domestic courts on the limitation of the right to privacy in the name of protecting the rights of others.[188] By contrast, in *Haas v. Switzerland* the Court shared the government's view that the restriction on access to lethal medicine is designed to protect public health and safety and to prevent crime, since the risks of abuse inherent in a system that facilitates access to assisted suicide

187 On the weaknesses of indicating such a protection target, in particular the incompatibility with the principle of proportionality, see more in: Stevie Martin, *Assisted Suicide and the European Convention on Human Rights,* (Routledge, 2021), 43, 76–123.

188 Pretty v. UK, par. 69, 78.

should not be underestimated.[189] In these cases, however, the issue of classifying legitimate aim is not considered extensively, nor does it refer to the public interest.

Not only does such reticence raise the question of the nature of the argument, but also of its legitimacy in the light of the legitimate aims of the Convention. *Prima facie* it is the protection of the rights and freedoms of others or, as the Court wishes when indicating this value rather enigmatically, in combination with the protection of health and safety.[190] However, such an extrapolation seems a bit far-fetched, especially because of the indeterminacy of the concern and the group it affects as well as its characteristics. Identifying the vulnerable group and those thus susceptible to pressure in terms of deciding to end their lives so as not to become a burden on others is only the beginning of explaining what the Court and national courts are in fact trying to protect by upholding the ban on assisted suicide or facilitating euthanasia. The Court's thesis here is that the depenalisation of assisted suicide would, in effect, create social pressure[191] and a socially acceptable attitude, recognised by domestic legal order, approving the "removal of the burden" from loved ones by the ill or incapacitated person. The key to understanding the essence of this argument is to delve into the structure and nature of this social pressure which can create the impression of a compulsion to die prematurely among those considered weak and vulnerable. This is the fear of creating a generally acceptable attitude in society and the conviction of the appropriateness of such a decision: the emergence of a social norm permitting such acts and consequently creating a certain standard of behaviour and a transferable pattern of such determined attitude, both of the ill and their relatives. The European courts are therefore making the point that such a precedent would have a dangerous effect and that it is therefore imperative not to allow this type of change to the current law on assisted suicide, because such a change would quickly create a cultural and moral attitude which would endanger the lives of those who, freely and consciously, do not wish to make such a decision within the framework of their individual choices. The aim of restricting the right to bodily autonomy is not so much the right of others to life as the unwillingness to create a new cultural attitude of moral choice which is contrary to the hitherto accepted and respected principle of reverence for life. The Court's statement in the *Hass* case about the State's obligations to protect the rights of others from the perspective of Article 2 of the Convention seems to move in this direction.

Reasons for further clarification of the nature of this argumentation can be found in the relatively few, but prominent statements contained in the judgments in end-of-life cases, which explicitly refer to moral issues. This level is much deeper in the opinions of judges of the British Supreme Court. They

189 Pretty v. UK, par. 58.
190 Pretty v. UK, par. 74.
191 There is even the term "duty to die" in the literature – Zannoni, "Right or duty." 183.

are, however, significant because they indicate the grounds for decisions on the protection of the weak and vulnerable, the risks of assessing the quality of human life and the obligation to protect the attitude of absolute respect for human life, which is essential in society.[192] They also expose the attempts to rationalise the chosen moral attitude[193] and highlight the endless search for other justifications.[194]

These voices pinpoint the moral implications of the decision, as well as the basis of the decision embedded in social and moral values.[195] This argumentation can be regarded as an attempt to define a moral minimum for the functioning of the community – and therefore a sufficient rationale for limiting the right to autonomy, even in such extreme and serious situations as the right to self-determination of people who are suffering and dying. It is also noted that there is an extraordinary difficulty in adjudicating such cases because of the far-reaching consequences – the sacrifice of the applicant's autonomy for the protection of other persons considered vulnerable[196] and doubts as to the moral consequences of this line of reasoning. Therefore the path of making a moral choice explicitly is not followed and, if it happens, it does not lead to the conclusion about the rightness of sacrificing the autonomy of an ill person for the sake of social good. However, this does not change the fact that this very tool, included within the methods defined here as teleological, has proved to be the most effective means of persuasion in cases where other methods were insufficient. Its utilitarian character and strongly persuasive formulation of the protection of the appointed category of the weak and vulnerable seems to function best – as of yet – as a reason for limiting the right to self-determination in a substantive assessment of the content of bodily autonomy.

192 Lady Hale said an extremely important sentence in the *Purdy* case (§ 68): "It is not for society to tell people what to value about their own lives. But it may be justifiable for society to insist that we value their lives even if they do not."

193 Lord Neuberger's opinion in *Nicklinson* case, which carefully considered the moral argumentation on the permissibility of participation in the taking of life. He recognised that argument based on the sanctity, or primacy of other human lives, or even undervaluation someone's life replicates the concerns about the lives of the weak and vulnerable (§ 90, 91) – that is, it allows the analysis to move from the plane of ethical considerations to the safe ground of legitimate aim in the form of the rights of others, the good of society in protecting its other members.

194 Lord Sumption in Nicklinson, par. 208–9. He quotes Justice Hoffman LJ on this point, who in the *Airedale NHS Trust v. Bland* [1993] AC 789, 826C-E in the Court of Appeal pointed: "we have a strong feeling that there is an intrinsic value in human life, irrespective of whether it is valuable to the person concerned or indeed to anyone else. . . . In a case like this we should not try to analyse the rationality of such feelings. What matters is that, in one form or another, they form part of almost everyone's intuitive values. No law which ignores them can possibly hope to be acceptable."

195 The relative importance of the right to commit suicide and the right of the vulnerable to be protected from overt or covert pressure to kill themselves is inevitably sensitive to a state's most fundamental collective moral and social values.

196 Lord Sumption in Nicklinson, par. 233.

Summary

A closer look at the ECtHR's reasoning in cases assessing the admissibility of medically induced termination of patients' lives as concerning complex ethical and legal matters in ECtHR case law prompts several observations. Although there have been many rulings on these issues, it would be difficult to consider them as decisive for the shape of domestic regulations or actions. Instead, the Court chooses a number of argumentative tools from each of the distinguished groups and makes use of statements and references to the notion of the best interest and the category of the vulnerable as useful means of argumentation. The combination of tools *ad auctoritatem* is particularly noteworthy, especially the repeated reference to the margin of appreciation in multiple respects, owing to the lack of consensus in several areas identified by the ECtHR. As in other cases discussed in this book, the flipside of the non-existent European consensus is the phenomenon of migration for the purpose of exercising the right beyond the scope permitted in the country of residence. Medical knowledge and experience of medical personnel is a strong authority in end-of-life matters. In the arguments of the ECtHR, it is they who most often provide the rationale for decisions on withdrawal of life-sustaining treatment. Argumentation with appeal to epistemic authority is also possible thanks to the use of the concept of the best interest of patient, which is a primary and unquestionable value according to the ECtHR's arguments. This method of argumentation, however, leaves room for, among other things, the grey zone noted in the dissenting voices and questions of fear of paternalistic treatment in extreme decisions,[197] especially as it concerns persons who are incapable of expressing their own will.

As far as the deontological argumentation is concerned, attention is drawn first of all to the identification of the State's positive obligations in the sphere of the protection of life and privacy, whether in the sphere of the creation of a legal framework, the rightful decision-making process or the possibility of judicial review. So far, only the finding of a violation of procedural obligations in this sphere has led to a decision that the State had indeed violated Article 8 of the Convention. At the same time, in its arguments, the Court incremented the right to privacy, adopting the strategy of assumption of the existence of the right to die in dignity without finding a violation of this right (*Pretty v. the UK*), or without finding a substantive violation (*Haas v. Switzerland)*. Such statements, however, are of great importance in shaping subsequent decisions based on the assumed scope of the right to self-determination, as well as the legal framework and decisions remaining at the discretion of domestic authorities.

197 Also indicated by Dougherty, "The Common Good." 162–3.

It is, however, extremely interesting and innovative that the Court's justifications make use of an instruction from the field of teleological ways of reasoning, by a reference to the need to protect the group of ***weak and vulnerable*** persons, that is, members of society hypothetically exposed to indirect social pressure, if the right to euthanasia and legalisation of assistance in committing suicide became a socially acceptable practice. The protection of the group thus defined became a counterbalance to the individual interest of persons wishing to die and effectively prejudged the reasoning of the state for maintaining a legal regulation prohibiting such practices. This strategy of identifying socially (but also morally) undesirable secondary effects of such a decision and the potential for excessive extrapolation of the applicant's demand is somewhat questionable, both dogmatically and axiologically, but it is convincing on utilitarian grounds – the most morally neutral ones. With this argumentative tool, it can be observed that the justification is sought by the courts in the realities of social life by appealing to the motives that such persons may have, and thus – indirectly – to develop a certain attitude of socially approved consent to the quicker and induced death of suffering and ill individuals. This way constitutes a search for a brake on the in-built rules and scopes of rights. Accordingly, the public interest is identified with the protection against social pressure on a hypothetical group of persons exposed to future social attitudes caused by a possible precedent of permissibility of assisted suicide. It relates to concern for other members of society and a paradigm shift in the protection of life and, in this sense, this defence can be regarded as one of the elements of the moral minimum of social life. This becomes perfectly clear in the line of argumentation of the British court, which preceded the ECtHR judgment and was upheld as to its conclusions by the ECtHR especially in the *Pretty* case and in the *Nicklinson and Lamb* case. Seeking justification in social life, in the motivations of others, and consequently in the impact on those around them and those adversely affected by the change of attitude towards them is an argument for respect for human life as such – for if, as Jackson wrote in his classic work: the *'idea that God alone should have the power to decide the moment of an individual's death'*[198] is no longer an axiom, there is a need for proof, for rationalisation of what has so far been considered fundamental and obvious. The rationalisations and arguments used as part of the teleological approach refer to observations and evaluations primary to the rules of law. They remain completely outside the interpretation of the law, relate to observations of society and possible undesirable effects or suffering and despite the rationalising efforts are the expression of moral choices made. Certain gaps in the argumentation referring to the protection of the weak and vulnerable indicate that it is not possible to present a

198 Emily Jackson, John Keown, *Debating Euthanasia*, (Hart Publishing, 2012), 37.

fully rational explanation for the limits of autonomy. Rather, it is simply a rhetorical device to illustrate the choice made, which is after all the moral choice par excellence. In these cases, therefore, the Court translates concern for the common good – what is good for us but for moral reasons – into empirical language; social realities and a matter of public interest.[199]

Bibliography

Bortz, Walter M. "The trajectory of dying. Functional status in the last year of life." *Journal of American Geriatric Society* 38 (1990): 146–150.

Brown, Teneille Ruth. "Medical futility and religious free exercise." *First Amendment Law Review* 15 (2016): 43–95.

Coggon, John. "Ignoring the moral and intellectual shape of the law after bland: The unintended side-effect of a sorry compromise." *Legal Studies* 27(1) (2007): 110–125.

Dougherty, Charles J. "The common good, terminal illness and euthanasia." *Issues in Law and Medicine* 9(2) (1993–1994): 151–165.

Freeman, Michael. "Denying death its dominion: Thoughts on the dianne pretty case." *Medical Law Review* 10(3) (2002): 245–270.

Gerards, Janneke. "Margin of appreciation and incrementalism in the case law of the European Court of Human Rights." *Human Rights Law Review* 18(3) (2018): 495–515.

Gorsuch, Neil M. "Right to assisted suicide and euthanasia." *Harvard Journal of Law & Public Policy* 23(3) (2000): 599–710.

Heywood, Rob and Alexandra Mullock. "The value of life in English law: Revered but not sacred?" *Legal Studies* 36(4) (2016): 658–682.

Insa, Francisco and Pablo Requena Meana. "Is medical futility an ethical or clinical concept?" *National Catholic Bioethics Quarterly* 2 (2017): 261–273.

Jackson, Emily and John Keown. *Debating Euthanasia*. Hart Publishing, 2012.

Jecker, Nancy S. and Robert A. Pearlman. "Medical futility: Who decides?" *Archives of Internal Medicine* 152 (1992): 1140–1144.

Kamisar, Yale. "Some non-religious views against proposed mercy-killing legislation." *Minnesota Law Review* 42 (1958): 969–1042.

Keown, John. *Euthanasia, Ethics and Public Policy – An Argument against Legalisation*. Cambridge University Press, 2002.

Keown, John. *The Law and Ethics of Medicine: Essays on the Inviolability of Human Life*. Oxford University Press, 2012.

Lee, Robert G. and Derek Morgan. "Regulating risk society: Stigmata cases, scientific citizenship & (and) biomedical diplomacy." *Sydney Law. Review*, 297 (2001): 297–318.

Martin, Stevie. *Assisted Suicide and the European Convention on Human Rights*. Routledge, 2021.

McCloskey, Bernard. "The right to life – Human rights at British and death." *Commonwealth Law Bulletin* 37(2) (2011): 219–240.

199 Ibidem, p. 159.

Mohindra, Raj K. "Medical futility: A conceptual model." *Journal of Medical Ethics* 33 (2007): 71–75.
Pedain, Antje. "The human rights dimension of the diane pretty case." *Cambridge Law Journal* 62(1) (2003): 181–206.
Sartori, Daria. "End-of-life issues and the European Court of Human Rights. The value of personal autonomy within a 'proceduralized' review." *Questions of International Law* 52 (2018): 23–43.
Schauer, Frederick. "Slippery slopes." *Harvard Law Review* 99(2) (1985): 361–383.
Taylor, Helen J. "What are the "best interests"? A critical evaluation of 'best interest' decision-making in clinical practice." *Medical Law Review* 24(2) (2016): 176–205.
Wada, Emily. "A pretty picture: The margin of appreciation and the right to assisted suicide." *Loyola of Los Angeles International and Comparative Law Review* 27(2) (2005): 281–287.
Williams, Glanville. *The Sanctity of Life and the Criminal Law*. Alfred A. Knopf, 1957.
Zannoni, Diego. "Right or duty to live? Euthanasia and assisted suicide from the perspective of the European convention on human rights." *European Journal of Legal* Studies 12(2) (2020): 181–212.

Conclusion

On the importance of argumentation

Legal practitioners tend to treat judicial reasoning as pronouncements governed by rules of logic and designated paths of interpretation aimed at indicating the rationale behind a decision based on legal norms. Its goal is to indicate the most logical way of solving a conflict or a problem, that is, the way that is best embedded in the system of legal rules. As Oliver Wendell Holmes wrote:

> the training of lawyers is a training in logic. The processes of analogy, discrimination, and deduction are those in which they are most at home. The language of judicial decision is mainly the language of logic. And the logical method and form flatter that longing for certainty and for repose which is in every human mind.[1]

And this is also how we used to approach the judicial reasoning contained in the decisions of the European Court of Human Rights. However, a closer inspection of the structure and content of the argumentation contained therein in the cases discussed in our book reveals that under the layer of established tools of interpretation and logic used by the ECtHR, there also lies another sphere of reasoning, and the tools employed perform functions other than interpretation.

The choice of cases detailed in this book relates to the limits of life, that is, the good protected at the highest level by law and in accordance with cultural or religious dictates, and fundamentally excluded from permissible human interference. These boundaries are drawn in the light of the conflicting exercise of the right to decide about oneself or one's life in the context of having offspring. The collision makes it perfectly clear how much the establishment of boundaries – or even the indication that they will not be drawn – eludes logical

1 Oliver Wendell Holmes, "The path of the law." (originally: 1897 *Harvard Law Review* 10, in: *Judges on Judging*, ed. David M. O'Brien, (CQ Press, 2004), 54.

DOI: 10.4324/9781003375999-7

inference based solely on legal norms. For these are cases in which it is apparent that, as the previously cited Holmes wrote further:

> certainty generally is illusion, and repose is not the destiny of man. Behind the logical forms lies a judgment as to relative worth and importance of competing legislative grounds, often an inarticulate and unconscious judgment, it is true, and yet the very root and nerve of the whole proceeding.[2]

Precisely, the rationalisation – that is, presenting by means of logic and interpretation – of arguments of ethical nature or, more commonly, the refusal to take a clear position on the content of rights in the face of a conflict of values seem to be the key objective in the observed ways of reasoning.

Certain regularities can be found in the analysed judgments, both in terms of the manner of conducting the argumentation and the intended effect of a given mode of argumentation. In the broadest terms, they aim at two objectives: either to avoid pronouncements on the substantive content of the right to self-determination of its private life or the right to life, or to affirm the admissibility of a limitation of these rights on the grounds of a legitimate aims defined *de novo* for the special purposes of those cases by the Court. The Court generally tends to avoid presenting an assessment based on value judgments and ultimately on the preference for one of the values. Accordingly, given the high moral sensitivity of the issues under consideration, the Court sometimes "obfuscates" the unambiguous meaning of the decision by means of argumentative devices. In other cases, the ways of reasoning used focus on the opposite: they strengthen the argumentation based solely on logic and the search for the meaning of norms, appealing to the world of social practice and the projection of the development of human attitudes, but at the same time appealing to the world of values. The means employed by the Court in such situations must be very persuasive, often referring to the non-legal sphere and sometimes used in unexpected contexts.

Irrespective of the fact that the Court avoids taking a definitive stance on moral issues, it employs legal and non-legal reasoning in the cases we have examined to substantiate its rulings, stemming from an ingrained universal social sensibility. Our book is an attempt to shed some light on this argumentation. We tried to expose the Courts' aims: convincing the audience of the rightness of the decision and to present the sphere of ethical assessments, frequently based on compassion and concern for shaping social attitudes, and difficult to express in the language of law. The Court rationalises and strives to encapsulate within the structure of judicial reasoning issues that fall outside its scope, sometimes making judgments of a moral nature, although this word is rarely used in the analysed justifications.

2 Ibidem.

At the same time, the Court's actions have an effect that cannot be compared with that of any other court and the ECtHR is fully aware of this. Although the applicant's individual case is to be decided, when it makes the point in *Pretty v. UK*, it does state at the same time that

> judgments issued in individual cases establish precedents albeit to a greater or lesser extent and a decision in this case could not, either in theory or practice, be framed in such a way as to prevent application in later cases.

In doing so, it expresses concern for the future effects of its possible ruling, which may affect the content of other judicial rulings. When, on the other hand, it points out that the British law penalising assisted suicide was designed to safeguard life by protecting the weak and vulnerable and that it is the State's task to assess the risks of potential abuse, it also expresses concern that its decision should not have the effect of disregarding or appearing to disregard such risks. It thus refers to the universal effect of creating undesirable social attitudes following its decision, although such an outcome is, after all, remote and goes well beyond the dispute subject to adjudication. The immediate consequence of the judgment is just a small fragment – the beginning of what the judgment entails, a cornerstone in the construction of the social effect of social, cultural meanings and attitudes. The message contained in judicial reasoning must therefore be expressed with great care, and the Court is aware of the indirect effect it produces. Therefore, in the judgments under review, the Court is very prudent in its statements, often using phrases that do not predetermine its position in any way for the future. In the *Pretty v. UK* case the Court stated that it was "not prepared to exclude that this constitutes an interference with her right to respect for private life as guaranteed under Article 8 § 1 of the Convention."[3] It has ruled similarly in other decisions, such as *Boso v. Italy*, where the Court considered that it was not required to determine whether the foetus may qualify for protection under the first sentence of Article 2. These are examples of such formulations, which do not exclude the approval of the claims raised by the parties, but also do not resolve anything. In this way, the Court, with extreme prudence and full awareness of the effect of all its assertions – and not only of the decisions themselves – seeks to formulate an assessment on the content and scope of the rights and claims of the applicants in such sensitive cases that will not preclude other outcomes that can be reached in the future.

Our study aimed to identify recurring patterns of argumentation used by the ECtHR in its case law with a view to persuading the addressee of a decision or judgment. While describing their relation to different methods of

3 Pretty v. UK, par. 67.

interpretation (classic as well as those specific for human rights law), it has to be said that they are of dual nature.

Some of them are based on methods or other interpretative devices. The best example is the tool of the margin of appreciation, which is frequently employed by the Court. Doubts concerning its application (resulting from the lack of its definition, of clear criteria of application, effects or type of cases where it should be used) – repeatedly cited in the literature on the subject – mean that, in our opinion, this device plays more of an argumentative than an interpretative role. This is well illustrated by the decisions handed down in cases concerning the admissibility of abortion, in which the subject of the margin of appreciation evolved over the years. The Court thus used this construct to present its current view of the case rather than to interpret the content of the Convention norms.

However, the Court also relies on other ways of reasoning, indirectly related to interpretative tools. Among these, we can distinguish the procedural and incremental arguments most frequently reiterated in the reviewed cases, intended to argue that the case is decided in compliance with all legal requirements and at the same time convincingly constructing a new substance of the rights guaranteed under the Convention. However, the Court also employs alternative tools, especially in combination with recourse to the concept of groups of persons who deserve special protection, which, in our view, are extremely important and categorised as teleological tools.

Thus, the hypothesis we put forward in Chapter 2, stating that whenever we deal with the Court's judgments we will be confronted with two levels of terminological concepts: traditional methods of interpretation and repetitive patterns (ways) of argumentation aimed at convincing the audience of the validity of the decision-should be considered proven. However, the hypothesis is made more precise by indicating that there may be a more far-reaching relationship between interpretation and argumentation, since both aim *de facto* at extracting from the legal norms in force the definitive substance of an adjudication in an individual case.

Argumentative tools

The focus of our work was to isolate recurring patterns or ways of argumentation used by the ECtHR in its case law with a view to persuading the addressee of a decision or judgment, regardless of whether they are simultaneously used as interpretative tools or constitute separate argumentative constructs. In our book, we focused on distinguishing the following recurrent tools of argumentation: arguments referring to authority (arguments appealing to external [non-ECHR] sources of law; margin of appreciation; and arguments appealing to epistemic authority, such as the knowledge of medical practitioners), deontological argumentation (incrementalism, proceduralism, as well as plasticity and assimilation of concepts used to describe and qualify behaviour) as well as teleological argumentation, consisting in the examination and evaluation of secondary effects, like the socially unfavourable phenomena resulting from the exercise/non-exercise of rights or freedoms.

This division is largely based on methods observed and described in rhetoric, that is, the art of argumentation. It is not easy to extract and describe each of the individual tools of argumentation used by the ECtHR. This is due, for example, to the fact that the Court uses the same conceptual grid regardless of the arguments it chooses to use.[4] For example, in *Evans v. UK*, the ECtHR focused on proceduralisation as the main axis of argumentation, while it "did not abandon" statements referring to the balancing of conflicting interests, which is characteristic of substantial review. Moreover, the difficulty in analysing the tools of argumentation adopted by the Court is increased by the fact that the arguments intermingle. This is clearly evident in the euthanasia cases, particularly *Lambert v. France*, and in the cases relating to abortion, in particular *A., B. and C. v. Ireland*. There, the Court gives a detailed account of the legislative work that resulted in the adoption of specific set of regulations that found application in the situation of the applicants. It provides a detailed description of the procedure and the position taken by the legitimate body, namely the parliament. On the one hand, the Court thus demonstrates the State's compliance with its procedural obligations by verifying the quality and grounding of the legislative decisions in widely held ethical views by examining the course of the legislative process. On the other hand, this argumentation is functionally similar to the use of the margin of appreciation and produces the same effect, such as fostering the conviction in the recipients that the solution of the problem made by the State was fully legitimate and that the verification carried out by the Court can only confirm its correctness and its entrenchment in the socially documented conviction of its (local) rightness.

In the cases we analysed in this study, the Court makes by far the most frequent use of ways of reasoning based on proceduralisation, incrementalism, margin of appreciation, and on appeals to the need to look after the interests of vulnerable persons.

These ways of reasoning can be distinguished, yet it should be noted that they are usually used in combination, which, in our opinion, enhances their argumentative effectiveness. Thus, they usually appear together in the pair of incrementalism and proceduralisation. Consequently, by indicating positive obligations, proceduralisation serves to indicate what elements constitute a right guaranteed under the Convention, often in a broader dimension than the case at hand. Hence, incrementalism is the mirror image of proceduralisation. This is true both in end-of-life cases (constant expansion of the catalogue of State's obligations to ensure the right to die with dignity) and abortion cases (gradual shaping of the scope of a pregnant woman's rights by assessing the State's legal framework and decision-making process). Building an argument

4 Cf. i.a. Bomhoff, Zucca, "Evans v. UK." 430.

based on the margin of appreciation serves as another example. This tool itself would not have such a persuasive effect were it not for the appropriately chosen subject matter, and this is often defined by the use of plasticity of terms. We encounter this type of argumentation, among others, in all cases concerning the admissibility of abortion, in which the importance of using specific expressions to describe a pregnant woman (*mother, mother-to-be*) and a foetus (*unborn child*) is fully evident.

Why does the ECtHR opt for certain ways of reasoning?

As in relation to methods and tools of interpretation, the Court does not follow a single logic for selecting argumentative tools when considering its cases. One can share the view expressed in the literature in another context that "it seems that the Court relies on a 'pick and choose' approach, selecting those arguments that it considers useful in reasoning its judgments."[5] It must be remembered, however, that this apparent lack of coherence should be viewed in the context of achieving the primary goal of the reasoning, which is convincing the audience of the correctness of the decision.

In choosing particular tools of argumentation, the Court is mindful of the necessity to achieve its persuasive objectives in relation to particular audiences. Thus, balancing the argumentation through the use of various tools is one way of persuading governments that the ECtHR operates within its remit and does not exceed it, which in turn is essential to induce them to respect the judgments.[6] This effect is successfully achieved through the use of procedural argumentation (such as cases concerning access to abortion, like *Tysiąc v. Poland*, where the Court assessed the fulfilment of State's positive obligations, examining the applicable law and assessing the decision-making process in relation to the applicant's right to privacy), at least in principle perceived as more neutral (because it does not directly refer to the substantive content of the law), and incrementalism, which aims to ensure predictability of decisions (as in the *R.R v. Poland* case, where the Court formulated new procedural obligations that fit in with pregnant women's right to privacy). At the same time, however, the Court reasons in such a way as to avoid the accusation of imposing its worldview on States, precisely by not using the premise of public morality and by not making explicit statements on morally sensitive issues.

Secondly, the chosen ways of reasoning are intended to weaken the criticism of the judgment by unsatisfied public opinion and the applicants themselves. A special role is played here by incrementalism, which is widely used

5 This view is expressed by Gerards in relation to proceduralisation tactics, however we consider it to be relevant to the issue of reasoning as a whole. See: Gerards, "Precedural Review." 159.

6 As to the allegation that one of the challenges faced by the ECtHR is the constant need to answer the question "whether it has gone outside (its) area of restraint." cf. Arden, "An English judge." 29.

especially in cases where the ruling does not confirm any infringement of law and therefore is not to the liking of the applicants. For although judgments do not always uphold the claims of the applicants, they often contain formulations through which the Court decodes the content of the given norm for the future and which meets the needs required by the applicants and people in a situation similar to them. Such an aim was realised when the Court in the case *Evans v. UK* established the existence of a right to become genetic parents while simultaneously not finding the violation of that right in the adjudicated case. A similar role is played by pragmatic arguments appealing to the "right to travel" present in cases concerning euthanasia, medically assisted procreation, as well as in abortion cases. The "right to travel," seen as a sign of the exercise of rights outside the country and noticed by the Court in all the categories of cases discussed, is used in a subsidiary way as an argumentative tool, although it is difficult to classify it conclusively. This argument is hybrid in nature; it is, in a sense, the reverse of the margin of appreciation, but it serves an essentially teleological function, drawing the audience's attention to the fact that a right – despite certain constraints in the country to which the complaint relates – can be exercised in an easy and accessible manner. Thus, the violation of the complainant's right is of lesser importance. This type of reasoning resonates in cases *A., B. and C. v. Ireland* and *H.S. and Others v. Austria*.

The third extremely important persuasive aim pursued by the Court by means of its reasoning is the choice of such ways of argumentation that are in line with the Court's role as the guardian of human rights in that they, on the one hand, protect minorities against arbitrary decisions of the majority and, on the other, aim at shaping certain social attitudes. In view of the small number of judgments in which the Court decided in favour of the applicants in matters falling within the scope of the analysis, there are few compelling arguments that fulfil this first objective. On the other hand, incrementalism and teleological arguments used by the Court play an important role in shaping social attitudes.

Moreover, the choice of argumentation is not without significance for the judges themselves. Our analysis confirmed that focusing on procedural argumentation – perceived as being of a more "neutral" character – makes it possible to seek a positive reception from States, but also to find consensual solutions shared by all the judges in situations where there is a serious risk of an ideological discord. It can be assumed that it is precisely the procedural approach that has allowed unanimous decisions in many cases concerning assisted suicide (*Pretty v. the UK, Haas v. Switzerland, Koch v. Germany*), as well as in a number of cases concerning the withholding of life support (*Ada Rossi v. Italy, Sanles Sanles v. Spain*). A vestige of such a quest for compromise by way of a procedural approach can be found in the separate opinion of Judge Casadevall in *Gard v. the United Kingdom*, in which the judge indicates "difficulties with the part of the Court judgment," in which it denies the need for the child patient's application to be heard separately from the mother's plea. In turn, the unusually strong dissenting opinion in *Lambert v. France* fundamentally undermined such an approach as one avoiding consideration of the substantive right to life protection.

Consensualism – universalism

At the same time, the Court's case law attempts to find a consensual vision of what the States subordinate to the jurisdiction of the ECtHR are prepared to consider as the content of protected rights. This is not an easy task, especially when it is necessary to move from the stage of general formulations to resolving concrete doubts as to the scope of the human rights, and especially collisions between them. This becomes most difficult when the issues to be resolved are worldview-related and deal with such a sensitive subject as life and the attitude towards it. It is almost impossible to find agreement on matters so fundamentally moral, nor is it possible to conduct an argument about them which would be subject to the rules of logic and the interpretation of norms.

The ways of reasoning intend to make it possible for the Court to convince its audience, and this audience is heterogeneous. In the cases discussed in this study, one can easily see the Court's efforts to find a platform acceptable to the diverse audience, both individuals and States. One such effort involves pointing out that, while it is true that an activity cannot be performed in the State party's territory, it can be exercised by the applicant outside its borders. Although this reasoning is only mentioned in the justifications, it is an important element in seeking compromise where there is none. An excellent example illustrating such an endeavour is the Court's clear position on the possibility to undergo a specific medical procedure abroad if it is impossible to do so domestically (such as in *S.H. v. Austria, A., B. and C. v. Ireland*). Undoubtedly, this argumentative device is aimed at softening the perception of judgments in the eyes of the public in cases where the Court did not uphold the arguments of applicants in an extremely distressing personal situation. The purpose of the argument is to indicate that a change in the position of the Court may be expected in the future, and additionally that the judgment itself does not prevent the realisation of the individual's interests abroad if such opportunity exists.

Employing a particular method of reasoning may be conditioned by the fact that it is individual governments that resort to a particular type of argumentation, often doing so on the basis of relevant decisions of domestic courts.[7] In this regard, the role of the UK and Irish courts has been particularly significant in medically assisted procreation as well as end-of-life or abortion cases. They have made it clear that certain adjudications remain the domain of the domestic legislature and not the court and, in doing so, have clearly prompted the ECtHR to take a procedural approach to the case (such as in *Evans v. UK, A., B. and C. v. Ireland*). Similarly, the extensive reasoning of the French State in

7 See, for instance, Nussberger, "Procedural Review." 176.

the *Lambert* case has resulted in the adjudication being justified by reference entirely to procedural arguments and appeal to epistemic authority positions.

In the context of this observation and given the diversity of the arguments put forward by the States, it seems that the ways of reasoning may also carry national overtones. Thus, in the case law developed on the basis of applications concerning the right to assisted suicide, the protection of the weak and vulnerable resounds clearly as an argument taken from the rulings of domestic courts (*Pretty v. the United Kingdom* and *Nicklinson and Lamb v. the United Kingdom*). Similarly, the ruling in *A., B. and C. v. Ireland* makes explicit reference to the well-established position of Irish society on the termination of pregnancy. It thus upholds a certain legal position and scope of the right to abortion, although the same scope and content of the right to privacy does not necessarily apply in other cases.

A crucial role in the search for compromise and in finding a universal standard involves incrementalism, which would allow for identification of new elements protected within the framework guaranteed by the Convention. It consists in developing the scope of the right, even without finding its infringement in a specific case. Under this way of reasoning, the Court and the domestic courts engage in a complex and dynamic dialogue, seeking to define mutually approvable positions in all categories of cases discussed in this book. Development of the scope of a pregnant woman's right to privacy is clearly demonstrated – especially in abortion cases. Relevant formulations of this right are also found in cases where there is no substantive resolution. A good example is the case of *Boso v. Italy*, in which the Court deemed the provisions allowing abortion on the grounds of risk to the woman's health to be in compliance with the provisions of the Convention, although the case concerned the rights of the father (which the Court did not find violated). And, in *A., B. and C v. Ireland*, in relation to applicants A. and B., the Court found that the prohibition of the abortion for reasons of health or well-being leads to the interference with their right to respect for their private lives,[8] although, in the opinion of the Court, the interference in these cases remained within the limits of admissibility. In the case of *R.R. v. Poland*, the Court – as if on a side note – defined the right to privacy anew besides the existing elements of the right to privacy, holding that the notion of private life applies to decision either to have or not to have a child or to become parents. This is a conclusion taken from a case dealing with issues other than access to abortion.[9] Confirmation of the existence of such a right in this case appears to be a step towards extending the right to respect for private life in the context of the decision to terminate a pregnancy, although it did not form the basis of the ruling on the applicant's complaints.[10] Again, the use of incrementalism and the gradual development

8 A., B. and C. v. Ireland, par. 216.
9 Evans v. the United Kingdom, par. 71.
10 R.R. v. Poland, par. 180.

of the scope of the right to privacy in this aspect is well illustrated in cases involving the right to die with dignity. The rulings in *Pretty v. the UK* and *Hass v. Switzerland* are good examples of this.

In the vast majority of cases examined in the book,[11] the extension of the scope to include the new element did not lead to the conclusion that there had been a substantive infringement of the right. This made it possible to prevent conflict on the grounds of the established scope. However, these statements were made and constitute the body of jurisprudence – they therefore provide the foundation for further proceedings, where they are expected to be cited, also for the purpose of establishing an infringement of law, such as in a much more categorical context.

Therefore, this way of reasoning is particularly indicative of the Court's intention and aim, which is to shape the justifications dialogically and to gradually develop the meaning of the rights whose scope it decides upon. The Court is aware that its statements are intended not only to respect socially established attitudes and approaches, but also to shape them among a broader audience. Therefore, it does not make statements concerning world views; it does not value them, that is, it does not question or single out any of them. This is very evident when it comes to the issue of abortion, which clearly has divided European countries into two – albeit obviously not equally sized – camps. Instead, it attempts to address the reasons and procedures that led to the contested regulations, avoiding statements about their moral foundations and merely indicating their existence. Respect for the ethical order presented and protected by the domestic legislation and decisions of the authorities requires the initiation of a dialogue by finding a platform on which the dispute will be possible without criticism or questioning of the moral assumptions themselves. This approach makes it possible to equip the recipient with the attitude of commitment to look for a common consensual solution to the practical problem, and thus to the underlying dilemma and conflict of values.

The margin of appreciation, in turn, is meant to leave room for differences where agreement is not necessary. In fact, the margin of appreciation is used precisely as an instrument to show that the agreement as to the content of Article 8 and Article 2 of the Convention – two provisions most frequently referred to in the respective applications – is not absolutely needed, and that changes in the interpretation of these provisions are permissible. The margin of appreciation in respect of the cases in question is no longer just a way of interpreting the Convention norms and searching for their scope, but a strategy for convincing people of the position adopted in the adjudication. This aim is especially subordinate to the definition of the object of the margin. In cases concerning the admissibility of abortion, it is easy to see how the subject

11 Still, it must be added that in a small number of cases discussed in the book, the emergence of a new element of a right protected under the Convention led to establishing an infringement (Dickson v. UK, Mennesson v. France).

of the Court's application of this device is changing, along with the notion of consensus among European states, which constitutes its element. In our book we identify three subjects of margin of appreciation in abortion cases: the first one, concerning the will of the parties to consider the foetus as a subject of the right to life (cases decided by the Commission: *Brüggemann and Scheuten v. Germany, X v. the UK, H. v. Norway*); the second, pertaining to the assessment of when life actually begins (*A., B. and C. v. Ireland*, the meaning of the concept drawn from *Vo v. France)*; and the third, concerning the freedom of the State to balance the interests of the woman and foetus, implicit in the wording of public interest (*A., B. and C. v. Ireland*, further developed in *R.R v. Poland* and *P. and S. v. Poland*). This noticeable evolution indicates the subordination of the use of the margin of appreciation device to serve rhetorical and argumentative purposes. When properly applied, the margin of appreciation tool makes it possible to demonstrate, wherever needed, that there is no need for the Court's interference, and the Court's declared "moral sensitivity" of the decided cases as an exposure to worldview and moral issues is, as it were, of primary importance to the subsequent findings and provides an excellent context for establishing the object of the States' discretion. The Court stops short of delving into the structure of either the moral or the legal conflict that may arise.

Equally creative is the Court's treatment of the argument concerning the lack of consensus at the level of the States on the assumptions concerning both the legal solutions adopted and their axiological foundations, such as the fundamental element conditioning the granting of the margin of appreciation. The various ways of applying it, as shown here, are subordinated to the objective of deciding on an infringement of the right to privacy. Indeed, it is no longer an instrument to interpret the Convention norms, but to justify that they mean different things in different States, which in turn serves to argue the reason why the Court did not determine any violation.

Worldview neutrality – pragmatism

What draws attention in the cases we are discussing is the almost complete lack of appeal to moral considerations. The Court does not present its clear position in relation to the ethical aspects of the decided cases, which would be possible if the legitimacy of introducing limitations to the rights and freedoms of individuals in the analysed areas was examined against the premise of morality. Nevertheless, its position in this respect can be read indirectly from the arguments used. The consequence of resorting to some of them is that the ECtHR makes significant moral and ethical pronouncements. Others, on the other hand, aim at avoiding such a statement or presenting it as narrowly as possible.

It is true that in a number of cases the Court does acknowledge that the case concerns a particularly sensitive issue, but in none of the analysed rulings did it explain what moral sensitivity would mean. It thus avoids explicitly identifying the moral dimension of the case and gives itself the option of making partial pronouncements. In this context, it expresses its approval for example, for: a) the use of assisted procreation techniques abroad, which are not permitted in Austria for moral reasons (*S.H. and Others v. Austria*); b) surrogacy, which is *de facto* prohibited in France – also for moral reasons – by requiring that its legal effects be taken into account in the domestic legal system, provided that it has been carried out lawfully abroad (*Mennesson v. France*); and c) the protection of the potential for life of embryos – which clearly demonstrates a moral stance – by accepting domestic regulations prohibiting their transfer for the purposes of scientific research (*Parrillo v. Italy*). Similarly, in cases involving allegations of inadmissibility of abortions, the Court does not pronounce on the permissibility of abortion. Instead, it confines itself to acknowledging – as regards Irish cases – the entrenchment of the protection afforded under Irish law to the right to life of the unborn which was based on profound moral values concerning the nature of life which are reflected in the stance of the majority of the Irish people while at the same time accepts that domestic law allows for performing the abortion abroad and even formulates certain information obligations upon authorities in this regard.[12] In these matters it avoids setting a moral minimum on a general level at all costs.

A similar outcome is reached after delving deeply into domestic legal arrangements, procedures and decision-making processes. The Court in some of these cases – such as *A., B. and C. v. Ireland* and *Lambert v. France* – reproduces and analyses with great insight and care not only the regulations involved, but the process that led to their adoption, the rationale and arguments of the drafters, the consultations, as well as the administrative, medical and judicial procedures applied with respect to the applicants. The Court thus focuses on the procedural side, examining decision-making at the State level and – although only to the extent of examining the decision-making procedure – with regard to the applicant's individual case. Such an analysis is intended to examine whether the law and decision-making process are designed to optimise protection of substantive rights. Ultimately, however, it usually brings about the possibility of adjudication and justification without the need for verification of the substantive content of the applicant's rights. By replacing such an evaluation with reconstruction of the legislative process in particular and by indicating its democratic legitimacy (*A., B. and C v. Ireland*) in the views of the competent authorities (*Lambert v. France*), as well as by the creation of a catalogue of positive obligations, that is to say, an indication of efforts seeking to create the conditions for the exercise of the rights guaranteed by the Convention within the framework of the State (such as with *Koch v. Germany* and *Haas v. Switzerland*), it is often possible to give the impression that the evaluation is objective, although in fact it is only a partial response to the claims raised in the applications.

12 A., B. and C. v. Ireland, par. 222.

A fundamentally pragmatic approach is also presented by the Court with respect to the distinctive tool of argumentation based on the margin of appreciation. In a certain special way, this mechanism is complemented by another construct, its reverse, such as the phenomenon of migration for the purpose of realisation of certain demanded rights in European countries other than the country of origin, as observed and, according to the Court, relevant for the protection of Convention rights. Abortion tourism is a good example of this because it leads to the creation of a coherent and repeatable concept of the "right to travel" – that is, accepting the practice of undergoing a particular medical procedure abroad (*A., B. and C. v. UK*). This reasoning is also present in other cases discussed in the work (*H.S. and Others v. Austria*). Arguing through the right to travel is an excellent means of withholding a finding as to the merits when the right can be exercised elsewhere. The effect of the dependence of the scope of the right on the place where it is exercised is discreetly omitted here, yet the effect of the actual possibility to benefit from a broader scope than in the country of origin is noticed. This is a purely pragmatic solution, referring to the actual effects of and opportunities to exercise the right, and not to its substantive content.

Pragmatism is most prominently used by the Court when defining the permissible limits of exercising the right, that is, when delving into the substantive assessment. In some cases concerning assisted suicide (*Pretty v. UK* and *Nicklinson and Lamb v. UK*) and medically assisted procreation (*S. H. and Others v. Austria*), under the influence of the State party's actions and arguments, it outlines the limits of the realisation of the right under Article 8 of the Convention, indicating the restriction of the protection of the rights and freedoms of others as the legitimate aim. This is perfectly understandable from the neutral worldview perspective and the liberal doctrine underlying the axiological system of conventional protection. According to classic liberal approach, only harm to another person can constitute a reason for restricting freedom.[13] The choice of this legitimate aim is therefore the only one that can be taken into account in cases concerning such a fundamental right as the right to private life. It is important that in abortion cases the question of the balance between the rights of the woman and the foetus has been left out of the assessment due to the axiological entanglement of the dispute about the priority of their respective goods. The cases have been decided from the perspective of the fulfilment of positive obligations. Conversely, in the two remaining categories – the cases of termination of life and medically assisted procreation – although it is difficult to find those who, by exercising their right to suicide or by medically assisted parenthood, directly cause, or are even likely to cause, harm to other persons, the Court decided to adjudicate those cases with the use of the legitimate aim of "protection of others." In order to introduce such a legitimate aim, the Court is forced to define a group of

13 John Stuart Mill, *On Liberty*, (London 1859).

individuals who are hypothetically threatened by the exercise of the right under Article 8. This is possible by combining the unquestionable and strongest premise of protecting the rights of others with resorting to an argumentative strategy of considering the possible negative social effects of the decision. By using such reasoning about the undesirable future implications of certain decisions, including the development of potentially unwelcome human attitudes and behaviour under the influence of authorising a particular outcome, the Court effectively persuades the need to limit the exercise of the right to privacy by creating an image of the threats faced by the community and especially its most vulnerable members. This persuasion evades the risks of ethical evaluation and the charge of moral majoritarianism in deciding on the limitations. It makes it possible to abandon ethical appeals altogether. It makes use of purely practical considerations, common sense and appeals to the emotional side. It is a question of concern for those who require it, and who, for particular reasons, are described by the Court as vulnerable to the possible abuse of rights that might arise if the applicants' claims were upheld. The ECtHR followed this line of reasoning, among others, in *Pretty v. UK*, sharing and reiterating the reasoning of the UK court and drawing attention to its precedent-setting nature and the necessary caution when making decisions that will inevitably result in certain legal, but also by extension social consequences. It thus refers to social practice, pointing out the fear of decisions and of harm to people which may potentially be enforced as a result of the creation of a certain social attitude of permitting behaviour which may expose the weak to take desperate and detrimental steps due to the impact and pressure of that attitude.

In fact, the Court thus makes the public interest and the good of the entire community tangible, although it almost never referred to this category explicitly in the cases in question, since it is a concept that falls outside the catalogue of legitimate aims contained in Article 8 of the Convention. Moreover, even an indirect reference to the public interest, such as the good of the community as a whole, would certainly give rise to accusations of moral majoritarianism – imposing the will of the majority on the individual – thus depriving him or her of the exercise of certain right. On the same grounds, there is no place for morals, public morals, and other goods and values, as they are not comparable to the human right to self-determination. But this one principle implies duty of a very wide scope which is sometimes difficult to be intuitively determined. Here, the Court ventures into the territory of pragmatic but also highly hypothetical assessments.

This is an invaluable argumentative tool, although, as indicated in the relevant literature[14] and discussed in our study, it raises numerous questions.

14 Bossuyt, "Categorical Rights and Vulnerable Groups." 717–8, 726–34, M. O'Boyle, "The notion of 'vulnerable groups' in the case law of the European Court of Human Rights." Report delivered for *Conference on the Constitutional Protection of vulnerable groups: a judicial dialogue*, Santiago Chile 2015, Peroni, Timmer, "Vulnerable Groups." 1056–85.

Hence, axiological and dogmatic doubts are raised by the hypothetical character of the identification of the group deserving protection special or juxtaposing it with the specific interests of the applicant, as well as by the heterogeneity of the group deserving protection. The only thing they have in common is the exposure to harm by the possible recognition of the applicants' claims and ad hoc creation of such a group for the purpose of persuasion, which is difficult to conceal. However, this device opens the way for appeals to common sense, indicating purely practical and plausible outcomes of possible decisions, as well as appeals to collective responsibility and a sense of concern, which is very convincing. On the other hand, it allows for an argument to be carried out on completely morally neutral ground, omitting ethical considerations through pragmatism and references to social practice.

This observation leads us to formulate a conclusion, or rather a supplement thereto, about the replacement of morality by the concept of human rights in the contemporary legal discourse. In current legal discussions on the subject, human rights have replaced morality and refer to moral theory, sometimes expressing the nostalgia of present-day society for lost moral values[15] it pretends to substitute the moral and ethical discourse. Yet under conditions of pluralism of values and attitudes, as well as the firmly established liberal view of human beings and their rights as moral claims and moral entitlements possessed by persons,[16] it is extremely difficult to adjudicate in situations of conflict of rights at the normative level. If the good means respect for and protection of individual rights – and these are universal, innate and unalienable, being derived from the human dignity and worth of every human being – the formulation of permissible limits of human behaviour encounters formidable obstacles.

The only logic that can be followed is that of the fear of harming another human being – this creates a normative system based on the personal responsibility of living in the community with others under the basic moral rule: to behave in a way that is not harmful to others. And this single principal system is evident in cases described in our book, even if sometimes it is not explicitly articulated. Thus, instead of the concept of moral limitation of the right to decide about life and death, we are given the solution that sets limits to the right to self-determination due to the necessity to protect the rights of others.

Other ways of reasoning singled out in our work (argument from authority or plasticity of concepts) have merely an ornamental or auxiliary character in the cases discussed herein. When assessed separately they do not produce a noticeable effect in the form of creating reasoning that independently persuades

15 Haule, "Some reflections." 367–95, 368; Frederic Megret, "International human rights law theory." in *Research Handbook on the Theory and History of International Law*, ed. Alexander Orakhelashvili, (Edward Elgar Publishing, 2020), 168.

16 Richard Wasserstrom, "Rights, human rights, and racial discrimination." *Journal of Philosophy* 61 (20) (1964): 628–41.

to the given decision. Undoubtedly, however, their use together with the appropriate selection of documents, positions or words can perfectly strengthen the intended effect. In the field of medically assisted procreation, this can be seen in the Court's use of reasoning based on the reference to binding and non-binding acts of international law, which allowed to strengthen, for instance, the thesis on the considerable liberty of states in shaping the adopted solutions. In the context of abortion, this is particularly evident in the use of arguments based on the plasticity of concepts, which allowed the Court to avoid emotional involvement through the use of words such as "mother" or "unborn child", in favour of more neutral ones: "woman" and "foetus".

What do recurrent ways of reasoning mean for the human rights case law?

Our book also provides insight into something more than just reasoning in the Court's oeuvre. Certain consequences of the judgments on the substance of rights and the direction of the development of jurisprudence are outlined, and we seek to define the functions of this kind of reasoning.

Incrementalism – gradual build-up of significance, predictability of judgments

The reasoning used by the Court and drawing on incrementalism has profound implications in terms of shaping the scope of rights and freedoms and influencing States to introduce specific arrangements favourable to individuals.

As an example, we can point to the inclusion of the right to recognition of the legal bond with both the biological and the legal parent as a consequence of birth of a child by surrogacy under a contract concluded abroad in the scope of Article 8 of the Convention, starting with *Mennesson v. France*. In this particular case, the Court's pronouncement translated positively into the fate of individual applicants. From the other side, the conclusion concerning the need for States to recognise the effects of foreign surrogacy, even in the absence of authorisation of surrogacy in their own legislation,[17] has far-reaching consequences in that the Court expressed its acceptance of such procedures and obliged States to introduce practical regulations in that regard.[18]

In its reasoning in cases concerning euthanasia, the Court has incremented the right to privacy by applying the strategy of assumption as to the existence of a right to die with dignity without finding a violation of that right (*Pretty v. the UK*), or without finding substantive infringement of that right (*Haas v.*

17 Paul Beaumont, Katarina Trimmings, "The European Court of Human Rights in Paradiso and Campanelli v. Italy and the way forward for regulating cross-border surrogacy." University of Aberdeen, Working Paper no. 2017/3, p. 12, available at: www.abdn.ac.uk/law/documents/cpil%20working%20paper%20no%202017_3.pdf.

18 Ibidem, p. 11.

Switzerland). However, determinations like these are of utmost importance when it comes to shaping subsequent decisions based on the presumed scope of the right to self-determination, as well as the legal framework and decisions left to the discretion of domestic authorities. Therefore, we see a gradual shaping of the right, already referred to, albeit in the form of "even assuming" until establishment the right to *facilitate the act of suicide with dignity.*[19]

Consequently, one observable outcome of the application of this technique is the predictability of subsequent judgments, built on previously carefully constructed foundations, though without finding a violation of the disputed right (or finding violations for other reasons). In employing the incrementalism, the Court, in a way, indicates and anticipates how and where the development of the right is heading, and thus what elements are required for recognising it as worthy of protection.

Proceduralisation – meaning the right through the lenses of procedural requirements

The intensity of the ECtHR's use of procedural reasoning supports the thesis expressed in the literature that the Court is more inclined to attach value to the quality of legislative process in hard cases with a high degree of sensitivity.[20]

Argumentation referring to the assessment of the State's fulfilment of its procedural obligations comes to the fore in cases arising out of legal disputes having strong ethical undertones. At the same time, the Court grants States a wide or even very wide margin of discretion in these cases. So, it can be hypothesised that there is a strong link between proceduralisation and margin of appreciation.

The application of procedural arguments by way of examination of the fulfilment of procedural obligations (requirements) obviously leads to different outcomes. Firstly, the Court may hold the States responsible for infringements against particular rights in cases where it would not have been able to hold them responsible for a substantive violation of the right (such a conclusion is manifested in the literature in relation to procedural obligations under Articles 2 and 3), or the finding of a substantive violation would involve taking a morally conditioned position. This was the situation in the abortion-related cases (*A., B. and C. v. Ireland, Tysiąc v. Poland, R. R. v. Poland* and *P. and S. v. Poland*) and in the cases relating to assisted suicide and euthanasia (*Lambert v. France*). To date, the Court has limited itself to finding a violation of the rights guaranteed by Article 8 only in those situations where it found non-compliance with positive obligations in the area of ensuring a proper decision-making process and the possibility to appeal to a court.

19 Haas v. Switzerland, par. 61.
20 Kleinlein, "The Procedural Approach." 95.

Secondly, the Court chose to employ proceduralisation in each of the three areas examined, in cases which apparently required it to make its own in-depth balancing of the applicants' interests. There, it recognised the State's drawing of the "bright line" (the terminology explicitly used in *Evans v. UK* and referred by the Court itself to *Pretty v. UK*[21]), namely the formulation of clear legal principles, even if they do not provide for the possibility of regulating exceptional situations differently, to "serve both to produce legal certainty and to maintain public confidence in the law in a sensitive field." The protection of those values – such as certainty and confidence – was placed above the legitimacy of the Court's independent balancing of conflicting interests in the individual circumstances of cases.[22]

Accordingly, it may be concluded that the Court's use of procedural reasoning in the cases in question led to conclusions that differed from those presented in relation to the use of procedural reasoning in the overall jurisprudence. Authors argue that procedural argumentation cannot replace substantive control, serving only as an auxiliary reasoning at most.[23] By contrast, in the reviewed cases, this reasoning constituted an equally important element of the justifications. It can be pointed out, for example, that, based on the assumptions of proceduralisation, the Court has held that the fact that some legislation does not provide for the weighing of competing interests in each individual case is not per se contrary to the Convention requirements (so, for example, in *Evans v. UK* and *Pretty v. UK*).

Although there is a general perception that resorting to proceduralisation-based reasoning is of a more "neutral" character, the Court's use of procedural tactics does not always lead to smoothing the relationship between the ECtHR and the respondent State, as best exemplified by the years-long non-enforcement of abortion-related decisions against Poland. On the other hand, a mere finding of a procedural violation of the Convention may often be insufficient and disappointing for the applicant.[24] This is where the Court's conclusions, formulated using incremental arguments, can meet the expectations of applicants and persons in a similar situation.

Undoubtedly, the analysis of the judgments shows that the procedural approach has served to augment the scope of the Court's review in situations where it would grant states a wide margin of appreciation or in situations

21 Evans v. UK, par. 65 and 68 and Joint Dissenting Opinion of Judges Türmen, Tsatsa-Nikolovska, Spielmann and Ziemele, par. 1 and 8.

22 The use of the afore-mentioned formulation was suggested by the arguments of the British government, which in turn had based it on the judgment of Lord Griffitsh in the House of Lords case of *Attorney General v. Observer Ltd.* (no. 2) of 1998, compare Bomhoff, Zucca, "Evans v. UK." 439.

23 Nussberger, "Procedural Review." 174–5.

24 Nussberger, "Procedural Review." 166.

where it would be beyond the Court's competence to engage in the adjudication in the substantive aspect of the right in question.[25]

Clearly, the intensity of the use of the different types of arguments in a case – including those pertaining to procedures – will depend on the result that the Court wishes to achieve by appealing to the individual arguments. If the Court wants to redefine substantive standards, then less attention will be paid to procedural reasoning.

Meanwhile, the nature of positive obligations allows the ECtHR's judgments also to retain their subsidiary character vis-à-vis national legislative and judicial actions without substantive adjudication on end-of-life issues.[26]

Margin of appreciation – shaping the right at home

The wide margin of appreciation granted to States by the Court in cases involving moral considerations leads to the recognition and approval of a wide variety of national solutions. By means of this mode of argumentation, the Court is certainly not pursuing the aim advocated in the doctrine in respect of its jurisprudence, namely the harmonisation of law.[27]

In none of the cases reviewed, in which national legislation was called into question, did the Court find the existence of European consensus reflecting at least in principle a common moral standard. Establishing the existence of such a consensus would undoubtedly have an impact on limiting the margin of appreciation granted to those States whose legislation does not coincide with it. Granting States such a wide margin of discretion, as was done in *H.S. and Others v. Austria*, prompts the conclusion that almost any decision of the legislature, irrespective of its consistency and rationality, will fall within that margin.[28]

The reasoning used by the Court, built on references to the margin of appreciation, proves that it has accepted that States have the right to reflect certain views on moral and ethical issues in their legislation and to shape

25 Arnardóttir, "Organized Retreat." 6. An example of cases in which it would be impossible for the Court to pronounce on the merits of the case without engaging the procedural obligations approach are cases under Article 2 of the ECHR in which the circumstances leading to death occurred outside the temporal scope of the Court's competence in relation to the given country.

26 British jurisprudence takes a similar position on the scope of positive obligations, particularly in the sphere of Article 2. In the *Pretty* case, Lord Cornhill drew attention to the social and cultural contingencies and thus social relativism of positive obligations, stating that actions in the sphere of positive obligations are more judgmental, different in individual states, more dependent on the opinions and beliefs of the people and less susceptible to any universal injunction.

27 Such a postulate can be found, for instance, in Christos L. Rozakis, "The European Judge as Comparatist." *Tulane Law Review* 80(1) (2005): 257–80.

28 Cf. earlier comments on the coherence of the Austrian government's argumentation, see Hoof, Pennings, "The consequences." 667.

provisions in such a way as to be consistent with those views. The close association of the width of the margin of appreciation with the moral views of society, as was the case in *H.S. and Others v. Austria* and *A., B. and C v. Ireland*, deserves special mention. Clearly, the Court leaves it up to the national authorities, and in particular the parliaments of the Member States, to resolve ethical issues and conflicts in this area. Meanwhile, it pays close attention to the way the decision is reached: the consultation processes (*Lambert v. France*), the participation of the public and parliament in resolving the issues giving rise to the complaint (referendum – *A., B. and C. v. Ireland*), or the process of considering the rights and claims of the applicant in court proceedings (*Koch v. Germany*). In this respect, therefore, the State's demonstration of its thoroughness in examining the social background and the views held in society is a very strong argument in disputes – all the stronger the more difficult it is to resolve a worldview dilemma.

The need to protect specific groups of persons as a limit of right to self-determination

Throughout our book, we have assumed that when deciding on morally sensitive cases, the Court uses the premise of public morality as a legitimate aim for restricting the rights and freedoms of individuals very infrequently, hardly ever in fact. Be it in euthanasia or medically assisted procreation cases, the rationale it accepts is the protection of the rights and freedoms of others. In cases involving medically assisted procreation, the Court also makes auxiliary reference to the premise of protection of public health (*S.H. and Others v. Austria*) and occasionally the premise of protection of public order (*Paradiso and Campanelli v. Italy*). Defining the group whose interests – values belonging to whom – are protected by these premises is crucial for the Court's assessment of the application of these premises, instead of the seemingly appropriate premise of public morality.

It seems relatively easy to identify the interests that are protected under the premises of public health and public order. However, it may be difficult to identify the interests that are protected under the premise of "rights and freedoms of others." The key question that arises here is how concrete the identification of other persons must be for the balancing test to be reliable. In both categories of cases in which such a legitimate aim has been formulated, namely the end-of-life and medically assisted procreation cases, the rights and freedoms of persons concern a hypothetical group of wronged persons, a category that represents an extrapolation of the Court's fears about the possible and future harm that would be caused by extending the limits beyond the national decisions. The protection of the group so defined counterbalanced the individual interest of the applicants and effectively led to the limitation of their rights. As we pointed out previously, this strategy of determining the socially undesirable effects of a ruling is quite controversial, albeit convincing on pragmatic grounds. This tactic reveals that the courts seek justification in the realities of social life, referring to the motives which may guide such persons, and thus – indirectly – to develop a certain attitude of socially approved consent to certain behaviours. When it comes to marking the limit of the right to assisted suicide, it is the fear of pressure being exerted on weak and vulnerable persons to end their lives. Similarly, in the medically assisted procreation cases, the Court abstractly identifies a circle of "other persons," such as unspecified disadvantaged women or children potentially born as a result of the surrogacy technique. In either case, such a designation of a hypothetical group appears insufficiently precise to provide a background and reference for evaluating the interference into the applicants' rights by balancing their rights against those of this abstract group of persons. However, the Court accepts the governments' argument that it is precisely the protection of these potential victims that will justify the interference with the applicants' rights by the need to ensure the protection of the rights of other persons, identified as groups deserving special attention. Identification of these groups is without doubt an element contributing to the position of a judicial authority in the context of moral standpoint on the issue of admissibility of specific actions by referring to social practice.

This pragmatic instrument of reasoning through the indication of possible risks of a contradictory decision seems to be one the most interesting among those discussed in the study. It may mark a certain tendency to use different ways of reasoning and to look for consensus where it is particularly difficult to do so. However, from the point of view of the consequences for the system of protection, it should be noted that there is a risk of creating such a group ad hoc for the purposes of almost any adjudication, not only within the scope of the discussed cases. This may produce unexpected effects and limitations of rights not yet considered. From the point of view of the stability of jurisprudence and its predictability, this is in fact a sort of game-changer. The argument derived from the need to protect the rights of others is a powerful one; it has the most unquestionable justification in the human rights order, and the values represented by the legitimate aim thus formulated are capable of counterbalancing any right guaranteed under the Convention, among all those that may be restricted under the Convention norms. This is neither dogmatically nor ideologically questionable. Yet for this very reason, constructing a group of hypothetically vulnerable persons for the purpose of arguing about the limits of the exercise of a right – and in particular of the rights guaranteed by Article 8 – is a move with consequences that are difficult to foresee.

Conclusion

As the analysis we have carried out demonstrates, in all the cases it has decided, the Court employed several ways of reasoning at once. Some of them have been known for a long time and take the form of methods or tools of interpretation. Our study shows, however, that they are used primarily as means of convincing people of the decisions rendered, and thus they are derivative of the decision. They serve to substantiate it, and not only to give meaning to the norms of the Convention. In addition, their use is much broader and includes not only law, but also social practice and decision-making processes.

The use of particular ways of reasoning is demonstrated in great detail against the background of cases involving moral dilemmas.

By applying some of the argumentative devices, the Court clearly strives to avoid taking a position on issues of a morally sensitive nature. This will be the result of proceduralisation and appeals to authority, including the margin of appreciation.

In turn, other ways of reasoning favour the possibility of presenting the Court's view on certain moral issues, although such pronouncements are constructed with great prudence and usually indirectly. Undoubtedly, these ways include incrementalism, which consists in extracting new constitutive elements of the right vested in the applicants, arguments referring to potential secondary effects on groups deserving special attention, or the Court's use of flexible terms describing its attitude towards specific entities or phenomena (a foetus, rather than an unborn child; a woman, rather than a mother wishing to undergo an abortion). These last two lines of argument allow the Court to indirectly present its position in relation to ethical issues.

A prominent outcome of our study is the conclusion that although the Court generally avoids pronouncing directly on significant moral issues, it does not remain indifferent to the need to foster desirable social attitudes. Its single most important action in this regard is the development of the concept of "vulnerable groups" or "groups deserving special protection." One major advantage of these concepts is the creation of a moral and empathetic duty of care towards others, which, according to this case law, is enshrined in the Convention's order of human rights. If the limitation of the right to self-determination involves the protection of a group potentially exposed to the indirect effects of such a broad conception of the right, then such a limitation implies treating the duty to coexist within society more broadly than apparent *prima facie*. Hence, if in a neutral and liberal setting human rights supersede the ethical order, then the conclusion can be read from the case law in these particularly sensitive cases that, within the protection of human rights, only they alone can act as boundaries for the realisation of individual claims. However, designing limitations based on the rights and freedoms of others may go beyond action directly aimed at violating them. The relationship between the exercise of the right under Article 8 and the potential outcome of harming some hypothetical group of persons as a consequence of accepting the moral and social stance adopted is still rather vague and intriguing, but it seems to set clear limits as to individual action.

Thus, notwithstanding the fact that the Court has not been assigned the role to pronounce on moral issues with authority, it remains the "Conscience of Europe."[29] As opposed to the traditional conscience, however, the Court – in its capacity as the most effective international tribunal – must rationalise its rulings and convince all those subject to its jurisdiction of its arguments.

29 *The Conscience of Europe. 50 Years of the European Court of Human Rights*, Council of Europe 2010, Kanstantsin Dzehtsiarou, "The Conscience of Europe that Landed in Strasbourg: A Circle of Life of the European Court of Human Rights." *The European Convention on Human Rights Law Review* 1 (2020): 1–6.

Bibliography

Arden, Lady Justice. *An English Judge in Europe*. www.judiciary.uk/wp-content/uploads/JCO/Documents/Speeches/lj-arden-an-english-judge-in-europe.pdf

Arnardóttir, Oddný M. "Organized retreat? The move from 'substantive' to 'procedural' review in the ECtHR's case law on the margin of appreciation." *ESIL Conference Paper Series* 5(4) (2015).

Beaumont, Paul and Katarina Trimmings. "The European Court of Human Rights in Paradiso and Campanelli v. Italy and the way forward for regulating cross-border surrogacy." *University of Aberdeen, Working Paper No.* 2017/3, p. 12. www.abdn.ac.uk/law/documents/cpil%20working%20paper%20no%202017_3.pdf.

Bomhoff, Jacco and Lorenzo Zucca. "Evans v. UK – European Court of Human Rights: The tragedy of Ms Evans: Conflicts and incommensurability of rights, Evans v. the United Kingdom, fourth section judgment of 7 March 2006, application no. 6339/05." *European Constitutional Law Review* 2(3) (2016): 424–442.

Bossuyt, Marc. "Categorical rights and vulnerable groups: Moving away from the universal human being." *The George Washington International Law Review* 48 (2016): 717–742.

Dzehtsiarou, Kanstantsin. "The conscience of Europe that landed in strasbourg: A circle of life of the European Court of Human Rights." *The European Convention on Human Rights Law Review* 1 (2020): 1–6.

Gerards, Janneke. "Procedural review by the ECtHR: A typology." In *Procedural Review in European Fundamental Rights Cases*, edited by Janneke Gerards and Eva Brems, 127–160. Cambridge University Press, 2017.

Haule, Romuald R. "Some reflections on the foundation of human rights – Are human rights an alternative to moral values?" *Max Planck Yearbook of United Nations Law Online* 10(1) (2006): 367–395.

Holmes, Oliver Wendell. "The path of the law." (originally: 1897 *Harvard Law Review* 10) In *Judges on Judging*, collected and edited by David M. O'Brien. CQ Press, 2004.

Kleinlein, Thomas. "The procedural approach of the European Court of Human Rights: Between subsidiarity and dynamic evolution." *International & Comparative Law Quarterly* 68 (2019): 91–110.

Megret, Frederic. "International human rights law theory." In *Research Handbook on the Theory and History of International Law*, edited by Alexander Orakhelashvili. Edward Elgar Publishing, 2020.

Mill, John Stuart. *On Liberty*. J. W. Parker and Son, 1859.

Nussberger, Angelika. "Procedural review by the ECHR: View from the court." In *Procedural Review in European Fundamental Rights Cases*, edited by Janneke Gerards and Eva Brems, 161–176. Cambridge University Press, 2017.

O'Boyle, Michael. "The notion of 'vulnerable groups' in the case law of the European Court of Human Rights." *Report Delivered for Conference on the Constitutional Protection of Vulnerable Groups: A Judicial Dialogue*. Santiago Chile, 2015.

Peroni, Lourdes and Alexandra Timmer. "Vulnerable groups: The promise of an emerging concept in European human rights convention law." *Inteurnational Journal of Constitutional Law* 11 (2013): 1056–1085.

Rozakis, Christos L. "The European judge as comparatist." *Tulane Law Review* 80(1) (2005): 257–280.

The Conscience of Europe. *50 Years of the European Court of Human Rights*. Council of Europe, 2010.

Van Hoof, Wannes and Guido Pennings. "The consequences of S.H. and Others v. Austria for legislation on gamete donation in Europe: An ethical analysis of the European Court of Human Rights judgments." *Reprod Biomed Online* 25(7) (2012): 665–669.

Wasserstrom, Richard. "Rights, human rights, and racial discrimination." *Journal of Philosophy* 61(20) (1964): 628–641.

Index

For Product Safety Concerns and Information please contact our EU
representative GPSR@taylorandfrancis.com
Taylor & Francis Verlag GmbH, Kaufingerstraße 24, 80331 München, Germany

www.ingramcontent.com/pod-product-compliance
Lightning Source LLC
LaVergne TN
LVHW021126300926
849160LV00010B/879
9781032452227